BRADFORD WEST GWILLIMBURY P. L.

959
.604
2
Nhe

Aug. 23, 2016

33328900204450

The Khmer Rouge : ideology, militarism,

D0206017

THE KHMER ROUGE

THE KHMER ROUGE

Ideology, Militarism, and the Revolution That Consumed a Generation

Boraden Nhem

PSI Guides to Terrorists, Insurgents, and Armed Groups
James J. F. Forest, Series Editor

 PRAEGER

DISCARDED
BRADFORD WG
PUBLIC LIBRARY

AN IMPRINT OF ABC-CLIO, LLC
Santa Barbara, California • Denver, Colorado • Oxford, England

Bradford WG Public Library
425 Holland St. W.
Bradford, ON L3Z 0J2

Copyright 2013 by Boraden Nhem

All rights reserved. No part of this publication may be reproduced, stored in a
retrieval system, or transmitted, in any form or by any means, electronic, mechanical,
photocopying, recording, or otherwise, except for the inclusion of brief quotations in a
review, without prior permission in writing from the publisher.

Library of Congress Cataloging-in-Publication Data

Nhem, Boraden.
    The Khmer Rouge : ideology, militarism, and the revolution that consumed a
generation / Boraden Nhem.
        pages cm. — (PSI guides to terrorists, insurgents, and armed groups)
    Includes bibliographical references and index.

    ISBN 978-0-313-39337-2 (hardcopy : alk. paper) — ISBN 978-0-313-39338-9
(ebook)   1. Parti communiste du Kampuchea.   2. Pol Pot.   3. Genocide—
Cambodia.   4. Cambodia—History—Civil War, 1970–1975.   5. Cambodia—
History—1975–1979.   6. Cambodia—History—1979–   7. Cambodia—
Politics and government—1979–   8. Cambodia—Politics and government—
20th century.   I. Title.
    DS554.8.N55   2013
    959.604′2—dc23   2013011127

ISBN: 978-0-313-39337-2
EISBN: 978-0-313-39338-9

17   16   15   14   13   1   2   3   4   5

This book is also available on the World Wide Web as an eBook.
Visit www.abc-clio.com for details.

Praeger
An Imprint of ABC-CLIO, LLC

ABC-CLIO, LLC
130 Cremona Drive, P.O. Box 1911
Santa Barbara, California 93116-1911

This book is printed on acid-free paper ∞

Manufactured in the United States of America

Contents

Preface:
The Era of Artillery
Bombardment

It was a morning in July 2009 and I was sitting inside the U.S. Embassy to apply for a visa. I had by then been studying in the United States for four years, but I still needed a visa every time I returned. As the interviews took some time, people always had to wait, during which time we often befriended the others waiting. That day, a middle-aged man approached me and started a conversation. I learnt that he was applying for an immigrant visa to meet his fiancée, who was waiting in the States. He probably must have thought I was applying for the same visa as well, and that I had a fiancée waiting for me in the States too, which was curious considering the fact that I must have looked too young. He finally asked me this question and I answered that no, I was pursuing my academic career in the United States which would then be my fifth year of study after an extra year of study in France. Both he and his friends were awed by the history of my study, which, to me, was only a humble achievement.

He then uttered a line I have never forgotten: "[Sigh] The children of this new era are not like our era, we were Children of the Artillery Bombardment Era." This line is simple, but it dug deep into my consciousness and my thoughts. In one short and simple line, this man had just described the life of the general Cambodian population during the 30 years of civil war. To my knowledge, no Western author has ever used a phrase similar to that line, or any phrase that can rival it, in summarizing the hardship endured by the Cambodian people during the 30 years of war. The line also implied a break between two eras, a break created by the "Win-Win Policy" of Prime Minister Hun Sen.

The description was not new, and elders always spoke to me about it, except that I never paid much attention simply because I thought it to be too banal.

In 2009, however, I was seeking a phrase that would describe the history of Cambodia during that period and what the man said just shook me to my core. During the war, even small children could tell the different types of planes, whether the planes were reconnaissance, bombers, or fighter planes, by just listening to the sound of their approach, and they even knew the model of the plane. This was one of the skills acquired by children who grew up in the midst of intense war.

The Cambodian Civil War shaped the lives of all the people involved, but not just a few years of their lives. For many people during that generation, their entire life related to war. If one tries to make a metaphor, it is as though these people worked their whole lives in war and then gained peace (after 1998) as their pension in retirement. Essentially, the war consumed this entire generation. What caused this tragedy? This one simple question has produced a wealth of books and research and this current book seeks to offer a novel explanation.

WHAT WILL THIS BOOK BRING TO THE LITERATURE ON THE KHMER ROUGE?

The Khmer Rouge was in power for less than five years and more than half of those years were spent fighting against the Vietnamese. The first attack took the Vietnamese by surprise and the Khmer Rouge killed at least hundreds of Vietnamese villagers during their raid. Vietnam soon retaliated and for most of 1977, the two armies skirmished back and forth. Refugees as well as cadres on the execution list began to pour into Vietnam. Vietnam soon gained the upper hand in the East Zone, which led Pol Pot to believe that commanders of the East Zone conspired with the Vietnamese to bring him down. This led to a major purge, culminating in the collapse of the regime.

But the most infamous legacy of the Khmer Rouge is genocide. The Khmer Rouge had been carrying out their "cleansing policy" ever since the first day they marched into the capital city on April 17, 1975. Moreover, their administration of the country was simplistic by modern administration standards and their military operations were too ambitious. Their record of almost four years in power was probably the worst in Cambodian history. Such a notorious regime then became the subject of much research by scholars and former diplomats in Cambodia, as well as by French nationals who stayed behind during the last few days of the Khmer Republic. Despite the large volume of research, however, there are still gaps in the literature.

INDIVIDUALS VS. ORGANIZATION

First of all, the literature has focused mostly on individuals, especially Saloth Sar, alias Pol Pot, who appeared to singlehandedly carry out the atrocities and who then attacked Vietnam with a small number of his inner circle. To a great extent, this was true. But the conditions and the environment in which decisions were made were never examined in detail. How could Pol Pot receive the support of his subordinates when he implemented his dangerously narrow-minded policies? This requires a closer examination about the nature of the organization that he was leading.

The majority of the literature follows only the life of Pol Pot. This makes a great story, but if one wants to study the war termination experience, then the story is only half complete. In retrospect, to succeed, Pol Pot needed an organization. And as will be seen in this book, Pol Pot salvaged an old organization, built on it, eliminated the traces of the old organization and then implemented his agenda once that organization helped propel him to power. However, Pol Pot was successful only because most of his policy fitted the circumstances that surrounded him. In the last years of his life, circumstances changed dramatically, but Pol Pot still clung to his ideology that was extreme and exclusionary, and which had also become outdated. Then the organization rejected him and the war ended in 1998. Pol Pot and some of his extremist colleagues then tried to reverse the flow. This was not successful and it only delayed, not prevented, the end of the war.

The evidence also reveals that it was the Win-Win Policy (WWP) devised by Prime Minister Hun Sen that actually ended the war. One of the keys to the success of the WWP was, in my own opinion, its focus on the "political-military organization" of the Khmer Rouge, and not just on any individuals. No matter who Pol Pot was, if he had no organization and no army, how could he claim to have his voice heard, or to achieve anything of any scale?

The innovative Win-Win Policy motivated me to choose a different approach that has not yet been explored by other authors. But what do I mean when I say I want to study the "evolution" and the "dynamics" of the "organization" of the Khmer Rouge? How do I weigh the relative importance of "agents" or "individuals" and "structure" or "organization" in determining the outcome?

When one studies the subject of organization, one has to ask the question about what is more important, individuals or organization? This question is known in academic circles as the "agent-structure" debate, which is beyond the scope of my research here. In this book, I assume that individuals and organizations interact with each other to produce the final outcome. Neither can be considered being more important than the other. Of course, individuals create organizations. But as Karl Marx famously put it "men make their own history, but they do not make it in the circumstances of their own choosing." Individual decisions need to take into account the complex environment and the decisions of other individuals, both of which jointly determine the outcomes. People make plans, but plans may not all be realized, depending on the circumstances. My main contribution to the literature is the examination of the "organizational aspect" of the Khmer Rouge to complement the existing and already vast, but individual-oriented, narrative of the Khmer Rouge.

Before proceeding to the explanation of what I mean by "organization," I wish to make one clarification. The term "organization" is translated to Khmer as *angkar*. Coincidentally, the Khmer Rouge also used the code words *angkar* or *angkar leu* (superior or higher organization) as a disguise for their political machine, the Communist Party of Kampuchea (CPK). In this book, my goal is to study the Khmer Rouge as an "organization" and the reader will see that I consider organization as the key explanatory variable. However, this argument is not necessarily meant to imply that the Khmer Rouge called itself *angkar* or "organization" because the members knew the advantages of a sophisticated organization. Therefore, to avoid confusion, throughout this book, I will use *angkar* or *angkar leu*, without translation, to describe how the Khmer Rouge named themselves, and the term "organization" will be used as a general term.

WHAT IS AN "ORGANIZATION"?

Ever since human beings came together and lived as groups, organizations needed to be built in order to increase efficiency in using limited resources to fulfill their goals. An organized structure was also necessary to maximize results by way of high productivity, and also as a way of ensuring the survival of the group in the event of attrition of its members. An organization is an interconnected system linking smaller parts together to work for the "mission" of the whole. All organizations are built to fulfill a certain mission or purpose. Without a mission or purpose, the organization will become less useful for society or the group that has created it, and will no longer be cost effective. An organization without a mission would also lose support among its members, and members would call for its abolition. When the mission ends or the purpose erodes, an organization will then scramble to find a new mission or purpose, so that it can continue to justify its existence.

A school board, a political party, a government, a religion, and the military are only a few examples of organizations. The military is probably one of the most sophisticated forms of organization humans have ever created. Its mission is to fight and win wars and to protect the nation that created it. As an organization that is prone to a high rate of attrition, the military necessarily has a long and systematic chain of command to try to circumvent this problem. It also has a strict internal set of rules to keep members in line. Amidst chaos on the battlefield, one simply cannot afford to allow democratic decision making or options regarding whether to join action; the commander has absolute power. Often, that power is curbed within the established just war principles, but the authority cannot be discussed in the middle of the fight.

An organization that is built for a certain mission will therefore find it difficult to perform the function of another. For example, when the military controls the civilian government in the event of a coup, the outcome tends to be disastrous, mainly because the military organization is not designed to run a civilian government or to manage the economy. The management of the economy requires consultation and feedback and the decisions are mainly made by a board with representation from different stakeholders. Most of the time, compromise is the norm, something that the military cannot accept or understand.

Throughout history, charismatic leaders always seemed to singlehandedly lead their troops to great victory without the help of anyone else. The main problem with this story is that the charisma and the cult of personality itself mask the organizational machine behind it. It is evident throughout history that the groups who came to power were usually not the ones who started something, but the ones who were well organized. In Tsarist Russia, it was not Lenin who started the revolutionary fervor, it was the Bolsheviks, who were simply better organized than Kerensky, who actually enjoyed the spoils of the revolution. In World War II, Gen. Patton could move fast mainly because the logistics arrangement was right, not because of his fiery personality alone. The same thing can also be said of Alexander the Great and the army that conquered Persia and parts of India.

Good organization is also the reason why colonial troops could easily subdue local forces, in spite of the fact that local forces had numerical superiority. The colonial troops were fewer in number, but they were much more professional and better organized than the numerically superior, but unorganized locals. It is no surprise, therefore, that once the local forces learned how to organize and consolidate their power through unity of command, especially after World War II, they easily defeated the colonial powers.

Moreover, organizations will be rewarded with resources in order to fulfill their missions. Organizations that can perform their function well, or the ones whose mission is crucial to society, will receive many resources, while the ones that do not perform their function, or whose function is no longer important, will see their resources stripped away.

To function properly, efficiently, and effectively, organizations take advantage of routines and establish the so-called "standard operating procedures" (SOP)[1] that are essentially a repertoire of actions to be taken when a certain situation occurs.[2] This way, the members of that organization can easily cope with all situations by using the corresponding SOP. Their response to a complex environment then becomes a reflex, making it easier to get the job done. Members do not have to spend much time thinking and deciding, because the SOPs are readily available. To achieve this, the organization will need to build up large repertoires of SOPs for all the common situations that might occur. These might be developed from experiences over the life span of the organization, from trial-and-error, or from deductive theories. It is an important investment for an organization to build enough repertoires to be able to function smoothly.

For example, as a case study taken from a military organization, a truck carrying a platoon that was moving along a narrow road was suddenly ambushed. The soldiers, the officers and the drivers saw no enemy and they knew only that they were being shot at from the bushes alongside the road. If the organization is a poor one, and there is no good SOP, then the soldiers will be a sitting duck and most people will simply panic in such a stressful situation. Sooner or later, that unit will be annihilated. A good organization, on the other hand, will train the soldiers in advance on what to do if they are ambushed.

Some units would just drive through the site assuming the enemy has already chosen better terrain, so flight would be better than fight. In other units, soldiers would be ordered to dismount immediately and move into cover near the bushes in case there is ambush. In both cases, SOPs become a reflex. Once ambushed, the soldiers need not think about the options, they just need to follow what their organization considers the best course of action. People who have been in combat know that quick reflexes can save lives, and SOPs are designed to do just that.

But at the same time, organizations need to adapt to ever-changing situations and complexities in their environment.[3] Organizations that cannot learn and adapt to new circumstances (which may require a new mission and SOPs) are considered to be "stagnated," whereas the ones that do learn and adapt are called "innovative" organizations. Nonetheless, because of the investment in building repertoires and the cost associated with change, organizations tend to be rigid. The fact that some military organizations still retained cavalry units well into the 20th century is an example of rigid organizations that refuse to recognize changes in modern weaponry.[4] Such organizations tend to stick to their rigid norms and original missions, often with the belief that there is an existing repertoire and SOP somewhere that can actually solve the new problems. People who are well trained in one field will have a tendency to find it hard to comprehend the necessities of another field. So goes the classic dictum: "Those who are trained to use hammers will see that all problems look like nails." There is also the saying, "where you stand depends on where you sit." Unsurprisingly, during the Cuban Missile Crisis, Ambassador Thompson and McNamara (civilian leader of defense) advocated negotiation while the military categorically called for either an invasion of Cuba or surgical airstrikes.[5]

In another example, the military organization of the United States was built to win war with regular, large units. Therefore, the United States optimized this ideology by focusing solely on increasing firepower without restraint. During the Vietnam War, the U.S. military organization that was designed for conventional warfare was frustrated when the National Liberation Front and the Vietnamese People's Army (NLF/VPA)[6] used guerilla tactics, something that the American military organization was not built to counter.[7] The organization blocked any attempts to change its mission from conventional warfare to guerilla warfare, simply because this would have necessitated a reorganization of the U.S. military in Vietnam, a reorganization that the U.S. commanders were not prepared to accept.

In the case of the British military organization, which was primarily a colonial army, its main mission was precisely to counter small-scale insurrections in the periphery of its empire.[8] Thus, the track record of the British tends to be better than their American counterpart in guerilla warfare. On the other hand, the British would not stand a chance against Germany in World War I and World War II in a conventional battle, mainly because their organization was not built for such a mission. Britain always needed to bring France on board if it needed to intervene in Europe, and vice versa.[9]

These factors are very important in understanding the dynamics of organizations and how they evolve. Most of the time, whether an organization fails or succeeds depends on how well it copes with the changing environment, and whether it can build an appropriate set of SOPs to function properly and to fulfill its mission.

"KHMER ROUGE" OR HOW I SEE COLORS IN THIS BOOK

The name "Khmer Rouge" is itself controversial. Any reader of the literature on the Khmer Rouge will immediately notice that many books on the subject always avoid using the title "Khmer Rouge," while this book and many other books by Cambodian authors never shy away from using the term "Khmer Rouge." So what is the issue here?

It might be premature to talk about the Khmer Rouge at this point, but due to the different names that will be used later, I believe that readers should at least have some notions about what to expect. As noted, the use of this name is shrouded in controversy, and historians disagree on how this group should be called. But first we need to survey the evolutionary process of the group. My argument here is that the term "Khmer Rouge" could capture the whole life span of the organization, even though the Khmer Rouge themselves never like that name.

The first leftist movement in Cambodia was the Kampuchean People's Revolutionary Party (KPRP) in which a man named Saloth Sar, alias Pol Pot, was just a minor member. In the 1960s, Prince Sihanouk began using the term "Khmer Rouge" (French meaning "Red Khmer," Khmer being a term for ethnic Cambodian) to describe the Cambodian leftist movements in Cambodia. This term was used in tandem with the term "Khmer Bleu" (Blue Khmer) to denote the right-wing politicians. This second term would later be eclipsed by the name Khmer Rouge.

In the same period, after the KPRP cadres were in tatters due to the treachery of Siv Heng (the second man in the KPRP), Pol Pot emerged within the party and secretly renamed the KPRP to become "Pak Communist Kampuchea" or, translated into English, "the Communist Party of Kampuchea" (CPK). Some historians suggest this new party was born out of a transitional party, the Workers' Party of Kampuchea (WPK), which existed for only a few years. The existence of the CPK was not known to the world until Pol Pot declared it in a public speech in 1977, two years after he was in power.

In 1970, a coup deposed Prince Sihanouk, and the leftists immediately joined with the prince's government-in-exile, Gouvernement Royal d'Unité National Khmer (GRUNK) or Royal Government of National Union of Kampuchea with the Forces d'Unité National Khmer (FUNK) as the armed wing of this organization. The CPK or Khmer Rouge hijacked this name and worked under the names GRUNK and FUNK in order to use Prince Sihanouk's popularity to draw recruits.

When the Khmer Rouge took power in 1975, the GRUNK came to an end soon after. In fact, the GRUNK remained nominal from the beginning. After

1975, the Khmer Rouge called itself Democratic Kampuchea (DK). When it was defeated by the Kampuchea Solidarity Front for National Salvation (KSFNS)[10] and the Vietnamese army in 1979, the Khmer Rouge agreed to a marriage of expediency with other resistance movements under Prince Sihanouk, who by then had his own army. DK then became part of the Coalition Government of Democratic Kampuchea (CGDK). The name Democratic Kampuchea was necessary at that time, despite its history of brutality, because its "Sponsors" were able to preserve its seat at the United Nations.

After the Paris Peace Agreement was signed in 1991, the CGDK was abolished and all parties to the Cambodian civil war came together to compete in the election organized by the United Nations. After a few incidents, the Khmer Rouge boycotted the election and went back to guerilla campaigning. Most Western historians concluded that the Khmer Rouge continued to use the term "DK" until its demise in 1998. However, field surveys show that most, if not all, Khmer Rouge soldiers discontinued the use of this term after the Or-Ral area broke away from Pol Pot. This was perhaps due to the fact that many of them wanted to disassociate themselves from the organization. They either addressed themselves by the name of their units (divisions, regiments, etc.) or they did not use the term at all. When the second man in Pol Pot's inner circle, Ieng Sary, broke away from the Khmer Rouge in 1995, he tried to create a new organization and named it the Democratic National Union Movement (DNUM) in 1996. After that, the DK no longer existed in any meaningful way and the organization did not have any chance of coming to power. Ta Mok, the last hardliner, also relinquished the term DK and did not cling to any meaningful official name toward the end of the revolution.

However, one thing is clear. Just like many well-known and infamous names in history, the term "Khmer Rouge" was popularized not by the Khmer Rouge, but by its opponents. The term was widely used along with the term *pouk Pol Pot* (Pol Pot's cliques) to describe the Khmer Rouge fighters. As a result, the terms DK, KPRP, GRUNK, CPK, or CGDK are different names that described different combinations or groups of people at different times. But we need a term that can capture Pol Pot, his inner circle, and the bulk of the fighting forces that constituted a coherent organization. If we do not use an overarching term, readers might lose track of the organization and tend to think that the organizations were different, based on different names. This organization was a significant belligerent in the Cambodian civil war, and the war could not have ended without terminating this organization first. Only the term "Khmer Rouge," however imperfect it might be, can play such a role.

In literature concerning the Khmer Rouge, historians are divided over how to use this name. The Documentation Center of Cambodia published a literature review by renowned scholars on the subject in 2000.[11] In this debate, one group of historians considered the term "Khmer Rouge" meaningless. David Chandler used party membership as judgment of an organization, thus claiming that only the CPK and DK names can be used. Julio Jeldres, despite the fact that he agreed the term "Khmer Rouge" was coined by Prince Sihanouk, said the prince did not use the term very often and cautioned that the term cannot be used to encompass all communist movements in Cambodia. Jeldres also mentioned that the Khmer Rouge themselves never liked the term. Chhang Youk, director of the Documentation Center of Cambodia, opined that as a matter of legality and official public discussion, the term Khmer Rouge should not be used. Steve Heder even went further to deny the use of the term Khmer Rouge altogether, because it is "a vague term of abuse, suggesting above all a genocidal or at least murderous nature. As such, it can be a dangerously inaccurate political label."[12]

I concur with Chhang Youk who argued that we should not confuse historical terms and the terms appropriate only for the court of law, which is necessary in the context of the Extraordinary Chambers in the Court of Cambodia (ECCC). The ECCC is also known casually in Cambodia as the "Khmer Rouge Tribunal," which reinforces my point earlier that the term Khmer Rouge had become part of the Khmer lexicon for quite some time already. However, I disagree with Heder that the term always suggests genocidal or murderous acts. Three points are noteworthy here.

First, field research with former officers of the Kampuchea People Revolutionary Armed Forces (KPRAF) of the People's Republic of Kampuchea (PRK), the forces that deposed the Khmer Rouge in 1979, reveals two different terms. The term "Khmer Rouge" referred to the fighters and soldiers, as counterparts. Whenever they talked about the "Khmer Rouge," it was always a discussion of tactics, combat, and encounters with these forces. The genocide and murder, on the other hand, came up when talking about *ror borb Pol Pot* (Pol Pot regime), *pouk Pol Pot* (Pol Pot's cliques), or the *tchum noan Pol Pot* (Pol Pot era). These terms denote the Khmer Rouge between 1975 and 1979.

Second, during the integration process starting in 1995, the forces were still addressed as "former Khmer Rouge" until after integration. At that time, the term Khmer Rouge was preferred to *pouk Pol Pot*, the latter being much more cruel and relating to genocide and murder. A careful analysis of the government's rhetoric in mid-1995 shows that the term "Khmer Rouge" was used to distinguish between professional fighters and the extremists under Pol Pot. The Win-Win Policy of Prime Minister Hun Sen actually distinguished clearly between Pol Pot's extremists and those who were disillusioned by Pol Pot's ideology, and who were perhaps never implicated in the genocide of 1975–79. This policy successfully suggested to the former Khmer Rouge that integration with the government would not bring disaster. Therefore, Khmer Rouge is an umbrella term that does not necessarily denote genocide.

Third, many Khmer Rouge fighters joined the organization in the 1980s only, and therefore were not implicated in the genocide that took place between 1975 and 1979. On the other hand, most of the local administration chiefs of DK who might be implicated in the genocide simply vanished into the countryside after 1979 and were not present in the Khmer Rouge fighting forces.

However, despite this factional divide within the Khmer Rouge, I still use this term because it describes a group whose members had the following common characteristics:

- Some members had been combatants since the beginning of the struggle in the 1960s. They remained with DK until integration in the 1990s.
- Many new members grew up and joined the movement after 1979 only.
- All were strong believers in anti-Vietnamese ideology. Many retained this ideology after the DK days. They were too young to remember the atrocities committed during the DK regime, but they were old enough to see Vietnamese troops in Cambodia. Therefore, they strongly believed in Pol Pot's anti-Vietnamese rhetoric.
- Those who strongly believed in Pol Pot's propaganda. This group was a significant actor in the Cambodian civil war. The war ended when they ceased to exist. The splinter groups that integrated with the government after dissociating themselves from Pol Pot were called "former Khmer Rouge."

Therefore, the term Khmer Rouge is both meaningful and neutral, as many members of this group were not necessarily perpetrators of genocide. This group had been in existence since the 1960s, and continued its existence during many different periods while raising new recruits. After the election in 1993, which it boycotted, the group splintered and the term Khmer Rouge denoted an organization whose members began to desert.

The explanation in this book is not meant to relinquish the responsibility of the perpetrators of genocide between 1975 and 1979, and many members of the Khmer Rouge were indeed implicated in the atrocities. But it is only fitting that everyone is presumed innocent until proved guilty. Determining who is guilty and who is not is the sole responsibility of the ECCC. I do not intend to interfere in that process.

My point is simply that some of the Khmer Rouge, especially those who joined after 1979, could not have been implicated in the genocide that occurred between 1975 and 1979. Other members of the Khmer Rouge also lost their relatives under the DK regime but they considered a fight against the Vietnamese a more serious threat that transcended their personal sentiments. After the Vietnamese totally withdrew all their forces in 1989, this latter group of fighters lost their purpose and began to distance themselves from Pol Pot, yet they had no chance of escape. It was not until the Win-Win Policy provided a safe exit that these people were able to escape from the "Khmer Rouge." In sum, the term "Khmer Rouge" is not a synonym for "genocide." Only a thorough examination of the Khmer Rouge as an organization, from the beginning until the end, will reveal this difference. This more accurate taxonomy is one of the aims of this book. As a result, the term Khmer Rouge used in this book is not a derogatory term.

I also agree with historians such as Craig Etcheson and Helen Jarvis that the term Khmer Rouge has different meanings in different periods. But in this book, I would add that although the term Khmer Rouge refers to different things in different periods, the core was always Pol Pot and his inner circle whose fighters retained the above common characteristics. Here I follow Jarvis in the definition of the Khmer Rouge, which I think is quite comprehensive,[13] with some modifications during the last period.

Before the coup in 1970, the Khmer Rouge referred to all Cambodian communist fighting forces; between 1970 and 1976, the CPK sought refuge under the name GRUNK and FUNK to hijack legitimacy from Prince Sihanouk; between 1976 and 1979, this term referred to the government in power, the DK; between 1979 and 1993, the Khmer Rouge referred to a branch of the CGDK; between 1993 and 1998, the Khmer Rouge was the main guerilla force that was fighting against the new coalition government in Phnom Penh. During this last period, the Khmer Rouge was an organization that had lost its purpose when it no longer saw any Vietnamese troops in Cambodia, and had by then experienced the free market system. The Khmer Rouge between 1993 and 1998 is a story of a continuous, diminishing organization.

ACKNOWLEDGMENT

This book could not have been completed without the help and cooperation of many people, directly or indirectly. Regarding the early period of the Khmer Rouge, I relied mostly on the works of previous researchers, especially Becker, Chanda, Chandler, Kiernan, Meyer, Mosyakov, and Ponchaud. What I have done in this book is to summarize the literature and then analyze it through "the organizational lens." In terms of information, I think there is little room to improve on these works further, unless new archives are made public.

Another important part of my book is the material taken from the collections of the Documentation Center of Cambodia (or DC-Cam) that holds many documents related to the period of Democratic Kampuchea. Some of the photos in this book come from DC-Cam collections. I would like to express my deep thanks to Mr. Chhang Youk, director of DC-Cam, for his support and facilitation for my research.

For the years between 1979 and 1993, I relied on interviews with former officers of both the Khmer Rouge and the KPRAF. This is also a novel aspect of this book, since not many books have analyzed this period. However, during this time, research on the Khmer Rouge can be both interesting and frustrating due to the lack of information and archival materials. The substitute was interviews, but these too were difficult due to the fact that the ECCC (Khmer Rouge Tribunal) is now in process. Many people who I interviewed were never implicated in any crime, but they were still very cautious.

Many former officers of the KPRAF, on the other hand, requested that both their names and if possible, the names of their former foes (Khmer Rouge fighters), which they described in the interviews, be left anonymous. We then agreed that in such cases, only the name of the units would be identified, and individual names would remain anonymous upon request. I omitted the names out of respect for these officers and soldiers and I believe they would be better authors of their own biographies.

I would like to thank the former Khmer Rouge officers and soldiers as well as former officers of the KPRAF who provided me with insightful interviews. Many of the KPRAF are the unsung heroes of the nation and they are an important part of my book. Throughout this book, I will put only "former commander," "former officer," "former soldiers," "former cadre" and so forth instead of the real names. Anyone interested in fact-checking can contact me personally for the details of the interviews.

I would like to thank unnamed, former Khmer Rouge veterans of Region 20, Region 23, forces in Takeo, and former veterans of Khmer Rouge divisions after 1979. For the Khmer Rouge military, DC-Cam had already conducted interviews with many other units and I draw mostly from these sources. I also would like to thank Gen. (RET.) Dien Del who agreed to be interviewed. These interviews gave me a better understanding of the early operations of the armed forces of the Khmer Republic, as well as how the Khmer Rouge was perceived at the time. On the KPRAF's side, I would like to thank unnamed, former veterans of divisions 4, 6, 179, 286, sub-operational region (provincial garrison) of Siem Reap, Pursat, Battambang, Banteay Meanchey, Preah Vihear, military regions 4 and 5.

From 1993 until 1998, which was the era of the Win-Win Policy of Samdech Prime Minister Hun Sen, I am greatly indebted to Gen. Tea Banh, deputy prime minister and minister of national defense, who provided guidance on how I should approach the subject. As an important operator of the Win-Win Policy, Gen. Tea Banh's insights were unrivaled especially regarding his firsthand meeting with commanders of Khmer Rouge units who wished to dissociate themselves from Pol Pot.

I would also like to express my deep gratitude to Lt. Gen. Nem Sowath who was an assistant to Gen. Tea Banh during the Win-Win Policy era. General Sowath allowed me access to his private collection as well as the use of a considerable amount of this collection in my book. I wish to thank him for his support. The section on the Win-Win Policy is another novel aspect of my book, an aspect that has never been the subject of discussion by Western authors. This book will endeavor to show that the Cambodian civil war was terminated by this Cambodian policy. I would like to express my deep gratitude toward Gen. Tea Banh and Lt. Gen. Nem Sowath for their support of my historical work. I am very fortunate to have such considerate commanders.

Many other scholars also helped me with the researches in various parts of my book. I am greatly indebted to my professor, Dr. Stuart Kaufman, who was my foremost professor in security studies. Most of the campaign analyses that I have put into this book as well as my knowledge on organization theory were much influenced by my discussions with him over the years. The section on peacekeeping operations in Cambodia received great help from Dr. Harry Yarger who supervised my research at the U.S. Army War College's

Peacekeeping and Stability Operations Institute in 2009–2010. The section on the Khmer Rouge after 1979 greatly benefited from my conversations with Dr. Diep Sophal who also provided me with many archival documents.

Last but certainly not least, I wish to express my thanks to Dr. Mike Minehan who agreed to go through my manuscripts to correct any grammatical mistakes as well as to look out for any points that are not clear. Writing a book is difficult in the sense that we write about something that we, the authors, know by heart and can easily understand without much explanation, all the while forgetting that we actually write for someone else to read. Thus, an uninformed outsider is necessary to fulfill that role. Dr. Minehan was so kind to agree to all my requests without complaint. I am very fortunate to have such a great friend.

I am also indebted to my editors, Dr. James Forest and Mr. Steve Catalano, whose patience never ran out, even with the repeated delays on my manuscript delivery. Dr. Forest, in particular, gave me invaluable comments on each of the chapters in this book.

My students also deserve credit for being wonderful research assistants. Ly Meng, You Ratanaksamrith, Ly Sok Heng, and Sek Sophal did very well in arranging the archives from DC-Cam for me to work with. Ratanaksamrith, in particular, was very helpful in digitizing the maps used in this book. Ly Meng, Ly Sok Heng, and Sek Sophal also prepared the transcripts of the interviews. They are all part of a great team.

This book received help and support from many sources, however, needless to say, the views expressed in this book are solely my own, drawn from my objective academic analysis and are in no way representative of the official positions of the ministry of national defense of Cambodia. Also, the success of this book will be the success of everyone who helped me in the process, but I still assume all responsibility for any unintentional errors that might have occurred.

Acronyms

ANS	Armée Nationale Sihanoukiste
ARVN	Army of the Republic of Vietnam (South Vietnamese Army)
ASEAN	Association of South East Asian Nations
AXO	Abandoned Explosive Ordnance
CGDK	Coalition Government of Democratic Kampuchea
CIA	Central Intelligence Agency
CMAC	Cambodian Mines Action Center
CPK	Communist Party of Kampuchea
CPP	Cambodian People's Party
DRVN	Democratic Republic of Vietnam (North Vietnam)
ECCC	Extraordinary Chambers in the Court of Cambodia (Khmer Rouge Tribunal)
FANK	Forces Armées Nationales Khmères (English: Khmer Natonal Armed Forces)
FARK	Forces Armées Royales Khmères (English: Royal Khmer Armed Forces)
FUNCINPEC	Front Uni National pour un Cambodge Indépendant, Neutre, Pacifique, et Coopératif (English: National United Front for an Independent, Neutral, Peaceful, and Cooperative Cambodia)
FUNK	Front Uni National du Kampuchea (English: National United Front of Kampuchea)
GNU	Government of National Union
GRUNK	Gouvernement Royal d'Union Nationale du Kampuchea (English: Royal Government of National Union of Kampuchea)
ICP	Indochina Communist Party
KPNLF	Khmer People's National Liberation Front

KPRA/KPRAF	Kampuchean People Revolutionary Army/Kampuchean People Revolutionary Armed Forces (of the PRK)
KPRP	Kampuchean People's Revolutionary Party
KPRP-1980s	Kampuchean People's Revolutionary Party—Post 1979
KRA	Kampuchea Revolutionary Army (of the Khmer Rouge)
KSAFNS	Kampuchea Solidarity Armed Forces for National Salvation
KSFNS	Kampuchea Solidarity Front for National Salvation
NAC	National Army of Cambodia (of the SOC)
NATO	North Atlantic Treaty Organization
NLF	National Liberation Front
NPE	Neutral Political Environment
NPMEC	National Center for Peacekeeping Forces, Mines, and ERW Clearance
PAVN (or VPA)	People's Army of Vietnam (North Vietnamese Army, later the unified army), also known as Vietnamese People's Army
PPA	Paris Peace Accord/Agreement
PRK	People's Republic of Kampuchea
RCAF	Royal Cambodian Armed Forces (Post-1993)
RPG	Rocket-Propelled Grenade
RVN	Republic of Vietnam (South Vietnam)
SNC	Supreme National Council of Cambodia
SOC	State of Cambodia
SOP	Standard/Standing Operating/Operations Procedures
SRSG	Special Representative of the Secretary-General
SRV	Socialist Republic of Vietnam (unified Vietnam)
UNAMIC	United Nations Advance Mission in Cambodia
UNO	United Nations Organization
UNTAC	United Nations Transitional Authority in Cambodia
UXO	Unexploded Ordnance
WPK	Workers' Party of Kampuchea
WWP	Win-Win Policy

1

~∞∞∞~

The Forgotten Front
in a Forgotten War

The rise of the Cambodian left, from which the Khmer Rouge grew, can be traced back to the proliferation of ideas, ideologies, and the rise of the independence movements against the French. Among the movements in the three countries in Indochina, the Vietnamese left was probably the best organized, while the Cambodian left retained only a skeletal structure. The movement in Vietnam organized itself as the Indochina Communist Party (ICP). The name itself seems to encompass all movements in Indochina, and that became a subject of debate throughout its history.

Between 1930 and 1954, a section of the ICP became the founding members of the future Cambodian left. This was created to represent the leftist movement in Cambodia.[1] The establishment of the ICP was spearheaded by the Vietnam communist movement, which sought to unify the effort of the independence movements in Cambodia, Laos, and Vietnam against the French. But this is a highly controversial subject that requires some clarification.

When Pol Pot, the notorious leader of the Khmer Rouge, came to power, he expressed his view that the movement (the ICP and the section responsible for the Cambodian left) was nothing more than a façade for a hidden agenda of Vietnam to absorb all of Indochina after independence.[2] That would become the basis of his anti-Vietnamese ideology, which embodied and came to define what the Khmer Rouge is all about. In fact, in the early days, the Cambodian left had indeed worked under the auspices of the ICP and cooperated closely with the Vietnamese simply because the organizational structure of the Cambodian left was still not very sophisticated.

Nonetheless, there is also a competing view that claimed that the founder of the Vietnamese independence movement, Ho Chi Minh, objected to the label "Indochina" recommended by the COMINTERN in October 1930, during the meeting of the central committee of the Vietnamese Communist Party in Hong Kong.[3] His main concern was that the unification of efforts of all the three countries could not be successful without a strong organizational structure in Cambodia and Laos.[4] Besides, such an overarching organization would only distract the Vietnamese movement from its main goal, which was Vietnamese independence. Despite this objection, however, the party was renamed the Indochina Communist Party during that 1930 meeting.

Then again, the ICP fluctuated between the two extremes: independent Cambodian section vs. unified effort of Cambodia-Laos-Vietnam. First of all, around 1932, after the French authority suppressed a section of the communist network in Cambodia, the ICP sent a letter to its Cambodian counterpart stressing that an independent section of the Cambodian left would endanger all independence movements in Indochina.[5] The ICP reminded its Cambodian comrades once again that the effort must be unified. Nevertheless, the ICP's stance then changed again in 1941. That year, after the death of King Monivong in April, the French installed Prince Sihanouk who was then only 18 years old as king, in the hope that the young king would be much easier to control. However, the French couldn't have been more wrong. This time, the ICP was preoccupied with international affairs that were rapidly changing.

Cambodia suddenly became a battleground for superpower competition. When World War II started, fascist Japan began its expansion into Southeast Asia, chasing out both the French and the British. Thailand, which despised both France and Britain for encroaching on its territory, quickly joined fascist Japan and then invaded Cambodia to take control of Battambang province and a large portion of Siem Reap province. The Japanese plan in Cambodia was to chase the French out of Indochina so that Japan could establish control. But in May–June 1940, the German blitzkrieg rolled through France and the new Vichy government became an ally of the Axis powers. Fascist Japan had to make do with this reality and even though Japan was the de facto power in Cambodia, the French still retained some power over the administration. Behind this façade, the competition for power between the French and the Japanese in Cambodia intensified. Japan even acquiesced in an attempted coup by the right-wing group led by Son Ngoc Thanh. When that coup failed, Japan denied any rumor of support or even involvement. Japan wanted to prioritize the solidarity between the fascist governments and Vichy France over the counterproductive competition in Indochina.[6] Faced with such reality, one had to accept the possibility that the superpowers would try to use any resistance movement they could find to further their interests, and the plan for any genuine independence would simply stall.

When superpowers swamped Indochina, it was unfeasible to try to gain independence by some big movement because there were too many powerful enemies. The ICP took note of these developments. In 1941, when King Sihanouk came to the throne, the ICP changed its stance from that of a unified and overarching structure to one of "interdependence" between independence movements in each country. The "League for the Independence of Vietnam," also known as Viet Minh, was established. As the name implied, this stood in contrast to the overarching nature of the ICP. The Viet Minh also called for the establishment of a similar movement in Cambodia and Laos while there would be only a loose federation of all movements to unify the effort for the independence of Indochina.[7] However, the ICP still observed that any trace of "party structure" in Cambodia was still nonexistent.

It wasn't until the end of World War II that traces of party structure in Cambodia began to appear. Another factor was that French colonialism in Vietnam (Tonkin, Annam, and Cochin China) and the protectorate in Cambodia were partly based on the myth of the "White Men's Superiority" to lull the locales into a sense of fatalism, a sense that resistance would be futile. The Japanese victory over the French and the British during the war actually destroyed that myth. Now the yellow-skinned people could also defeat the white-skinned people. That new belief spelled the end of colonialism in Indochina as it incited broad revolt against the colonial power.[8]

From 1946 to 1954, the struggle for independence against the French intensified and the Cambodian left grew when the ICP recruited the most radical elements of the Cambodian left.[9] The Khmer People's Revolutionary Party (KPRP) was created in June 1951. That was the ultimate authority of the Cambodian left and was led by Tou Samut (a cofounder with Son Ngoc Minh). At that time, Pol Pot (the main actor of the Khmer Rouge, whom we will return to later) was a mere student coming from the suburbs to study in Phnom Penh (the capital city of Cambodia). Other future leaders of the Khmer Rouge were still in school, either in the country or abroad. Members of the KPRP worked closely with the cadres of the Viet Minh, and the Viet Minh also maintained sanctuaries along the Cambodian-Vietnamese border.

Early in 1954, the siege of Dien Bien Phu began. The French hoped to draw the troops of the Vietnamese liberation movement to the isolated fortress along the Laotian-Vietnamese border and then defeat them en masse with superior firepower. But the French miscalculated the determination of the Vietnamese. The French were defeated and surrendered later that year. Soon after the fall of Dien Bien Phu, the Geneva Conference convened in the same year and produced the Geneva Accord that aimed to restore peace in Indochina with separate ceasefire agreements covering the three countries in Indochina: Cambodia, Laos, and Vietnam.

The conference reaffirmed the independence of Cambodia, which Prince Sihanouk had just forced the French to cede one year earlier in 1953. But even more important was the presence or absence of minor liberation movements at the conference. Prince Sihanouk succeeded in preventing the KPRP from participating in the conference, and unlike Laos, the Cambodian left could not secure a safe haven within Cambodia.[10]

Vietnamese forces withdrew from Cambodia after the conference and although they provided shelter for 2,000 of their allies in North Vietnam,[11] some members of the KPRP chose to stay behind in Cambodia. The latter were then faced with the newly independent Cambodian authority. Radical elements like Pol Pot used the concession during the Geneva Conference as proof of Vietnamese betrayal of the Cambodian revolution.[12] Even the officials who were supported by Vietnam after the Khmer Rouge fell still felt resentment about this further into the 1980s. Mosyakov claimed that they resented the fact that Vietnam left them on their own to face the ruling regime.[13]

Despite the call for peace and elections after the Geneva Conference, the specter of war was looming on the horizon as North Vietnam and South Vietnam disagreed over the necessity of an election to decide on the unification of Vietnam. The United States was also obsessed with the domino theory with South Vietnam as the pivotal state. According to that theory, should the domino of South Vietnam fall, so would all the other dominos in Southeast Asia. The American assistance to South Vietnam increased steadily and it culminated in 1965 when the first contingent of U.S. Marines was officially deployed to South Vietnam. The Vietnam War, or the Second Indochina Conflict, had begun.

Such a disturbing and ominous event could not escape the attention of Prince Sihanouk. In an attempt to shield his country from the looming disaster and to contain the war, Prince Sihanouk adhered to a neutrality policy and joined the nonaligned movement. Within the Kingdom of Cambodia, the Prince sought to establish a "corporatist-style" state with himself as the father figure. After independence and even today, Prince Sihanouk has been known as *Samdech Oeuv* (literally, king-father).

In 1955, he abdicated his throne in favor of his father and became head of state, where he thought the real power lay. Prince Sihanouk established the Sangkum Reastr Niyum party (literally, populist society) and won a landslide majority in the 1955 election. The KPRP also participated in the election, as did other minority right-wing parties. On his father's death five years later, Prince Sihanouk reclaimed the throne but kept the title of prince and head of state, as which he was thereafter known. The process of building a harmonious, corporatist state continued. The KPRP then broke down into two parts: one group took refuge in North Vietnam where the authority had appointed them to various official positions; another group stayed behind in Cambodia and went underground. Their prospect for power was bleak. They had no army, no broad popular support, and their public wing of the party was suppressed.

On October 11, 1959, the editor of the *Prachea-tchunn* newspaper ("People" newspaper), Nop Bophan, was shot and killed. Then, the second man in the party, Siv Heng, defected. Because of the treachery of Siv Heng, the second most important person in the KPRP, many leftists were sought out by the authority. The party's secretary general, Tou Samut, disappeared; most likely he was killed along with his two bodyguards.[14] Mosyakov claimed that according to Tep Ken, an ambassador of the People's Republic of Kampuchea (PRK), all party documents were lost in 1962 during a raid in which Tou Samut and his bodyguards were killed.[15]

Siv Heng belonged to the rural wing of the party and therefore had more knowledge about the leftist sympathizers in the countryside than those operating in the city, including Pol Pot and his colleagues.[16] The latter, therefore, were shielded from this attack because they were part of the urban wing. It is also more likely that Pol Pot was spared because he was a minor figure at that time, and Siv Heng had knowledge of only the most important leaders of the party.

As the Vietnam War escalated, Vietnam found more advantage in allying with Prince Sihanouk who was quite critical of the West with his anti-imperialist and anti-American rhetoric. Besides, Prince Sihanouk had real power. As a result, the leftist militants and sympathizers had two choices: either to seek refuge in North Vietnam where they were provided with jobs and settlement, or to stay in Cambodia on their own with no support from the Vietnamese. The leftist party in Cambodia seemed to have no prospect for taking power at that point. They had to wait until the Vietnam War spilled over the border.

THE VIETNAM WAR CROSSED THE BORDER

Although much revered by his people, Prince Sihanouk's role as head of Cambodian politics was a difficult one. This was because his policy of international neutrality was at odds with the escalation of the Vietnam War. Internally, most of the right wing that Prince Sihanouk absorbed began to undermine the leftists. They also pursued a policy of aiding the U.S. effort in Vietnam. Faced with enormous tension at home and a war that was spilling over the border, the issue of the armed forces of the National Liberation Front (NLF) and the Vietnamese People's Army (VPA) taking sanctuary in Cambodia could no longer be ignored. Yet, this issue ran squarely against the neutrality principle.

The decision-making process faced by Prince Sihanouk at that time was probably the most excruciating one. Some people today wrongly portray the prince as making reckless decisions to allow the VPA and the NLF sanctuaries in Cambodia, but he tried to preserve his nation's interest the best way he could. Yet, the Vietnam War seemed too much to handle. The policy of neutrality was meant to avoid dealing with the war directly, while at the same time deflecting antagonism from the actors involved. But as the war intensified in Vietnam, the NLF and the VPA began seeking refuge along the Cambodian-Vietnamese border and the Army of the Republic of Vietnam (ARVN) entered Cambodian territory without permission in 1963. As the war was then also being fought in Cambodian territory, neutrality could no longer be maintained without the use of force.

But to enforce strict neutrality, Cambodia would need to be capable of pushing all foreign troops out of Cambodian territory and that meant the United States/ARVN and the NLF/VPA. The Cambodian military was not strong enough to enforce neutrality against both at the same time. A much easier alternative would be to cooperate with one side against another. Prince Sihanouk's policy fluctuated between two extremes. At one time, he bent his neutrality policy to allow sanctuaries for the NLF/VPA and arms transit through Cambodian ports.[17] As Clymer noted, this was a rational move that could not be taken lightly.[18] Some historians also argue that the prince's decision to acquiesce to the NLF and VPA seeking refuge in Cambodia was also driven by rational calculations.[19] The prince probably saw the United States losing a "people's war" in Vietnam and reasoned that a communist victory would destroy Cambodia should Cambodia remain neutral or support the United States. Moreover, the United States was suspected of giving support to anti-Sihanouk elements. Therefore, helping the NLF/VPA became the most rational policy. It is always good to make alliances with the likely winner.

Prince Sihanouk also tried to achieve neutrality via international conferences, but to no avail. Before the war in Vietnam intensified, in 1962, Prince Sihanouk called for a Geneva Conference to ensure (and probably enforce) the sovereignty and neutrality of Cambodia in an attempt to make sure that Cambodian territory would not be used for war. It was quite a surprise that it was not the NLF/VPA who rejected this plan but it was the Americans who showed reluctance to support the conference. This was mainly because two of America's most important allies, Thailand and South Vietnam, refused to support the prince's initiative.[20] This refusal was perhaps due to the fact that any such conference would surely call for a confirmation of the exact borderline between Cambodia and neighboring countries, a move which Thailand and South Vietnam might not be prepared to embrace.

To make matters worse, on February 5, 1964, planes from the South Vietnamese military attacked a village two kilometers inside Cambodia, killing five people and wounding six, and on March 19, aircrafts as well as ARVN ground troops attack Chantrea village deep in Cambodian territory, killing 17 villagers and wounding 19.[21] In the second incident, American advisors were also on the ground, and the official version of the story was that the soldiers, in pursuing the NLF, were deficient in map reading and accidentally attacked the Cambodian village.

Such excuses would only fuel the rage of Prince Sihanouk who, at that time, was already considering a break in diplomatic relations with the United States amidst many disturbing developments. These included a U.S.-supported coup in Vietnam, the U.S. support of Thailand (Cambodia's arch enemy who had just lost a case at the International Court of Justice to Cambodia with regard to the Preah Vihear temple along the border in 1962), and the anti-Sihanouk broadcast from radio stations originating outside Cambodia by Son Ngoc Thanh, a rightist *Khmer Serei* who sought to undermine the prince. Whether some of these suspicions were accurate or not is irrelevant because of the result that they all added to Prince Sihanouk's suspicion of a secret plot by the United States to overthrow him.

This perception of American intrigue was further exacerbated by the fact that the United States unduly stalled for a conference that the prince had called one year earlier. That conference was adamantly objected to by Thailand and South Vietnam, and the United States followed these two allies and withheld support. The prince was infuriated. To make matters worse for the United States, North Vietnam and China actually agreed there should be such a conference, perhaps just to make the United States and her allies look much worse.

Sensing this problem, the United States finally agreed to the conference, but the United States took too long to decide and China persuaded the prince that the United States had no intention to decide on anything serious at the conference anyway. This appeared to be a very convincing assessment.[22] The United States, in turn, saw this refusal by China and North Vietnam as an opportunity to finally agree to the conference. But then it was too late. On April 26, 1965, a demonstration destroyed parts of the U.S. embassy in Phnom Penh and soon after, Cambodia broke diplomatic relations with the United States.[23]

Taking advantage of such favorable conditions, the Democratic Republic of Vietnam (DRVN), or North Vietnam, took every measure to ensure that no leftist movement in Cambodia created any trouble for the prince's rule. As one of the rational actors, the DRVN needed to favor the stability of Prince Sihanouk over a leftist revolution in Cambodia. The stance that the DRVN took after the Geneva Conference continued, perhaps in greater depth than before. The purge caused by Siv Heng's treachery had already shaken the Cambodian left to its core, and the political and diplomatic circumstances throughout the 1960s further debilitated the original party structure of this leftist movement.

It was amidst this confusion within the party that a small but influential group of new leaders emerged. These leaders would later establish the reign of terror in Cambodia from 1975–79 and bear the name "Khmer Rouge." In fact, the term "Khmer Rouge" started to appear in Prince Sihanouk's speech in the 1960s when he used the term to describe all Cambodian communists. "Khmer" is the Cambodian name of ethnic Cambodian, while "Rouge" is a French word meaning "Red," a popular denomination of all things communist.

Today, people recognize this term more than anything else in the history of Cambodian civil war and they identify it immediately with Pol Pot. But the original term covered all leftists. The name Khmer Rouge stuck with Pol Pot and his inner circle mainly because they were the first of this group to emerge with power from the war. The term also had its counterpart in the name "Khmer Bleu" (Blue Khmer), denoting the right wing.

However, in the 1960s, the Khmer Rouge was an insignificant movement. The Khmer Rouge might mount an occasional attack, but there was simply no prospect for this group to challenge the greatly popular Prince Sihanouk, whom many Cambodians in the country still viewed as "god-king". It was also this immense popularity that made both the Vietnamese and the United States, especially the Vietnamese communists after 1965, wary of any actions that might antagonize the prince. The organization of the Cambodian left suffered in the process.

REFORMED ORGANIZATION: WHAT'S IN A NAME? (AND DATE?)

The treachery of Siv Heng, which led to the death of party leader Tou Samuth, affected only the rural wing of the party because Siv Heng was a member of the rural wing. Pol Pot and his inner circle were able to escape this tragedy and they started to build up a leftist party to their liking. But more importantly, Vietnam seemed to miscalculate when it did not put people whom it could trust in the KPRP during this period. After all, Vietnam persuaded these people to take refuge and assume official positions in Vietnam. Taking this rare opportunity, Pol Pot and his closest confidants took over the KPRP command structure.

This is the entry point of one of the most mysterious, secretive, and controversial episodes of the communist movement in Cambodia. The controversy and confusion is concerned with the founding date of the communist party under Pol Pot, as well as the evolution of the KPRP.

When was the "communist party" in Cambodia established? There were at least three changes related to the name of the party. As we have seen, the KPRP was established in 1951. In the late 1950s, Siv Heng's treachery led to arrests and the disappearance of many members of the KPRP. During this time, Pol Pot returned from France (where he dropped out of school due to his involvement in politics) and worked as a junior member of the KPRP under Tou Samuth. After the upset in the 1955 general election and then again in 1958 where the Sangkum Reastr Niyum party of Prince Sihanouk won a landslide victory, the leftist party was seeking new, alternative policies.

According to one account, 21 members of the KPRP met at a secret location in Phnom Penh to draw up a new charter for a new party named the Worker's Party of Kampuchea (WPK).[24] Chandler claimed that various documents pointed to the fact that the WPK was considered a rival party to the Communist Party of Kampuchea (CPK) created by Pol Pot (see below).

After Tou Samuth disappeared in July 1962, Pol Pot was elected the new general secretary in 1963 in a meeting of no more than 20 senior leaders of the party, convened at the railway station in Phnom Penh. His colleagues, such as Nuon Chea and Ieng Sary, were also appointed to the central committee. About one-third of the 12 posts were occupied by people close to Pol Pot.[25] People such as Keo Meas, who was a veteran of the KPRP and a member of the central committee of the WPK, did not hold any important post. More importantly, with his allies at the helm, Pol Pot changed the direction of the party and had determined that armed insurrection was to be carried out in tandem with political action,[26] a clear break from the KPRP.

Pol Pot was the radical force of the KPRP and he gradually reshaped its ideology to his liking, especially in terms of being blatantly anti-Vietnamese. Mosyakov claims that according to a veteran of the KPRP, upon assuming the position of general secretary in 1963, Pol Pot changed the name from KPRP to the "Communist Party of Kampuchea (CPK)" in an attempt to relinquish all his ties to the ICP and the Vietnamese.[27] However, Chandler concurs with Carney that the KPRP was renamed WPK in 1960, and then the WPK was not renamed until 1966 when the WPK became the CPK.[28]

But one thing is clear. Officially, Pol Pot did not make the existence of the CPK known until 1977, when he publicly announced that the CPK was established on September 30, 1960.[29] Apparently, Pol Pot still considered the date that was identified by some historians as the first congress of the WPK as being, in fact, the founding date of the CPK. In later years, a veteran of the KPRP close to Vietnam, Keo Meas, was forced to confess that the WPK was created as an opposition party to the CPK.[30] Of course, the confession obtained from the tortured cannot be counted as true, but it did tell us what Pol Pot wanted to hear from the people he suspected were plotting against him.

In the middle of this confusion, and unless previously unknown archives are made public, or remaining firsthand witnesses can provide an alternative explanation, this issue of the founding date of the CPK, the existence of the WPK, as well as its relations with the CPK, can only be a matter of speculation. If it is indeed true, as claimed by veterans of the KPRP, that early party documents were lost during the raid that killed Tou Samut in 1962, then the true answers to these questions might be lost forever.

If we are to speculate, it seems that the KPRP was indeed changed to the WPK in 1960. Pol Pot might have been in disagreement, but he could not do anything since he was not strong enough at that time. Perhaps Pol Pot did not like the name WPK because "workers' party" was not as comprehensive as "communist's party," which also included farmers, the main part of the Cambodian revolution. It is therefore a matter of speculation that the WPK was the intermediate organization between the KPRP and the CPK, but Pol Pot needed to choose the founding date of the CPK as 1960 because that was the only time when a new party statute was adopted. If Pol Pot wanted to create the history of a new party, this is the only date that could work.

The choice of this date was very significant. By definition, those who were members before 1960 were not considered members, probably in an attempt to sever all ties and history with former members of the KPRP, and by extension, the ICP and Vietnam. But all of these remained secret until 1977. However, what was important and evident at the time was the fact that Pol Pot immediately changed the stance of the party from political struggle to armed struggle[31] regardless of the low level of popular support they might have enjoyed during the reign of Prince Sihanouk. A revolution that suddenly became an armed insurrection without sufficient political support risked running into sudden disaster, as happened to Che Guevara in Bolivia in 1967.[32] This was because the guerilla, being too weak in the initial stages, would be crushed by government forces. But in Cambodia, things were different, all of which were of significant importance to Pol Pot and his CPK.

ACCIDENTAL GUERILLAS

The first stroke of luck enjoyed by Pol Pot and his friends was that, unbeknownst to Prince Sihanouk, the regime's local administrators in some rural areas were excessively corrupt. Forced land evictions, kidnapping, extortion, and extrajudicial arrests were only some of the most outrageous excesses by some of the local administrators to oppress the people for the benefit of the administrators themselves. Such oppression drew resistance from local "accidental guerillas," a term coined by David Kilcullen to refer to guerilla groups which fight not for some utopian ideology but only to protect themselves from local threats.[33]

One prominent example was the defense minister of the People's Republic of Kampuchea (PRK), Gen. Tea Banh.[34] Gen. Tea Banh's real name was Tea Sangvan and he was first arrested by the local authority for the only reason that he dared to defy them when the village chief wanted to take his sister as mistress. Sangvan, the elder brother of the girl, openly defied the chief and decried his actions as unworthy of a village chief. This infuriated the chief who then charged Sangvan as a communist sympathizer and ordered his execution along with another person whom the chief also hated. Sangvan was the second to be shot but as a twist of fate, the bullet passed through his body and arm, leaving him with only a flesh wound.

After the ordeal, Sangvan escaped into the jungle with other resistance forces and started fighting against the local authority. He then changed his name to Tea Banh, "Banh" being a Khmer word meaning "to shoot," to celebrate his escape from death. He had no intention of deposing Prince Sihanouk, but only wanted to depose of the local authority. However, for the prince, from above, it was simply hard to distinguish between such movements which were genuinely ideology-free and Pol Pot's movement which was based on communist ideology.

Similar revolts suddenly sprung up in the mid-1960s in many places all over the country. Most of these were cases of accidental guerillas, such as the previous case. Most of the time, the leftists knew how to take advantage of the people's grievances. But what exacerbated the problem was the competition between the left-wing politicians and the right-wing politicians in the government under Prince Sihanouk. The most famous of these episodes was the event in 1967 in Samlot, in Battambang province, the place that Pol Pot considered to be the birth of the revolutionary armed struggle in Cambodia.

Even to this day, the province of Battambang is known as the rice bowl of Cambodia and the district of Samlot in particular is known for its fertile land

and high productivity. Between 1965 and 1966, the NLF/VPA sought to buy rice from the farmers to supply their troops. This would threaten the supply of rice needed by the Cambodian government for processing and export. As a neutral government, the Cambodian government needed its own exports. The government then set up "royal cooperative offices" and government officials from the national rice company would go out and compete with the NLF/VPA to buy rice and paddies from the farmers. But the office was not able to meet its purchase targets, and according to some estimates, at least one-fourth of the rice surplus was sold to the NLF/VPA.[35]

In 1967, the government tried to avoid further losses and implemented a new policy aimed at reducing the quantity of rice that was lost to the NLF. During this time, Prince Sihanouk left Cambodia for France for a medical checkup. Prime Minister Lon Nol, who was a former governor of Battambang province, led the operations. "Intervention groups" escorted by soldiers were sent to Battambang and other provinces to make sure that the people would not sell their rice and paddies to the NLF/VPA.[36] Prince Sihanouk had been concerned only about how to prevent the surplus of rice from flowing out of export channels, but the implementers abused their power.

The officials who went out and bought the rice from farmers lowered the price down to only one-third of the market price[37] and certainly lower than the price offered by the NLF/VPA.[38] Even from a rational, free-market perspective, cash-strapped farmers would certainly sell their surpluses to the NLF. But when the intervention groups could not meet their purchase goals, they started to use violence against the people. Just like the case of Tea Sangvan in Koh Kong, anyone resisting the authority was branded as a communist sympathizer and would face the consequences.

Furthermore, the military escorting the intervention groups also seized any piece of land it wanted, and started its own farming activities.[39] Martin lamented that this was simply a series of good decisions that became disastrous due to poor monitoring and continuous confusion.[40]

The story goes like this:[41] Actually, it was Lon Nol who wanted to see those lands filled with orange farms, pepper farms. . . and permitted the soldiers to implement that order. But when the soldiers[42] selected land accordingly, it was seized in an anarchic manner, totally ignoring whether or not those lands had owners. The people who went to protest were either turned away or beaten up. The authority told the people they had no written title to the land and therefore, there was nothing that could prove that they were owners.

That small segment of the military then used the youths from the "Youth of Sangkum Reastr Niyum" (a youth organization established for helping with community works) to work on the newly seized lands. The farmers considered those youths to be the same as the soldiers and attacked them as well as burned down an office of the Youth of Sangkum.[43]

In Phnom Penh, the talented, left-wing Cambodian students from France who agreed to hold cabinet positions under Prince Sihanouk's regime organized a demonstration against the right-wing prime minister. The main leaders of this group were Khieu Samphan, Hou Yuon, and Hu Nim. They were all very famous among the students and the teachers because they themselves were teachers, and Khieu Samphan also had a reputation for teaching poor students without remuneration.[44] On March 11, 1967, Khieu Samphan and other leftists in the regime organized a large demonstration demanding the resignation of Lon Nol. Prince Sihanouk also criticized Lon Nol for the handling of the situation in Samlot. On March 30, two ministers of the Lon Nol government were called to testify before the national assembly.[45]

The left wing was poised to outmaneuver the right wing. But before this could happen, on April 2, a violent uprising took place in Samlot when farmers attacked a military checkpoint, killing two soldiers and taking many weapons with them.[46] Days later, the military responded and killed many villagers as well as burned down many houses, forcing hundreds or even thousands to flee into the jungle and mountains nearby. These tit-for-tat skirmishes between the authority and the farmers continued for weeks, until Prince Sihanouk returned to Cambodia.

These disturbing developments no doubt defeated the purpose of Khieu Samphan's demonstration, if it was supposed to undermine the right wing in a political maneuver without inviting an unnecessary "red flag" response from Prince Sihanouk. After all the trio, Khieu Samphan—Hu Nim—Hou Yuon, comprised of moderate leftists who believed they could work with Prince Sihanouk, while radicals such as Pol Pot tended to favor armed insurrection over peaceful consultation. This was the reason why the trio agreed to work in the government in the first place. Whether or not the activities of the leftists in the city and the rural areas were coordinated was irrelevant. What was more important was that the uprising in Samlot was significant because according to Ben Kiernan, the new members of the CPK, especially Ieng Thirith (wife of Ieng Sary and sister-in-law of Pol Pot), were said to be present at the scene and might be involved with some of those activities as well.[47] One cannot help but think that all leftists were the same.

Prince Sihanouk, who had returned from France on March 9, saw these disturbing developments. He was also handed a detailed report on what had happened, including the misconduct by the local authority and the military. Following this, a small number of local officials were dismissed.[48] Prince Sihanouk tried to calm down the situation and issued a call for the people to come back to their homes. However, many people of Samlot still stayed behind in the jungle until 1975. Lon Nol also resigned from the position of prime minister on April 30, 1967.

Samlot was not the end, far from it. During that period, many other provinces also saw such uprisings, such as in Prey Veng, Kompung Cham, Kompung Thom, and Kampot. But another significant event after Samlot, which is also related to illegal seizure of land, was in the northeastern part of the country, in Rattanakkiri and Mondulkiri, the provinces known for land suitable for rubber plantations. These areas were inhabited by highland tribesmen who had been living on those lands continuously since ancient times. But in the late 1960s, the local authority started forcing the eviction of many people in La Ban Siek district so that the land could be used for rubber plantations.[49] Those who refused were branded communist sympathizers, which then legitimated a violent crackdown from the government. The highland people revolted and even though they did not have weapons to match the firepower of the authorities and the military, they knew the terrain and they used ancient weapons with deadly efficiency, such as traps made of bamboo stakes.

It was probably in the context of these simultaneous revolts, in addition to reports from some local authorities who bent the information to relinquish themselves from responsibilities, that the prince began blaming the left-wing members of his government for inciting the revolt. After all, the demonstration by Khieu Samphan occurred just before the violent uprising in Samlot and other places. Logically, these revolts could not be a mere coincidence: someone on the left must have conspired to undermine the Sangkum Reastr Niyum. On April 22, the prince publicly blamed the leftist moderate trio as the mastermind of Samlot and threatened to bring all of them before a military tribunal. On April 24, Hou Yuon and Khieu Samphan left the capital city and joined the communists in the jungle.[50] Hu Nim would soon follow after attempts to strip him of his parliamentary immunity. Cambodia was on the brink of a new policy shift.

HINDSIGHT ASSESSMENT

With the benefit of hindsight, what were the main factors that caused the situation to deteriorate in this way after 1967? One thing that is important to make clear and on which all historians agree is that Prince Sihanouk never wanted to hurt his people or do anything to offend them. It was his subordinates who were the source of the problem. The local authority did not dare hurt "the prince's people," whom he always called "children" in his corporatist state, because they knew the prince would not tolerate any misconduct. Therefore they changed tactics. Anyone who opposed them would be branded "communist sympathizers," in which case the prince would not object to a crackdown.

But the prince could have sensed this problem early and better distinguished between misconduct of local authorities and uprisings of the communists. The only problem was that when all local authorities reported the same thing about the revolts, it produced the specter of a communist conspiracy. Historians concurred that the people in each of the episodes above did not want to oppose the prince, but they were forced to resort to violence by corrupt local authorities.[51] In most instances, the people were armed with only ancient weapons such as sickles, knives, and axes. . . these were the only things they could improvise from their everyday agricultural tools. However, the unjust crackdown simply drove people away from the villages, making it extremely easy for the communists to enlist recruits.

The people were also faced with a second problem. Pol Pot and his colleagues piggybacked on these revolts to further their own agendas. In and around the areas of the revolts, true communist sympathizers would infiltrate the provincial towns and then clandestinely drop pamphlets denouncing Prince Sihanouk as a traitor or a puppet of the United States.[52] This accusation was both false and completely misleading for everyone except Pol Pot and his branch of the communists. No ordinary people would support what was said in the pamphlets and anyone caught with such pamphlets denouncing the beloved prince would be beaten up by the crowd. The NLF/VPA also would not want to make such offensive comments. The pamphlets were blatantly misleading, since Prince Sihanouk had severed diplomatic ties with the United States since 1965, a status quo that the NLF/VPA wanted to maintain.

However, for Pol Pot, deposing the monarchy in Cambodia had always been his ultimate goal. When he was in power, Pol Pot boasted in the publication of the official history of the party that he was always a staunch antiroyalist and considered Samlot as his personal struggle as well as providing self-sufficiency and autonomy for the CPK.[53]

Pol Pot knew that, at the time, there were still so many NLF/VPA soldiers around that he could not denounce the prince as serving communist Vietnam or his (Pol Pot's) relations with the Vietnamese would be strained prematurely. Therefore, he found it necessary to denounce the prince as a "puppet of the Americans," despite the fact that Cambodia had no diplomatic ties with the United States at the time.

Regardless of who spread the pamphlets, the actions furthered the suspicion of Prince Sihanouk of a communist conspiracy against him. Peaceful demonstrations in the capital city demanding the resignation of the prince's close subordinates and right-wing leaders, followed by the unprecedented violent uprising in Samlot as well as the anti-Sihanouk pamphlets, led to demonstrations in other provinces. For a logical observer, what more is necessary before calling these events a communist conspiracy?

Furthermore, the unhealthy competition and rivalry between the left wing and the right wing in the government prevented any meaningful monitoring activities by the central government on the local officials.

It was perhaps because of these reasons that after receiving a detailed report on the misconduct of local officials in Samlot, the prince condemned Lon Nol. But then, the prince shifted the blame to the left wing, more specifically, the moderate trio of Khieu Samphan, Hu Nim and Hou Yuon.[54] Perhaps this shift was due to the simultaneous developments that seemed to be provoked by the left.

Despite the fact that both the right wing and the left wing had a hand in the deepening crisis, it seemed that in the eyes of Prince Sihanouk, the left wing was to blame. After all, only the left wing organized a violent insurrection to overthrow the prince. This fear was perhaps compounded by the ferocity of the 1968 Tet Offensive in Vietnam. After these two significant events, Prince

Sihanouk began to withdraw support from the NLF/VPA, perhaps due to the fear that the communists were secretly plotting against him, using the Khmer communists while maintaining a friendly rhetoric on the surfaced.

Prince Sihanouk was not the only one suspecting the Khmer communists. We must remember that during this period, even North Vietnam had already lost control over the KPRP and thus, the armed insurrection was not caused by Vietnam but by Pol Pot, and it was difficult for both the prince and North Vietnam to be sure of what was really going on. The NLF/VPA, on their part, were in a dilemma. They might simply ignore the abuse by their Khmer communist comrades, in order to avoid straining relations between the two, but by doing so, they would antagonize Prince Sihanouk.

Then, a policy shift took place. Lon Nol and the right wing turned from villains to victims, the remaining moderate leftists became radicalized and took up arms, and the people who were the true victims suffered all the consequences. Not long afterwards, Lon Nol's position as prime minister was reinstated, along with the normalization of diplomatic relations with the United States. The prince began to move away from the NLF/VPA and toward the United States, despite having severed diplomatic ties since May 3, 1965. After Samlot, rhetoric against the communists increased, while the relations between Cambodia and the United States started to improve.

Diplomatic relations were reestablished on June 11, 1969, and in the last days of July, a letter was sent to invite President Nixon for an official visit to Cambodia. The press was also strictly controlled to avoid antagonizing the Americans.[55] Moreover, the prince also authorized an operation by some elements of the Forces Armées Royales Khmères (FARK—the armed forces under Prince Sihanouk's government) in the province of Rattanakiri in the northeast, to dislodge the NLF/VPA sanctuaries along the border.[56]

Several local battalions were involved in the operation, along with elements of other battalions. But Maj. Dien Diel, commander of the 4th Tactical Group in charge of reserve and support troops, maintained that the NLF/VPA still declined combat with the FARK until after the coup in 1970.[57] The prince also began to publicly decry the NLF/VPA's expansionism, and hinted that Cambodia would not protest if the U.S. Air Force bombed the "known" sanctuaries of the NLF/VPA on the border.[58]

NLF/VPA: TIME TO WORRY. . .

The instability in Cambodia was an ominous sign for the NLF and the VPA. The NLF/VPA could not be indifferent about this because the loss of sanctuaries in Cambodia would prove disastrous for their campaigns. Because they received support from Prince Sihanouk, who was immensely popular, they would not do anything that might alienate the prince. After Samlot, however, this cordial relationship could no longer be maintained. On July 5, 1969, Huynh Tan Phat, prime minister of the newly formed underground communist government, the Provisional Revolutionary Government of the Republic of South Vietnam, paid an official visit to Cambodia to conclude some economic and trade agreements. But the main objective of the visit was an attempt to defuse these disturbing developments. However, the visit failed when Prince Sihanouk later publicly announced that the NLF/VPA was not sincere in its promises.[59]

In retrospect, it is clear that the NLF/VPA actually did not have any intention to destabilize the reign of Prince Sihanouk. On the contrary, they even tried to discourage any movements that sought to destabilize the regime that enabled them (the NLF/VPA) to transit the border and establish sanctuaries. But it also shows that the NLF/VPA, by abandoning the Cambodian left, paradoxically allowed Pol Pot, and the new radicals who were not very well known to the Vietnamese and the ICP, to come to power.

Pol Pot secretly pushed for armed insurrection against the regime, without support from the Vietnamese. However, this seemed to succeed as it coincided with local resistance against the abuse of power by some local authorities. Unbeknownst to the prince, the right wing also plotted to undermine the left wing in the government, which led to the disappearance of Hou Yuon, Hu Nim, and Kheiu Samphan, the moderate leftists in the government. This was the cause of the main break in the relations between the NLF/VPA and Prince Sihanouk and that paved the way for renewed diplomatic relations and the shift of Prince Sihanouk's policy toward the United States.

According to Mosyakov, as the specter of a complete strategic reversal loomed large, the Vietnamese began to look to the remnant of the KPRP, now secretly renamed CPK, to find old allies.[60] They also began to reinsert former veterans of the KPRP, to whom they had given refuge and official positions in North Vietnam in the early years when the NLF/VPA found in Prince Sihanouk a more useful ally than the KPRP. The KPRP was perceived to have too little popular support, compared to Prince Sihanouk. Now, the KPRP was the only viable alternative. However, Pol Pot and his allies had reshaped the KPRP beyond recognition, and the Vietnamese were faced with a difficult choice: undermine Pol Pot and his CPK, or accord support, however temporary, to Pol Pot until victory.[61] The Vietnamese chose the first alternative. While some can call the Tet Offensive a political victory, or even a military one against the United States and South Vietnam, what followed, especially the Phoenix Program,[62] actually debilitated the NLF command structure, as most underground agents were exposed. The Vietnamese needed to push forward to maintain initiatives, and simply could not allow an internal purge to destroy their operations in Cambodia.

A review of the literature shows that at this point, the communist forces in Cambodia were under the leadership of four distinct groups. The first group was the radical group composed of Pol Pot and his allies such as Nuon Chea, Ieng Sary, and Ta Mok. These were the new generation of leaders who emerged after the treachery of Siv Heng destroyed the senior leadership of the KPRP. These people were staunchly anti-Vietnamese and their alliance with the

Vietnamese was only a marriage of convenience. However, violent demonstrations notwithstanding, they were simply too weak to take power without the NLF/VPA.

The second group was comprised of intellectuals who had returned from their study in France, who were moderate, and who believed that they could work with the government of Prince Sihanouk. Hou Yuon, Hu Nim, and Khieu Samphan were the most important members of this group. Most of these had served in the Cabinet as members of the government under Prime Minister Lon Nol, who was staunchly right-wing. During the struggle up until 1975, they served as the popular faces of the regime, masking Pol Pot's real power and intentions. Their reputation also drew mid-level cadres who were mostly school teachers. This would prove fruitful for a movement which tried to convince people to join its cause, mainly because teachers were highly skilled in the art of persuasion. This group was also anti-Vietnamese. However, except for Khieu Samphan, members of this group were quickly liquidated after the Khmer Rouge's "liberation" of Phnom Penh.

The other two groups were veterans of the KPRP. However, the third group consisted of the veterans who chose to stay behind and face purges of the regime in Phnom Penh. They welcomed the Vietnamese, unlike their radical precursors, but they also resented the Vietnamese for leaving them alone to face the regime. These people rejected the leadership of the cofounder Son Ngoc Minh (the other cofounder being Tou Samut who was killed during the Siv Heng treachery). This group survived the purge in 1975 and some of them, such as Sor Phim, became regional commanders (please see next chapter). The veterans of the KPRP in Cambodia were purged, starting in 1977, when they refused to participate in an overt war against Vietnam.

The fourth group also consisted of veterans of the KPRP, but they chose to stay in Vietnam after the Geneva Conference in 1954.[63] These people were trained in Vietnam and were reintroduced back into Cambodia when Prince Sihanouk shifted his position toward supporting the United States. These were moderate leftists who would maintain a moderate foreign policy and a friendly stance toward neighbors such as Vietnam and Thailand. After the Khmer Rouge victory in 1975, they were labeled as Vietnamese allies and were quickly purged following a false invitation to serve in the new government.

In sum, the Khmer Rouge in mid-1969 was a combination of different factions, and it was a rainbow organization with each group vying for power. However, all groups tacitly agreed to a marriage of convenience so that the struggle could be successful. Pol Pot and his radicals stayed behind the scene plotting to take power internally. The trio—Hou Yuon, Hu Nim, and Khieu Samphan—became public faces of the movement. After 1970, they were the main escorts of Prince Sihanouk during the trip across the "liberated zones." The veterans of the KPRP all served as field commanders with little concern for the intrigues of political leadership. Thus, the political wing of the Khmer Rouge consisted of those who believed in the new CPK and were committed to do anything to uphold that view. On the other hand, the veterans of the KPRP worked very well with the NLF/VPA to ensure success for the movement.

Later, it was the radicals who would come to bear the name "Khmer Rouge." Pol Pot was the main leader of this group. In fact, his real name was not even Pol Pot. Pol Pot was born "Saloth Sar" to a wealthy farmer in Prek Sbov district near the Kompung Thom provincial town. He had nine siblings (two sisters), all of whom suffered during the war. Saloth Chhay, one of Sar's brothers, died during a forced evacuation of Phnom Penh in 1975. No one would know that Saloth Sar was Pol Pot until seeing a poster of him on the wall of a cooperative kitchen.[64] This was a far cry from the personality of a boy named Saloth Sar whom everyone described as friendly and nice.

In Cambodia during the 1930s and 1940s, a new western-style education system emphasizing science had just been introduced into schools, and teaching aids were in short supply. Before that, the pagodas were the main educational institutions in Cambodia. When Saloth Sar grew up, he was able to study in Phnom Penh because one of his relatives named Meak was a concubine to King Sisowath Minivong.

After a period in a pagoda in Phnom Penh (Wat Botum Vatey), with the help of Meak, Sar could actually afford to enroll in a catholic school, Ecole Miche. This period of Saloth Sar's life is a matter of mystery and debate. Chandler mentioned that Pol Pot claimed he had stayed at the pagoda for four years while his relative said Sar spent only one year at the pagoda.[65] Chandler maintained that Saloth Sar was born in 1929 but that would mean he is younger than his quiet rival Nuon Chea who was born in 1927. The elder Nuon Chea would be a problem for the rise of the younger Pol Pot and Nuon Chea was described as a "personal friend" by Le Duan, a high-ranking Vietnamese communist.[66] Accordingly, Chandler speculated that Pol Pot twisted his biography to show that he was actually older than Nuon Chea, and was thus fit for command. Later, Nuon Chea would be transformed from being a veteran of the KPRP to a radical in Pol Pot's inner circle.

Sar's record at school was unremarkable. However, in 1949, he was part of the first batch of 100 students to receive a scholarship to study in France. Chandler speculated that perhaps Sar received that scholarship as a political favor from the Democratic Party which was in power at the time. In 1949, Ieng Sary, a future close associate of Pol Pot, also went to study in France.

Born to a Cambodian-Vietnamese farmer in South Vietnam, Ieng Sary's real name was Kim Trang. He went to live in Prey Veng province in Cambodia after his father's death and changed his name to Ieng Sary. Sary attended the prestigious Lycée Sisowath, an elite high school in Cambodia, which many future prime ministers and statesmen as well as other members of the royal family attended. He later met his wife there, Khiev Thirith (who later changed her name to Ieng Thirith). Khiev Thirith's sister was Khiev Ponnary, who was the first female to pass the exam for BAC II (high school diploma). She later married Saloth Sar in 1956; he was eight years younger than her. This effectively made Ieng Sary a relative of Pol Pot. Khiev Ponnary was an intellectual in Khmer literature and according to Chandler, she was probably behind all the sophisticated terminology, catchphrases, and proverbs used under Democratic Kampuchea.[67] As will be shown in the next chapter, that fact probably explains why the Khmer Rouge developed a sophisticated ideology, despite the almost total absence of intellectuals in its rank and file.

Sar continued his unremarkable academic career in France and came back without a degree. But Chandler noted that during his stay in France, Saloth Sar might have travelled to Yugoslavia (staying in Zagreb), during a time when Yugoslavia tried to dissociate itself from the Soviet Union.[68] With a drought and an apparent threat of Soviet intervention, Yugoslavia mobilized its people to defend the country, during the time of Sar's visit. Chandler speculated that this gave the young Saloth Sar ideas about mass mobilization which disastrously turned into a forced evacuation of Phnom Penh in 1975, and later the forced labor of all the people under his reign of terror.[69] Saloth Sar came back from France in 1957 and became a member of the KPRP, perhaps because he had been associated with communist students in France.[70] He immediately participated in the underground activities of the KPRP.

THE COUP OF MARCH 18, 1970: NEW LIFE FOR THE KHMER ROUGE!

Even after this improvement in command and control, the Khmer Rouge in 1969 was still much the same as what it had been before: a small organization with little popular support that could do nothing beyond occasional protests that turned violent. According to Nuon Chea, before 1970, only two regions maintained some trace of party structure: the southwest and the Kompung Chhnang area, although the eastern area could maintain some party structure because there were cadres such as Sor Phim in the area.[71]

The Khmer Rouge needed to wait until the sudden fortune that was provided by the coup of 1970. On August 14, 1969, a new "National Salvation" government, with the right-wing Lon Nol as prime minister, was established by Prince Sihanouk, perhaps as a sign of changing policy. The situation was still dire when Prince Sihanouk deployed a large formation of the FARK to Rattanakiri, Mondulkiri, Stung Treng, and Kratie in order to chase the Khmer Rouge forces and the NLF/VPA out of their border sanctuaries. The operations were also in response to the unrest which was suspected as having been motivated by communist sympathizers.

At that time, the Khmer Rouge was not much of a force to be reckoned with, although the NLF/VPA was still a formidable force. Nevertheless, the NLF/VPA declined most of the combat[72] and, according to a former FARK commander, most of the fighting was between FARK and the dissidents of the Khmer Loeu (highland people).[73] These Khmer Loeu tribesmen were known for their unquestioned loyalty and deadly efficiency in combat. When the Khmer Rouge came to power, some of them were chosen as Pol Pot's personal bodyguards, probably because Pol Pot had lived in the areas (Northeast) in the early 1960s.

It can be argued that the NLF/VPA was stunned by Prince Sihanouk's new stance. The NLF/VPA then chose a very careful balancing act. On the one hand, they now began to send in the old veterans of the KPRP and began to take more interest in the functioning of the KPRP which, unbeknownst to them, had already been renamed by Pol Pot since 1960 as the Communist Party of Kampuchea.[74] On the other hand, the NLF/VPA still tried not to do anything that might enrage the prince further. They probably hoped that the prince might change his mind later. This is evidenced by an attempted public relations campaign through the official visit of Huynh Tan Phat, prime minister of the Provisional Revolutionary Government of the Republic of South Vietnam in 1969. On the ground, the NLF/VPA also declined combat with the FARK. As a result, the Khmer Rouge was in need of assistance, but this assistance was nowhere to be found. But while most of the FARK was busy at the border, a small segment of the FARK in the capital was busy with something quite different.

After the 28th National Congress[75] on December 27, 1969, the cabinet office of Prince Sihanouk announced that the prince would go to France for a medical checkup. Accordingly, on January 6, the prince left Cambodia. On March 8, 1970, there were simultaneous demonstrations involving people in many districts of Svay Rieng province in protest against the NLF/VPA presence.[76] These events were not surprising considering that the prince had been publicly talking about the issue for quite some time and had already sought to reestablish diplomatic relations with the United States, which had been severed in 1965. This new stance was an attempt to counter the apparent threat from the NLF/VPA, perhaps after witnessing the ferocity of the Tet Offensive one year earlier.

On March 11, following the genuine demonstration in Svay Rieng, another demonstration was organized by the authority in Phnom Penh, aimed at denouncing the NLF/VPA presence in Cambodia.[77] During the event, the embassy of the DRVN (North Vietnam) and the Provisional Revolutionary Government of the Republic of South Vietnam were sacked, quite similar to what happened to the U.S. Embassy in 1965. However, Prince Sihanouk issued a condemnation of the demonstration, calling it "pro-American."[78]

On March 16, there was another demonstration in front of the national assembly accusing many people of allowing the NLF/VPA sanctuaries in Cambodia. Soon, some opportunists in the national assembly started criticizing many people in the government on the same ground.[79] Accusations then spilled over to Prince Sihanouk; various elements of the right wing accused the prince of being guilty of providing sanctuaries for the NLF/VPA, at which point the loudspeaker in front of the assembly went dead and the discussions were then confined within the closed door of the national assembly.[80]

There was a reason why accusations against Prince Sihanouk could not be uttered: the prince was still immensely popular. All those previous demonstrations against the NLF/VPA sanctuaries in Cambodia never mentioned Prince Sihanouk. On the contrary, when a member of the opportunist right wing tried to piggyback on those demonstrations by linking the name of the prince to the presence of the NLF/VPA on Cambodian soil, he was beaten up by the angry crowd and was only saved by intervention from the police.[81] The crowd might have even stormed the national assembly had the accusations against Prince Sihanouk continued publicly.

The national assembly continued with fiery debates for days and then the situation started to deteriorate. Soldiers began to take up positions on the night of March 16 and 17. Amidst the upheaval, Prince Sihanouk continued his official visit to Moscow. There were at least three accounts of what happened next.

Prince Sihanouk accused the Central Intelligence Agency (CIA) of being the mastermind behind the coup by supporting Lon Nol and Prince Sisowath Sirimatak in the coup. In his book published in 1972, *My War with the CIA*,[82] Prince Sihanouk traced the American covert intervention in Cambodia as well as the strategic bombing campaign in Cambodia that began in the mid-1960s. The coup, the prince argued, was simply an extension of such an interventionist policy.

The second account was given by Ros Chantraboth, who was a close friend of Lon Non, brother of Lon Nol, through personal interviews with Lon Non. According to him, even on the night of March 17, the two masterminds of the impending coup, Lon Nol and Prince Sisowath Sirimatak, were still hesitant. It was Lon Non who pushed for the coup through a ruse: he told Lon Nol that Sirimatak was ready to go while waiting for a green light from Lon Nol and in turn, he told Sirimatak that Lon Nol was ready.[83] Despite being a right-wing politician, Lon Nol was also known for his staunch support of Prince Sihanouk. Rumor had it that Prince Sisowath Sirimatak, descendant of the Sisowath lineage of the Cambodian monarchy, was not very happy with Prince Norodom Sihanouk's reign. Prince Sihanouk came from the Norodom lineage of the monarchy.[84]

According to the third account, the coup was engineered by some opportunistic right-wing politicians who took advantage of the anti-Vietnamese fervor following the sacking of their embassies. They also capitalized on Lon Nol's reluctance to sever his ties with the prince.[85] Some historians, such as Meyer, also concur that groups of right-wing politicians, especially in the national assembly, had a role to play in the coup.[86] The reason they chose Lon Nol was perhaps because he was popular in the military and he was also the prime minister at the time.[87]

On March 18, 1970, the legislature voted to remove Prince Sihanouk from power. The national assembly made this decision behind closed doors while paratroopers took up position around the national assembly.[88] From then on, things started to go downhill very quickly.

The coup cut short the official visit of Prince Sihanouk in Moscow. Prince Sihanouk then flew to Beijing where he held a secret meeting with Pham Van Dong (premier of the DRVN) and Zhou Enlai (premier of China) on March 21, 1970.[89] The main agenda of the meeting was probably a show of support for the prince to continue the fight in Cambodia against the coup plotters.

On March 23, Prince Sihanouk broadcast a message from Beijing calling for his "children" (denoting the Cambodian population) to go to the jungle and join the Marquis (a French term originated from the World War II resistance movement in France). The Government of National Union (GNU) was proclaimed.

In his book, *My War with the CIA*, the prince asserted that the idea of the GNU occurred to him while on a plane from Moscow to Beijing. Three days after the March, 23 broadcast, the prince maintained that he received support from the moderate leftist trio, whom he called "three of our outstanding intellectuals."[90] These three people were no other than Khieu Samphan, Hou Yuon, and Hu Nim, whom the prince had threatened to arrest following charges related to the troubles in Samlot in 1967. It was that event that had forced them into the jungle in the first place.

Now, both found in each other what they did not possess on their own. The moderate leftist trio needed the prince to gain legitimacy internally and externally. With the prince's name, they would be able to receive more outside aid as well as an unwavering source of recruits. They immediately agreed to proceed under the guidance of Prince Sihanouk. Similarly, Prince Sihanouk also needed his former rivals. His GNU could only be a government-in-exile because it remained in Beijing. Organizing his own armed forces might take a longer time. To many, the prince's past history with the trio was irrelevant, now that the rightists had shown their true character. Therefore, the prince saw the trio as more indispensable than ever. Besides, this trio already had a structure of armed forces on the ground. Unbeknownst to them, Pol Pot pulled all the strings.

On May 5, 1970, the combination of the GNU in China and the leftists in Cambodia produced what was known as the Royal Government of National Union of Kampuchea, more commonly known by its French version as Gouvernement Royal d'Union Nationale du Kampuchea or GRUNK. This was not a government-in-exile, but a full-fledged government with "liberated areas" in Cambodia, although the prince remained in Beijing. Prince Sihanouk was the head of state of the GRUNK, his close confidant Penn Nuth[91] was the prime minister, Khieu Samphan was deputy prime minister, minister of defense, commander-in-chief of the GRUNK armed forces (known in its casual name "*korng torp samdech oeuv*" or "armed forces of King-Father"), Hou Yuon was minister of cooperative, and Hu Nim was minister of propaganda.

In essence, the GRUNK was designed as a two-faced government from the start—the political wing stayed in Beijing while the military wing was in Cambodia, where the real military power lay. Sensing this treachery, Prince Sihanouk later asked repeatedly to come and stay in the liberated area, but his requests were denied. The reason was simple: although Khieu Samphan appeared to control the military, it was in fact Pol Pot who controlled it. The CPK was pulling the string behind the GRUNK's back. Finally, it was only after he threatened to resign that the prince was allowed to visit the liberated area, but even so, he was closely spied upon.[92]

When the Khmer Rouge came to many villages in 1968–70, what it found was an existing guerilla structure in all of those villages, most of them accidental guerillas. After the formation of the GRUNK with Prince Sihanouk at the head, however, scores of new recruits volunteered for the fight. All the Khmer Rouge then needed to do was to distribute weapons and organize an administration system.

From the time of the coup to the debacle of Operation Chenla II, which we will see below, the main activity of the Khmer Rouge was recruitment. The main recruitment pool consisted of three major groups: people oppressed by the local authority, supporters of Prince Sihanouk who decided to fight to return the prince to power, and those who were enraged by the American strategic bombing. In most instances, however, the Khmer Rouge used different ways both to entice and coerce people to join them.

For example, at the beginning, the major propaganda tool was a chant by the demonstrators: "Hail Samdech Oeuv,[93] I do not care if you do not go but I have already gone [to join the Marquis]."[94] All the chants would begin with "Samdech Oeuv," which signified the fact that the Khmer Rouge sought to exploit the prince's popularity to the fullest extent possible. However, after a while, the chant did not easily attract bystanders. After all, the chant seemed optional, "I don't care if you go." In war, where death can come at any time and in any place, many people will elect not to fight if they have the choice.

Probably in response to slow recruitment and to an increase in the number of potential recruits in the second category as well as people who were indifferent, the chant of the Khmer Rouge was transformed into a much more coercive one: "Hail Samdech Oeuv, whoever does not go [to join the Marquis], his/her house will be burned to ashes!" and "Hail Samdech Oeuv, whoever does not go [to join the Marquis] will be smashed to pieces!"[95] Following this coercive campaign, the villages became unsafe for anyone hostile to the Khmer Rouge and even bystanders could not stay. The local authority then fled to the provincial towns.

THE KHMER ROUGE COMES OF AGE

One of the misconceptions and misleading concepts about the history of the Khmer Rouge was the implicit assumption that the Khmer Rouge was immediately strong after 1970 and that the Khmer Republic was doomed from the start. It is true that the Khmer Rouge could tap into the large pool of recruits after the 1970 coup and that its use of Prince Sihanouk's reputation was very helpful internally and externally. Yet, one important question remained: how could these new recruits challenge the experienced Forces Armées Nationales Khmères[96] (FANK soldiers, formerly FARK under Prince Sihanouk)?

It was true that after the coup, new recruits started flowing in. Immediately after the coup, there were numerous demonstrations in different provinces demanding the return of Prince Sihanouk. In many places, people were told the prince had arrived and they all went to receive the prince, but nothing happened.[97] In most of the demonstrations, the newly formed FANK opened fire on the demonstrators, killing many people and wounding scores of others. Those demonstrators then went into hiding in the woods or jungle near their villages, fearing reprisal from soldiers who went into the villages to pursue the demonstrators. By then, in many villages, those who were outlawed by the Khmer Republic began to act as guerillas, and they received support from their families who remained inside the villages.[98]

At least in the beginning, the FANK could also tap into the minority urban youth who were antiroyalist, until excessive corruption destroyed them later.[99] Furthermore, the Khmer Republic also received the support of some Khmer Krom elements from South Vietnam and some of these were the best units. Khmer Krom was a name given to inhabitants of Cochin China, which the French granted to the newly established South Vietnam in 1949. The land was known in Khmer as "Kampuchea Krom" or Lower Cambodia. Kampuchea Krom had always been the subject of antagonism for many extremists in Cambodia toward Vietnam. In fact, the Khmer Rouge used Kampuchea Krom as a propaganda tool and as proof that Vietnam tried to "swallow Cambodia." But in 1970, the Khmer Republic considered the Khmer Rouge a more serious problem than South Vietnam, which was also fighting against communism, and which was also supported by the United States. The Khmer Republic received weaponry as well as units of the Khmer Krom fighters.[100] Some units were solely composed of the Khmer Krom and in some units, the Khmer Krom formed entire battalions.

But before the Khmer Republic could take advantage of this assistance, the NLF/VPA took the initiative. Under the pretext of helping Prince Sihanouk to take back power, the NLF/VPA preempted the situation, and sent their troops in overt operations on Cambodian soil. However, before the NLF/VPA could conduct large-scale operations, the United States and South Vietnam, in turn, preempted the NLF/VPA in a series of operations known as the "Cambodian Incursion" from May 1, 1970 to June 30, 1970. This was a series of 13 search-and-destroy operations in Cambodian territory to eliminate the NLF/VPA sanctuaries.[101] The operation was also meant to be a large-scale operation to root out the NLF/VPA in order to buy the FANK some time to prepare itself for the coming war.[102]

But the result was disastrous. The United States and the ARVN never remained in the occupied area, and their operations actually pushed the NLF/VPA across the Mekong River, overrunning most of the Cambodian provinces, which the Khmer Republic never recovered.[103] By the end of 1970, the Khmer Republic controlled less than 50 percent of the entire territory. The NLF/VPA crossed the Mekong River and overran all remote areas as well as provincial towns in the northeast. The close proximity of this area to North Vietnam and Laos made it the most difficult area for the Khmer Republic to contest. The Khmer Republic controlled only a handful of provincial towns, and some major national roads were also interrupted. In 1970, the Kompung Thom provincial

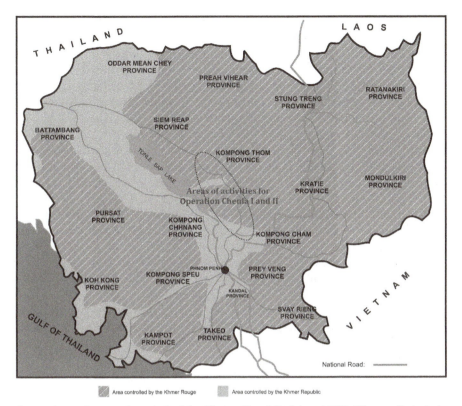

Approximated areas of control of the Khmer Republic (circa 1972). The small circle in the middle was the area of activities for Operation Chenla II of the FANK that ended in disaster. (Boraden Nhem)

town was cut off from land traffic and the Mekong River remained the only connection between Kompung Thom and the capital city. National Road number 6 between Kompung Cham and Kompung Thom was controlled by communist forces, especially the NLF/VPA bases at rubber plantations.

The first sweep by the NLF/VPA also forced the Khmer Republic from most of the rice-growing areas necessary to sustain the regime. At the same time, fresh recruits, new Khmer Krom units, and quantities of ammunition and weapons also arrived as part of American aid to the Khmer Republic.[104] The FANK general staff had determined that the time was ripe for an offensive. The first strategic objective was to open National Road 6 from Kompung Cham provincial town to Kompung Thom provincial town. Operation Chenla I was launched in late August 1970. The objective was to capture and consolidate the areas near Kompung Cham provincial town, from the district of Skoun to the district of Kompung Thmar (which is halfway between Kompung Cham and Kompung Thom). The FANK was considered too weak to hold territory beyond this point.

At the same time, this was puzzling because apart from the large scale of this operation, the FANK also conducted small-scale operations in other areas, thus reducing the forces that the FANK could muster to ensure complete victory of Chenla I.[105] This false sense of security was further heightened by the fact that the NLF/VPA still declined combat.[106] Maj. Dien Del who commanded one of the units during the operations observed that none of the units encountered any fixed positions that the NLF/VPA would defend. Their main bases of operation were well fortified and were located in the Chup rubber plantation and the Chamkar Andong plantation. Chenla I divided the forces into two groups, the first one fighting from Skoun, and the second group clearing National Road 7. By late 1970, Operation Chenla I had achieved its objectives and despite not being able to neutralize the NLF/VPA's sanctuaries in the rubber plantations, it ensured that the FANK could now resettle some of the refugees, as well as set up militias and self-defense forces in many areas under their control.

Then on the night of January 21–22, 1971, a group of perhaps 100 NLF/VPA commandos organized a fierce raid and attacked the Pochentong airport in Phnom Penh, destroying almost all of the military aircrafts at the air force base adjacent to the civilian airport.[107] Some of the units in the Chenla operation were transported back to Phnom Penh to respond to the new contingency. On February 8, Lon Nol was grilled in the parliament over the attack and suffered a stroke that night which left him partially paralyzed.[108] He was immediately evacuated for hospitalization in Hawaii. At this point, Operation Chenla I was de facto at an end. There were simply not enough forces to deal with the NLF/VPA in Chamkar Andong and the Chup plantation.[109]

When Lon Nol returned on April 12, 1971, he sought to regain the initiative lost during the commando attack in early 1971. Operation Chenla II was drawn up. However, the decision was a purely political one, made over the objection of the FANK general staff. Lon Nol wanted to upgrade the objective of the original Chenla I plan to also include the clearance of the road from Kompung Thmar district to Kompung Thom provincial town. The FANK general staff argued that the column was understrength and was not ready to stretch as far as Kompung Thom. Maj. Dien Del objected to the plan on the ground that it would stretch the forces too thinly, while the primary objective should be the Chamkar Andong and the Chup rubber plantation, which up to that point had not been touched. A long line of the FANK column could become easy prey for the NLF/VPA. The suggestion went unheeded and Maj. Dien Del left command for a staff course.

But there was a political reason why Lon Nol decided to carry out such a daring operation. The first reason was that Lon Nol wanted to reverse the drop in morale after Prince Sihanouk joined with the Khmer Rouge. He also wanted to mobilize the whole country for war in his concept of "mobilisation générale."[110] But according to Dien Del, the operation was also motivated by the visit of Prince Sirimatak in the United States, probably to request more aid.[111]

The success of Chenla II would certainly prove to the Americans that invest-ment in the Khmer Republic would return large yields. And as the final deci-sion fell under Lon Nol, on August 21, 1971, Operation Chenla II was launched.

The initial phase of the operation was successful and the FANK units linked with each other on October 25, 1971, and phase 1 of the operation, which was the offensive part, ended. Now it was a matter of defending and consolidating the territory. Barely hours into the second stage on October 26–27, 1971, the NLF/VPA launched their offensive from the Chamkar Andong plantation, sur-rounding the columns at Rumlong, and annihilated this formation.[112] This ef-fectively cut the FANK formation into two parts. What happened next was a full rout of all the FANK units involved in the operation. There were no clear statistics concerning losses, but Sak Sutsakhan put the number at 10 battalions of personnel lost, plus an additional battalion worth of armored vehicles.[113] Most of the best units of the FANK, especially the Khmer Krom units, were annihilated or routed during this debacle.[114]

Years later, Pol Pot wrote in the official history of the party that Opera-tion Chenla II was singlehandedly smashed by the Khmer Rouge forces.[115] This was not supported by facts, however. Although the Khmer Rouge had a large pool of recruits, most of their soldiers were poorly trained given the time constraints. It was also doubtful if they had training camps large enough, or enough instructors, to train a force big enough and capable enough to annihi-late the best units of the FANK (formerly FARK). Even the use of Vietnamese instructors from the NLF/VPA appeared to be unlikely due to language prob-lems, and again, personnel shortages. Interviews with former commanders of the FANK also reveal that they encountered skilled Vietnamese units, not the Khmer Rouge. Diel Del claimed that even in small attacks before 1973, the rockets (used for indirect fire such as mortars) that were used were Russian-made, indicating that the NLF/VPA were the users.[116] After 1973, he claimed, the rockets were Chinese-made, indicating that the Khmer Rouge had now mastered the battlefield. Unfortunately, there was no photographic evidence remaining to back up the claim.

The Khmer Republic was in tatters after Chenla II, and the strategy from 1972 to 1975 was purely defensive. Many other initiatives were later taken, but none rivaled the size of the Chenla II operation. The main problem was low morale and insufficient personnel. Corruption amidst the deteriorating military situation was also a debilitating problem for the Khmer Republic. Dien Del claimed that in 1973 he proposed to create an army composed of five remaining divisions, or a bare minimum of three divisions, to be reserved exclusively for offensive operations in an attempt to take back the initiative. However, the general staff refused and maintained those forces in static de-fense of insignificant positions, although positions that offered commercial benefits.[117] In another case, Ros Chantrabot maintained that any commander of the army had to "pay" the air force regularly; otherwise they would not receive close air support in times of need.[118]

The year 1973 finally came. The Paris Peace Accord was signed between the United States, South Vietnam, North Vietnam, and the Provisional Revolutionary Government of South Vietnam. The negotiation began in 1968 but had become stalled since then. In 1972, U.S. combat troops were withdrawing from South Vietnam, and the NLF/VPA started to conduct offensive operations and began to occupy territory. The NLF/VPA now no longer needed sanctuaries, rather, they needed to get out and fight. However, the American strategic bombing campaign hindered the final push of the NLF/VPA by causing mass casualties in the units that were fighting against the ARVN.[119]

In 1973, the DRVN, or North Vietnam, finally agreed to the peace accord which essentially stipulated that all parties were to cease hostilities and wait for the future election to decide the fate of Vietnam. The DRVN, of course, already maintained the upper hand militarily. The United States, on its part, no longer had any ground troops in Vietnam by the end of 1972, except for some advisors. The United States supported the peace accord only to be able to portray itself as a responsible ally who would not leave without ensuring its ally—South Vietnam—at least received a guarantee of peace.

In 1972, the NLF/VPA withdrew most of their forces from the sanctuaries in preparation for the final push to Saigon, and by 1973, their main concern was fighting with the ARVN openly. The NLF/VPA no longer needed sanctuaries in Cambodia because after 1973, there would be no more American bombers or ground troops to worry about. Gen. Giap's final stage of the People's War had begun.[120]

Journey in the Khmer Rouge–controlled zone, 1973. (©Documentation Center of Cambodia. Used by permission.)

The years 1972–73 were, therefore, the best time for the Khmer Rouge to mature. The Khmer Republic was on the defensive, the United States had already retreated, and the NLF/VPA was busy fighting in South Vietnam. The Khmer Rouge had already spent at least two years building its ranks and files and establishing a new communist system in the countryside. The Khmer Republic would soon meet its fate.

BEHIND ENEMY LINES

Immediately after the coup in 1970, many people all over the country came out in demonstrations to support the deposed prince. These demonstrations were met with violent crackdowns when the FANK used armored personnel carriers to crush the demonstrators. The soldiers of the Khmer Republic simply sprayed fire into the crowd, killing many people. In some accounts, hundreds of people were killed at one time.[121] Some of the demonstrators who survived did not immediately return to their homes. Instead, they had to flee into the woods near their villages.[122] But because the families of these runaway demonstrators were still in the villages, they helped their relatives, despite threats from the regime.[123]

Soon after, members of the Khmer Rouge came into these locales and recruited these youths and runaways who eagerly joined the Khmer Rouge, hoping to fight and bring Prince Sihanouk back to power.[124] The organization was designed and based on Chinese and Vietnamese guerilla units. The young people who ran away would now operate from out of their respective villages. They operated as "armed propaganda units," meaning that they had a dual mission—to educate people about their cause while retaining the ability to fight, should the situation demand it. The "educators" required little training and all they needed to do was to go from hamlet to hamlet singing the revolutionary songs dictated by the communists, along with some catchphrases and slogans.[125]

Those who distinguished themselves in working for the party would be promoted to *korng chhlorb* for their villages, meaning guerilla units, and now they had the right to own a gun, as well as other weapons that they had seized from the enemy. The mission of the *korng chhlorb* was to defend the villages. Gradually, the local authority of the Khmer Republic no longer dared to stay in those villages. The Khmer Rouge also established its own administration because the local authority of the Khmer Republic had already fled to the provincial towns. Each village also had its own "messenger" or "courier" who was given a bicycle for communication. If they needed to spread the word about the arrival of the FANK, this messenger would use the bike for fast communication. Many of those who went into the Khmer Rouge areas during that time always confirmed this mode of transportation.[126]

All these military units were under the command of a "committee" consisting of three distinct positions. The first position was the chief of the locale (held by one person), the second was the deputy chief (also held by one person), and the third was the member (which might be held by more than one person, each responsible for different areas). Sometimes, these committees were to be augmented with a political commissar appointed by the CPK. We will discuss this structure in detail below. But before we proceed, it is necessary to understand the Cambodian administration system first.

In Cambodia before the war, the smallest level of the territorial administration was the *phoum* (hamlet); the other levels were the *khum* (village), the *srok* (district), and the province. Cambodia at the time did not have any administrative unit above the province. Only the armed forces could create a "military region" which encompassed several provinces. The Khmer Rouge followed the existing administration system, but made two modifications. First of all, the province would be renamed "Region" followed by a one, two or sometimes three-digit number that was determined randomly. For example, most of Prey Veng was renamed Region 20 and Svay Rieng was renamed Region 23.

The second modification was the Zone. Before Democratic Kampuchea, a "zone" that encompassed many provinces existed only in the military domain under the form of "military region." The Khmer Republic also had zones under civilian administration, but they were all subservient to the military forces.[127] However, the Khmer Rouge also elevated the civilian administration to the zone level and then the party secretary was in charge of both the military and civilian administration in that zone.

The inner workings of the Khmer Rouge's civil-military administration could be discerned in a rare document from an alleged spy of the Khmer Republic, who had travelled deep into the Khmer Rouge liberated areas between 1972 and 1973.[128] It must have been a once-in-a-lifetime experience.

When the communist forces overran most of Cambodia after the 1970 coup, there was no more free movement between the capital city and the countryside. Scores of refugees from the American bombing campaign came into the city, but those who ran from the city to the countryside were carefully vetted because the only acceptable purpose for travel to the countryside was to join the GRUNK in order to return Prince Sihanouk to power. Without a proper letter of introduction from some party branch in the city, those who arrived from the city would be arrested.

This was the reason why, when going into the Khmer Rouge's sanctuary in 1972, Ith Sarin and his friends needed to be accompanied by an underground "political commissar" of the underground communist network in the capital. Sarin went to the countryside under the pretext of joining the revolution. Upon his entry into a Khmer Rouge–controlled area, he was received by the militiamen of the village. At that time, the village was under the control of a "chief of the front," essentially working as the chief of the village. In some new village, or a village that was not very close to the CPK, a political commissar was also appointed to work alongside the chief of the front.

Those who are not familiar with the Soviet system might not be aware of the importance of this position, the "political commissar." The political commissar was a very particular title and performed a unique function. During the October Revolution in Tsarist Russia in 1917, Lenin counted on desertion and mutiny within the Russian army to weaken and then overthrow the Tsar.[129] When the new communist party came to power, however, it had to make do with the military apparatus that had propelled it to power. In order to control these defectors, the party decided to establish a new position called "political commissar" which had a distinct rank separate from normal military personnel and also had a different career path.[130] It was specifically designed to ensure the loyalty of those who used to work under the Tsar. These political commissars also had the authority to cosign all military orders of the military commanders.[131]

When the system evolved in China, Vietnam, and other socialist countries however, the political commissar did not have the authority to cosign orders, rather, the political commissar would become the "messenger" of the party. The military commander, then, needed to listen to the political commissars, because these would be the ones who knew more about what the party wanted from the military. In the Cambodian system, in some cases, the commissar might come down to the company level. They were the official bearers of messages from the party, and they normally knew more than the military commanders did. Their main job was to keep the soldiers in line and to maintain party discipline.

Ith Sarin's account of the political commissar during his trip to the area controlled by the Khmer Rouge fitted this description. In one instance, Sarin met with a company commander (called *korng rooy* or "hundred-men unit") who mistook him for a party core member and went on and on about how Prince Sihanouk could not be allowed into the liberated zone, otherwise the CPK would be ruined. The company commander was then called into a private place by the political commissar. After this conversation, the company commander returned and never spoke about anything with Sarin again.

According to Sarin's observations, the farmers believed that when the revolutionary soldiers captured Phnom Penh, Prince Sihanouk would return to power. The Khmer Rouge also worked very hard to nurture this belief in order to recruit soldiers. The Communist Party of Kampuchea was not known to the average farmer, and the Khmer Rouge referred to the CPK simply as *Angkar* (literally translated from Khmer as "the organization"). Only full-fledged members ("core" members) would know the existence of the CPK. The educational materials for the new members also differed from those of the core members. For those who were new members, only standard materials were provided. The core members, on the other hand, had access to much more elaborate communist theory, one of which denounced the monarchy, something that directly touched upon Prince Sihanouk's stature. Moreover, each cadre did not reveal their real names. They were known only by their "revolutionary name" which was only one syllable, and sometimes it was a number.

Sarin was a very skilled analyst. During his brief stay with the Khmer Rouge, he observed that after the Chenla II debacle, the Khmer Rouge formalized its administration as follows:

1. South West Zone (Kampot, Koh Kong, Sihanouk Ville, Takeo, Kompung Chhnang, Kompung Speu, and Kandal). This Zone was led by Tchou Chet who was the party secretary, and Ta Mok was the military commander of the Zone. This was the largest area and the most important one according to Sarin because the Khmer Rouge reported that expenditure in this Zone was the highest, reaching 2 million Riels (Cambodian currency) in 1972 with a 135 Riels salary for each and every Khmer Rouge cadre.

2. East Zone (Kratie, Svay Rieng, Prey Veng, Kompung Cham).

3. North West Zone (Kompung Thom, Siem Reap-Oddar Meanchey).

4. Pursat-Battambang-Pailin.

5. Special Zone, established in late 1971 to manage the areas around Phnom Penh. This was the place where Sarin spent most of his time, and he later worked as commander of a mobile unit (probably a squad) of this Zone.

6. Preah Vihear, Stung Treng, Mondulkiri, and Rattanakiri were under direct control of the central committee of the CPK. Sarin was very sharp in noting that the area was strategic as it bordered three countries: Laos, Thailand, and Vietnam.

There was a party secretary at the Region level (equivalent of the province) and the district level. The party secretary was aided by a deputy party secretary and several members who were in charge of different areas—military, economy, and social welfare. The hamlet and village levels were defended by the local militias.

Sarin even participated in one session where Hou Yuon came to talk at a local gathering, addressing many issues. Sarin noted that only one of the banners welcoming Hou Yuon mentioned Prince Sihanouk as head of the GRUNK. All other banners displayed communist ideology. During that meeting, Hou Yuon admitted openly that relations between the Khmer Rouge and the Vietnamese were not particularly good, and that the Khmer Rouge tried very hard to become independent of the NLF/VPA. Life in the liberated zone was not very bad. After all, Hou Yuon ran the Zone like a modern government.

But of the information revealed by Sarin, none rivaled his chilling description of the CPK, which was called *angkar*. What he described was so unconventional that no one believed him at the time. Sarin observed that Prince Sihanouk was virtually powerless in a command system on the ground where all members of the group were not from Prince Sihanouk's inner circle. Prince Sihanouk and the GRUNK were only a front used by the Khmer Rouge (the CPK being the real player) to bolster its reputation.

According to Sarin, the members of the central committee of the CPK consisted of the following:

1. Khieu Samphan, who was deputy prime minister of the GRUNK and minister of defense; he also held the title of supreme commander of the military.
2. Saloth Sar, alias Pol Pot, first senior member, secretary general of the CPK.
3. Ieng Sary was the second man in the CPK.
4. Son Sen was the fourth person in the party.
5. Koy Thuon was the deputy minister of finance.
6. Hu Nim, minister of propaganda.
7. Tiv Ol, deputy minister of interior, in charge of rural management and cooperatives.
8. Khieu Ponnary, deputy minister of education, culture and youth.
9. Tchou Chet, deputy minister of health.
10. Sok Thourk, deputy minister of national security.
11. Pok Deurs Kumar, deputy minister of foreign affairs.

Khmer Rouge communist leaders during the struggle in 1971. Sitting from left to right: Nuon Chea, unknown, and Pol Pot. Standing from left: Koy Thuon. The banner behind the group reads: "Hooray! The Glorious Communist Party of Kampuchea." The cadres were well aware of the existence of the CPK but outsiders viewed the organization as GRUNK under Prince Sihanouk. The prince was only a figurehead with no real power. The CPK pulled all the strings. (©Documentation Center of Cambodia. Used by permission.)

INTELLIGENCE FAILURE

The real identity of Sarin is not very clear. Was he an adventurous, and subsequently disillusioned, school teacher who entered the Khmer Rouge–
controlled area out of curiosity? Or was he a spy of the Khmer Republic who
was sent into the area? In fact, in his book, Sarin was very precise about the
names of the Khmer Rouge cadres. In each case, he mentioned their real names
as well as their backgrounds, and where he could not, he demonstrated that he
had actually tried to go beyond the revolutionary name.

Most importantly, Sarin had noticed that the Khmer Rouge did not operate
alongside the Vietnamese. This was quite a surprise for many observers who
considered the Khmer Rouge and the NLF/VPA to be one and the same. Even
the CIA station in Cambodia at the time did not recognize the true relations
between the two.[132]

The Khmer Rouge and the Vietnamese only agreed to a marriage of expediency in a time of need. Even so, this apparent understanding was achieved only
at the top level. At the lower level, clashes usually occurred between central
and region/zone levels concerning the presence of Vietnamese troops.[133] In
the East Zone for example, people in some villages began to resent the Vietnamese presence, despite the latter's efforts to appease them.

In 1973, a major incident occurred when some of the Khmer Rouge cadres in
Region 25 encouraged the people to protest against the Vietnamese. These were
again purged by other Khmer Rouge in the Region, although the Vietnamese
finally agreed to move out into the woods while the Khmer Rouge maintained its
presence in the populated areas. Other zones also witnessed similar incidents.[134]

In sum, what Sarin described in his book was impeccable intelligence. It came
from good sources, it was clearly articulated, and it was disseminated in a timely
manner.[135] However, the intelligence report failed at the final stage of the intelligence cycle because it failed to convince the decision makers of the need to
take the report seriously, and to design actions based on it. The reason that it
failed was because the information stood squarely in contrast with the prevailing
assumptions at the time, assumptions which, in retrospect, we know were faulty.

But the general perception worked against him. Sarin's participation in
various Khmer Rouge activities was considered suspicious. His background
became shady and his real motives were questioned. Ith Sarin was arrested and
later killed in 1973.

Ultimately, it seemed that the only viable intelligence regarding the tumultuous
relations between Prince Sihanouk and Khmer Rouge was not taken seriously.
The Khmer Republic continued that flawed policy, staying on the defensive. Oc-
casionally, a small push by the FANK could capture a certain stronghold (like the
district of Amleing and Oudong in Kompung Speu), only for it to be recaptured
later by the Khmer Rouge.[136] The Khmer Republic seemed to suffer from a lack
of comprehensive strategic plans and the military operations did not satisfy any
strategic imperatives. Alas, even if they had a clear strategy, the Chenla II debacle had already drained their forces beyond the capability to sustain a long
campaign. The Khmer Republic was never able to escape from this vicious circle.

2

An Army That Has a State

Dear Party which I respect and value more than my life. Dear comrades and friends, I was wrong. But I never betrayed the Party. Before, I never answered but after I got severely beat up that I decided to make a false statement. I would like to sacrifice my life for the Party. I would like to request the Party not to arrest anyone whom I have wrongly accused in my confession letter. Our friends are innocent. I am neither part of the CIA nor the Khmer Serei. This is what I decide for the last time before I die. Dear Party and comrades, please spare my life. I am a communist militant and sacrifice my life for the Party. Ah Vorn, Ah Khet, Ah Kong Sophal all wrongly accused me as CIA, Khmer Serei, I am not involved with them. Brother! My wife and Comrade Nath's wife are all innocent. Phnom Penh, 15 December 1978—Sun Ty, alias Teanh.

[Postscript addressed to Duch, head of S-21 Security Prison]: Please Comrade, do not tear off this letter; this is my very last voice. Hooray! The great and glorious Communist Party of Kampuchea! Hooray! The great and glorious Kampuchean People's Revolutionary Party! Hooray! The bold and audacious Kampuchea People! Hooray! The Kampuchea People's Revolutionary Army[1]!

—Confession letter of Sun Ty, alias Teanh, chief of logistics office of the general staff HQ of the Kampuchean Revolutionary Army.[2]

THE BOYS IN BLACK CAME INTO THE CAPITAL

Since 1974, the talk of peace and negotiation circulated widely in Phnom Penh. The only trouble was that such calls came from the Khmer Republic which, at that time, controlled less than 10 percent of territory in Cambodia. The Khmer Rouge, on the other hand, did not respond, as it was busy organizing the big push to take the city. The Khmer Rouge's plan was to conquer the city before the Vietnamese forces captured Saigon, so that Pol Pot could claim his independence from Vietnam's assistance.[3] High casualties did not seem to bother Pol Pot, as long as he could take over Phnom Penh before Saigon fell.

But the officials of the Khmer Republic did not know that. The presence of Prince Sihanouk on the FUNK and as the head of state of the exiled government (GRUNK) lulled them into a false belief about the prince's eventual return. On the other hand, the Khmer Rouge leadership, and not just Pol Pot, used the prince only to gain legitimacy for their movement, without saying this publicly. The prince's name drew most of the Khmer Rouge recruits, but the Khmer Rouge leadership always viewed the prince as an obstacle to its power, as the prince's immense popularity could not be diminished. The prince also noticed this intrigue, but everything was already too late. He had no real power, and the Khmer Rouge leaders carefully cut him off from direct contact with the general populace.

The Khmer new year of 1975 marked the final offensive of the Khmer Rouge on Phnom Penh. In January, it cut off traffic on national road Number 5 at Neak Loeung, roughly 40 kilometers from Phnom Penh. The airport also came under constant rocket attack, making it all the more difficult for the private chartered planes hired by the U.S. government to land and supply the dying Khmer Republic.

When the situation seemed dire, Prince Sihanouk tried to make a last ditch attempt to come back to power by declaring that he would return on the condition that the "traitors" in the Khmer Republic were no longer in power.[4] It was allegedly reported that Lon Nol was paid a sum of $1 million to resign, which he did on April 1, 1975.[5] Sokham Khoy became the new president, who then declared that he was disposed to surrender power to Prince Sihanouk. On the night of April 11, the Khmer Republic was abolished and a high commission was established to prepare for the eventual return of Prince Sihanouk. This return was supported by the Americans, and had the prospect of being realized the next morning.

However, next morning, the development was ominous. According to Ros Chantrabot, at 4:00 A.M. on the morning of April 12, 1975, John Holdrige, the U.S. deputy chief of mission in China, informed that he was told such a deal could no longer be made and that Prince Sihanouk's return would not happen.[6] It was simply unthinkable to hope that the Khmer Rouge, who almost captured the city, would agree to a negotiation and the return of Prince Sihanouk. Not much later, President Ford declared that the situation in Cambodia was dire and it was probably too late to do anything; all remaining American personnel and citizens in Cambodia, as well as many high ranking officials of the Khmer Republic, were immediately evacuated by helicopters from Phnom Penh.

The situation began to deteriorate and a general sense of panic began to rise. Marine helicopters landed on the U.S. Embassy and evacuated the last remaining personnel of the embassy, as well as all American citizens from Cambodia.

Cambodians gathered near the Marines perimeter behind the U.S. Embassy, watching the Marines helicopters in the distance that carried the last remaining American citizens and personnel out of Cambodia. April 12, 1975. (©Roland Neveu. Used by permission.)

On April 14, 1975, traffic was interrupted on the road between the capital city and the Pochentong airport. Ever since the Khmer Rouge tightened the noose around Phnom Penh, Pochentong airport was the only place where the city could receive supplies. Phnom Penh was in the grip of fear on the night of April 16, 1975. The FANK had already broken into a full rout.

The morale in the city turned from bad to worse, and then a state of denial set in, based on the hope that "since the Khmer Rouge is also Khmer, then maybe everyone can work out a peaceful deal." Some Khmer Republic officials still clung to this belief until they were arrested by the Khmer Rouge.

One of the Khmer Republic's important figures, Lon Non, the brother of Lon Nol who had by then already left for Hawaii, still stayed behind. Lon Non was the commander of the elite "15th BI" (15th *Brigade d'Infantrie*, 15th Infantry Brigade), an elite brigade under direct command of the president. He had connections with some of the communists in Kompung Cham before the Khmer Republic, and still believed he could reason with the Khmer Rouge. In fact, Lon Non might have been in contact with Saloth Sar as well.[7] According to a report by a Khmer Rouge commander,[8] on the night of April 16–17, FANK divisions started to wave a white flag as surrender and Lon Non had ordered artillery fire from a 105-millimeter (mm) battery to signal the surrender.

Khmer Rouge soldiers marched into the General Staff HQ of the FANK. April 17, 1975. The letter on the gate read: "ÉTAT MAJOR GÉNÉRAL DES FANK" (FANK General Staff Headquarter). (©Documentation Center of Cambodia. Used by permission.)

At first light on April 17, rumor spread that the Khmer Rouge was marching into the city from all directions. The city was in complete silence. Around 7:00 A.M., a small group of young fighters dressed in black came into the city. They were supposed to be the "liberators" and their actions would determine whether the war would end violently or peacefully. The people began to rejoice when they saw that the young fighters were very friendly and certainly did not fit the profile that was described by the Khmer Republic.

Along the way, the liberators were greeted by people everywhere, and everyone laughed. The liberators told the people that the war had ended and they were on their way to negotiate a truce and accept the terms of surrender from the Khmer Republic. Groups of FANK soldiers carrying white flags were also walking into the city, apparently to meet up with the liberators and negotiate a truce to end the war.

The liberators wore black clothes, but those looked very clean. They carried a flag bearing a cross on a blue-and-red background. The flag had nothing related to communism, no hammer and sickle, no red star, and the red color seemed insufficient. . . The fighters seemed well groomed and well fed. The commander rode on the jeep, wearing a neat, black Polo shirt,[9] an expensive acquisition for a commander of the victorious army. Then it became clear why the liberators were so friendly. The commander of the liberators was recognized as Hem Keth Dara, a senior captain of the 15th BI.[10] He said that he would lead his force to the Ministry of Propaganda to negotiate peace.

Khmer Rouge soldier on a motorcycle carrying a handgun and a loudspeaker announced the evacuation of the capital, Monivong Boulevard, in front of the railway station. April 17, 1975. (©Roland Neveu. Used by permission.)

Around 9:00 A.M., those who were listening to the radio would hear the first message by the new authority. The commander announced three things about the liberation that the general population should know:

1. The party had achieved 100 percent victory all over the country.
2. Peace and normal life would return to society. The transition would be peaceful and just and impartial.
3. All people, "Excellencies," and officials please gather at the Ministry of Propaganda to prepare for negotiation and further orders.

The announcement was accompanied by messages from the Supreme Patriarchs of the two Buddhist sects, calling for calmness and peaceful negotiation. Gen. Mey Sichân, chief of operations of the FANK general staff headquarters, announced that all FANK forces had laid down their arms to begin the negotiation process.[11]

Around the same time, just about the time the first wave of liberators arrived at the Ministry of Propaganda to meet with Lon Non and representatives of the Khmer Republic, another group of liberators came in. Unlike the first one, however, this group was larger in number and came in from all directions. This second set was almost entirely composed of young fighters, dressed in old, black clothes. Most, if not all of them, wore a *krâma*, a type of traditional Cambodian towel that is a signature accessory of a typical farmer. The large majority of these unsmiling fighters carried the iconic AK-47, the signature weapon that all communist fighters love, and were supported by RPGs (rocket-propelled grenades) in almost every squad. At that time, a squad equipped with AK-47s and RPGs was the telltale sign of communist forces.

They walked silently into the city in small groups of two files, barrels pointing to the side of the road, always. They wore dark green caps, their combat gear was covered with scores of "Chinese-made grenades" and their shoes were the "Ho Chi Minh-style" improvised sandals made from truck tires.[12] These

Real Khmer Rouge soldiers started walking into the city late in the day. Here, the soldiers walked in two files, following the cadre and his radioman. April 17, 1975. (©Roland Neveu. Used by permission.)

shoes were cheap to make and were stealthy when walking. This appearance, in addition to their strict discipline, conveyed a sense of zero tolerance. A cadre walked in front along with his radioman or at the back of the formation. This was the commander of each respective unit.

This second wave of liberators neither made jokes nor laughed. They were all disconnected from the joy on the street, and they seemed to focus exclusively on their mission. And their first mission was to shut down the source of the first radio broadcast that had probably originated from the Ministry of Propaganda. Along the way, everyone wearing uniforms of the FANK or police were immediately stripped of their uniforms, insignia of rank and weapons, and were immediately rounded up awaiting further orders.

About half an hour later, before the people could rejoice about the news in the first broadcast, a second message was broadcast in a more angry tone. It seemed that a Khmer Rouge mobile radio station based in Steung Trang in Kompung Cham province was now the source of that second broadcast. The new station issued a four-point message:

1. The party had achieved 100 percent victory all over the country after defeating the Lon Nol traitors and their cliques.
2. This victory was achieved violently at gunpoint, not by negotiation.
3. The party has no need to negotiate with anyone or any party.
4. The traitors must suffer the consequences of their actions. No other people can take their place.

Lon Non and Hem Keth Dara were dragged out and executed near the Ministry of Propaganda. It was clear by 11:00 A.M. that the first liberators were imposters, a group led by the remaining Khmer Republic officials for a purpose that has still never been fully understood, even up until this day. Some claimed they went in just to confuse the victors, to make a false impression that they were some kind of internal network that helped liberate the city.[13] Perhaps they hoped that in the event of the return of Prince Sihanouk, they could present themselves as a victor, meaning that they should be entitled to the spoils of the new government. To this day, no one knows the real motive behind such a risky gamble. The gamble did not pay off, and Lon Non and his allies were killed by the Khmer Rouge.

The second wave of liberators who came in were the real Khmer Rouge, the fighters who came from the jungle, who originated from the farming classes and the oppressed, and who were committed to fight against the American allies who dropped bombs on their houses and villages.

The areas of responsibility of each unit were determined based on the region where they came from. For example, the Eastern Zone would come to occupy the east of the city and the Northeast Zone would come from the northeast, and they carried out orders within those areas.

Panic now replaced the earlier joy and jubilation. Those who were in military uniform or the police were immediately rounded up and disarmed. Later, they were forced into big trucks and were never to be seen again. Then the Khmer Rouge units that arrived at their destination started to implement the second stage of their order, which was mass evacuation of the population from the capital city.

By dusk, all Khmer Rouge units had reached their respective destinations and the evacuation order was now systematic. The Khmer Rouge actually prepared bicycles, motorcycles and minicars to carry speakers across the city to call for the general evacuation. However, the population in the capital city had swelled to over half a million people. There was a shortage of speakers, and the Khmer Rouge needed to use the soldiers to spread the news. The messages were disseminated by the Khmer Rouge and they contained the following orders:[14]

- All people should not make any unnecessary movement (i.e., curfew).
- Everyone should stay in their house.
- Everyone must prepare for a "temporary" evacuation outside of the city for three days only.
- The evacuation would be toward the countryside, at least three kilometers from the city.
- The evacuees must use only the roads that are designated by the party.
- No one should deviate or use other roads.
- There is no need to take large items of baggage because the evacuation is only temporary.
- The people have a three-day deadline to evacuate or face martial law.

The Khmer Rouge also provided some explanations for their commands:

The goal of the evacuation is to clean up hidden enemies who waited to overthrow the revolution.

The order to evacuate comes from Angkar and everyone needs to follow the principles set by the party.

The party must do this in order to protect the people's lives and the city from destruction by American bombers. The Americans were unable to destroy the revolution through combat, and they now sought to destroy us by bombing the city.

This time, the Americans will use bigger planes, so evacuation must be quick and swift.

The evacuation was a well-thought-out plan.[15] The Central Market was taken as the starting point for evacuation. Each partitioned sector would become the "spoils of war" of the respective Khmer Rouge's Zone and people were evacuated in all directions corresponding with the Khmer Rouge's Zones.[16] It was total chaos. Only one road was used for each direction. In reality, the crowd had to walk down the road on foot with whatever they had with them when they left the house. At the sight of this mass exodus, many people realized they would not be allowed to return to their home. The Khmer Rouge soldiers also

walked among the crowds and those who protested or deviated from the designated route were taken away and were never to be seen again. Within the confusion, many people walked toward their hometown in the countryside instead
of the designated provinces and zoning plan.[17] The Khmer Rouge soldiers then
decided to stop enforcing the final destination they should go to; the soldiers
only made sure the people did not deviate from the main road.

Checkpoints were also set up to check for former officials under the Lon Nol
regime as well as members of the FANK or police. According to one Khmer
Rouge commander, around 300 to 400 in total were rounded up each day.[18]
This was also in part because the routed FANK soldiers now came back into
the capital city, marching opposite of the crowds who were going out. They
were easy prey for the Khmer Rouge checkpoints.

Many people had by that point realized that there was no going back. There
was simply no temporary evacuation. Many people would never see their
homes again until 1979, many others never will.

The road was congested and the crowd barely moved. The new authority
then ordered a 15-day deadline for all the people to arrive at their destination
in the countryside. But walking hundreds of kilometers barefoot and on congested roads was simply impossible. When the deadline arrived, the Khmer
Rouge decided that to process things faster all the evacuees must stop after the
deadlines, and then they were to be included in the area where they were at the
time of the deadline. They would begin their new life there.

The evacuation of Phnom Penh on April 17, 1975 will remain one of the
most controversial and unscrupulous policies the Khmer Rouge has ever undertaken. It is also puzzling as to why the Khmer Rouge carried out such a
policy. What was the rationale behind this policy, if there was one at all?

The real reasons behind the stated purpose of the evacuation are still not
very clear to this day. But one can speculate on a few reasons why such a policy
was adopted. First of all, the Khmer Rouge was determined to reorganize society into a pure communist society with no classes. To do so would require
everyone to leave the city and live with the peasantry, which constituted the
majority of the people in Cambodia. Years of living under the decadent regime
of the Khmer Republic made people forget the true values of manual labor
which, according to the Khmer Rouge, was the true source of production.

Second, the Khmer Rouge believed in foreign subversion and espionage by
hostile countries and considered the evacuation the only way to root out those
subversive elements.[19] The Khmer Rouge leaders always claimed they had
thought of it in advance and actually announced it as one of the reasons Phnom
Penh was to be evacuated. Pol Pot believed that after the fall of Phnom Penh,
subversive elements would attempt to overthrow the regime, which called for a
preemptive policy, hence an evacuation.[20]

Third, the evacuation was a surprise for many Khmer Rouge senior leaders.
One thing is clear: not many people in the Khmer Rouge itself knew in advance
about the evacuation plan. According to some accounts, upon learning about

Khmer Rouge top leaders at the Pochentong airport. From left to right: Pol Pot, Nuon Chea, Ieng Sary, Son Sen. (©Documentation Center of Cambodia. Used by permission.)

the zoning system in which Phnom Penh was divided up into blocks to make it easier for the evacuation, Hou Yuon, the party secretary of the Special Zone, is said to have exclaimed, "This is Berlin!",[21] referring to the Berlin Wall. Not long after, he was executed for opposing the evacuation plan.

TIME-BOMB DECISIONS

After taking over the city and after the evacuation was completed, Khmer Rouge senior leaders went into the city. A ceremony at the Independence Monument was held to commemorate their fallen comrades. During the Khmer Rouge regime, no ordinary people would live in Phnom Penh. It was entirely a city for the cadres and senior leaders as well as the infamous security prison, the S-21. Some factories also resumed their function. The Khmer Rouge let the technicians of the old regime live for a while to teach them how to operate the machines and then replaced these technicians with workers who did not have any prior technical experience.

Upon taking over, the Khmer Rouge made a series of decisions that would soon lead to disaster. In fact, the regime became a large time bomb because of those decisions. The regime would collapse, and in a dramatic manner. It was only a matter of time.

Many important decisions will be examined here: the resignation of Prince Sihanouk, issues with regard to the history of the party, the Four Year Plan, the restructuring and upgrade of the revolutionary army (establishment of the Kampuchean Revolutionary Army), relations with Vietnam and China, and "enemy cleansing policy."

The Sihanouk situation is now ripe. He has no more air to propel him [us?] any further. So we decided to let him resign as he wished.
– Decision of the Central Committee of the CPK, March 30, 1976.

At the outset, the CPK that Pol Pot had created by changing the name of the KPRP in the 1960s was now in power. The CPK created a "revolutionary organization" (*Angkar Padevoat*) to rule the country. Thereafter, the people would live under an authority that they knew only by its abbreviated form *Angkar* (Khmer word for "organization") or *Angkar Leu* (higher Angkar).

As of September 1975, the central committee of the CPK was composed of the following members: Pol Pot, Nuon Chea, Sor Phim, Ieng Sary, Son Sen, Ta Mok, and Vorn Vet.[22] In 1977, three more members were added to the central committee: Khieu Samphan, Ke Pauk, and Nhim Ros. Among them, Pol Pot had studied in France, but had returned without a degree. Ieng Sary and Khieu Samphan had studied in France while Nuon Chea had studied in Thailand and Vietnam. All other members of the central committee were military commanders.

The new regime, which did not yet have an official name (besides GRUNK, which was a government-in-exile), convened a congress attended by 1,000 people to vote on a draft of a new constitution from December 15–19, 1975. The constitution was ratified on January 5, 1976. According to the new constitution, Cambodia was officially known as "Democratic Kampuchea." The constitution also talked about the establishment of a democratic government. It established a "People's Assembly," which was composed of 250 members. Among the 250 seats, 150 would represent the peasantry, 50 would represent the industrial workers and manufacturers, and another 50 would represent the Kampuchea Revolutionary Army (KRA).[23] The constitution made no reference to the existence of the CPK.[24] Just like many other institutions of Democratic Kampuchea, the People's Assembly was only a nominal institution and it never convened for anything except a single meeting in April 1976 to consider the resignation request of Prince Sihanouk from the position of head of state of Democratic Kampuchea.

At the state level, Prince Sihanouk remained the head of GRUNK, which existed until the proclamation of Democratic Kampuchea. The Khmer Rouge essentially used the prince only to gather support among the people, as well as the international actors. In July 1975, the Khmer Rouge requested the return of Prince Sihanouk to Cambodia. Upon his return, the prince was immediately appointed as head of state of Democratic Kampuchea and even presided over a cabinet meeting. But just like the cabinet that the prince presided over, the title head of state was nominal only. A few weeks later, the prince was forced to go to the United Nations where he successfully reclaimed the Cambodian seat at the UN for Democratic Kampuchea.[25] Not long after, his requests to go to the countryside to meet his compatriots were repeatedly denied,[26] and the prince finally decided to submit a request for resignation in 1976.

After an internal meeting in March 1976, the Standing Committee of the CPK accepted the prince's resignation when they thought they could no longer use the prince for their own gain. After all, the Khmer Rouge had already taken power. The Standing Committee then referred the matter to the People's Assembly, which convened for the first and last time in April 1976, to accept the resignation of the prince. The prince was to receive an annual pension of $8,000, but this was never disbursed.[27]

The life of Prince Sihanouk under the Khmer Republic was actually only a short distance away from death. The Khmer Rouge leaders never trusted the prince, and they feared that any contact between the prince and the people would eclipse Angkar's rule, due to the prince's immense popularity. Both the Khmer Rouge and Prince Sihanouk knew this, and both tried to outmaneuver the other. But ultimately, the Khmer Rouge won out. As early as 1973, the prince had already publicly voiced his disapproval of the way the Khmer Rouge treated him. Nayan Chanda noted that during a visit of a Swedish ambassador in Hanoi, the prince said that Ieng Sary was personally spying on him.[28] The Khmer Rouge, in turn, sought to keep him in Beijing, Hanoi and Pyongyang as much as they could so that the prince would never have the chance to see his people.

The prince's return to Cambodia after 1975 was a last ditch attempt to win back his people and power, but by then it was too late. The Khmer Rouge was already in power and as they broadcast on radio during the evacuation of Phnom Penh, their power was achieved "through force of arms." Most of the prince's relatives were sent to "cooperatives" and forced labor, where most of them perished.[29] Their connection with the royal family did not help but actually hurt them, in spite of all the services rendered by Prince Sihanouk to the regime. The prince himself might have been killed had it not been for the intervention of China. Nayan Chanda wrote that the ailing Mao still struggled with his weak voice to tell Ieng Thirith not to send Prince Sihanouk and his wife to the cooperative, which proved to be a lifesaver for the prince and his family.[30] After his resignation, the prince was held prisoner in his own palace, with no contact with the outside world, until January 1979 when Democratic Kampuchea collapsed.

EMPTY GOVERNMENT

One peculiar fact about Democratic Kampuchea was the nature of the cabinet ministries. The Khmer Rouge already had a sophisticated cabinet system with various ministries and ministers who were intellectuals. After 1975, however, most, if not all, intellectuals were severely purged. Hu Nim, who was perhaps the last of the intellectual cadres who were purged, was arrested and sent to S-21 on January 10, 1977. Many others vanished long before that. It seemed that the ministries that existed before 1975 mostly disappeared along with their ministers. After all, the ministries had no clear structures or permanent staff that could sustain the organization after the passing of the minister.

Under Democratic Kampuchea, many other ministries (apart from the crucial ones: defense, foreign affairs, industry, and economy) were established. Before 1976, Democratic Kampuchea did not exist, and the organization in power was the CPK. After Prince Sihanouk resigned, Khieu Samphan replaced Prince Sihanouk as the head of state in 1976.

Pol Pot became general secretary of the CPK and Nuon Chea became the deputy general secretary. The CPK would function in complete secrecy and its existence was not even known until after 1977. In the March 1976 decisions,[31] we know that the Central Committee had been discussing the organization of the new government and other institutions since May of that year. The People's Assembly was led by Nuon Chea, followed by Comrade Phim (Sor Phim) and Comrade Mok (Chhit Tchoeun, alias Ta Mok). Members of the government were:

- Comrade Pol (Saloth Sar, alias Pol Pot): Prime Minister.
- Comrade Van (Ieng Sary): Deputy Prime Minister, in charge of foreign affairs.
- Comrade Vorn (Vorn Vet): Deputy Prime Minister, in charge of economy and finance.
- Comrade Khieu (Son Sen): Deputy Prime Minister, in charge of defense.

Scores of other ministries were created, but all of them were nominal only and had no notable activities. The reason was simple: without enough

Nuon Chea during a lecture to Khmer Rouge cadres in Phnom Penh. From left to right, front row: Vorn Vet, Ta Mok, unknown, Ke Pauk, second row: Khieu Samphan, unknown, Ieng Sary and Son Sen. (©Documentation Center of Cambodia. Used by permission.)

intellectuals and competent staff to run the civilian administration, the ministries simply could not function. In contrast, Democratic Kampuchea tended to favor the establishment of a ministry only for some specific and ad hoc job. For example, we know that under Democratic Kampuchea there was a "ministry of state garment."[32] The CPK was still the organization behind the scenes and this was the organization that pulled all the strings.

CHANGER OF HISTORY, NOT HISTORY CHANGER

The second policy implemented by the CPK was to change history and determine the official historic dates of the party. On March 30, 1976, the Central Committee of the Communist Party of Kampuchea issued decisions on a variety of issues, one of which concerned the founding date of the party.[33]

First and foremost, Angkar determined that the founding year of the party was 1960, not 1951. The Central Committee had stated clearly in the decisions that they changed the party's founding date from 1951 to 1960 in order to emphasize the independence of its Communist Party from other political movements. "The party wanted to clear itself from false relationships with other communist parties and to distinguish itself," the document said. The CPK now started to undermine the existence of the KPRP and the WPK. In later years, senior cadres of the Khmer Rouge jailed at S-21 were forced to confess that they supported the KPRP and the WPK in order to undermine the CPK.[34]

The question of who were members of the CPK now became a problem for anyone who was member before 1960. This was an important turn of events because now, Pol Pot officially disowned himself from the KPRP and attempted to sever all relations between the CPK and the Vietnamese as well as other Cambodian communists. Only in September 1977, shortly before a trip to Beijing, did Pol Pot publicly declare the existence of the CPK and his position as premier of Democratic Kampuchea.

In itself, the decision to rewrite history had two objectives: to sever all ties with the Vietnamese in preparation for a war, and to radically reshape Cambodian society. According to a decision of the central committee of the CPK on March 30, 1976, the following two dates were officially the historic dates because of their significance to the party and the state:[35]

- January 17, 1968: the birth of the revolutionary army, the day on which armed struggle was carried out nationwide. This was actually the time of the riot in Samlot where the guerillas attacked the soldiers and took the guns.
- April 17, 1975: Independence Day, the largest, most important ceremony of all.

The Khmer Rouge also changed the meaning of the traditional Khmer New Year ceremony. The decision stated that the "Independence Day Ceremonies" were celebrated over three consecutive days, covering the Khmer New Year days (April 15–17). During this time, however, people were given a three-day break for "political indoctrination," not cultural and religious celebration.

It was the beginning of a movement to destroy the Cambodian culture and replace it with artificial ceremony, not unlike the Reign of Terror and extreme secularization of society under the French Revolution.

ALL BARRELS POINTING EASTWARD: CONFLICT WITH VIETNAM

As early as May 1975, the Khmer Rouge planned to take back Phu Quoc Island, known in Khmer as "Koh Tral," which was roughly 12 kilometers from the Cambodian coast of Kampot province (Region 35 under Democratic Kampuchea). The island had always been a point of contention and controversy, as it was a favorite target of many opportunist politicians, past and present. The island is often used to incite anti-Vietnamese sentiment for political gain. The Khmer Rouge, however, used force to pursue their fantasy.

On May 1, 1975, Meas Muth, commander of division 164 (a name that we shall see in the 1990s in a later chapter), ordered a battalion of soldiers (300 troops) led by Comrade Bo to invade the island.[36] The island was roughly 500 square kilometers, resulting in a force-to-space ratio of roughly 3 soldiers per 2 square kilometers. This ratio was simply too low for mounting either a successful attack or a defense.

The soldiers took some large plastic bottles and balloons to be used as improvised life vests in case the operation went awry. The soldiers had some heavy weapons, but knew nothing about either the topography of the island or the position of the Vietnamese army. Their reconnaissance mission took three days, during which time the Vietnamese army captured all of them except 30 soldiers who swam back to the Cambodian coast, using coconuts as improvised life vests.[37] Even a novice strategist could have predicted that the plan would become a disaster. But in 1975, the Khmer Rouge believed that since they had defeated the United States, anything was possible. Vietnam did not make any large-scale retaliation for the event and still maintained diplomatic relations with Democratic Kampuchea and kept its embassy in Phnom Penh.

Therefore, from the outset, the Khmer Rouge already considered Vietnam as enemy and took all precautionary measures as if a war had already broken out between the two countries. In a series of meetings in late 1975 and early 1976, the Central Committee of the CPK had determined that Vietnam had already encroached on Cambodian territory and gave hints that war with Vietnam was inevitable. These series of meetings shed light on two main issues: the relations between Democratic Kampuchea and Vietnam and the relations between Democratic Kampuchea and the People's Republic of China. These two topics are often issues of controversy and are usually explained by many casual conspiracy theories. To avoid confusion, in this book I will follow the chronological order of archival material before drawing a conclusion.

We know that on October 9, 1975, the central committee of the CPK conducted a meeting on various issues. On defense, the meeting did not attack Vietnam

as yet, but still recommended some precautionary measures. The most prominent issues on the agenda during this meeting were the assistance from China in
rebuilding the revolutionary army, as well as providing many types of equipment
such as radar and weapon factories.[38]

On February 22, March 30, and May 15, 1976, the Central Committee
and the Standing Committee of the CPK conducted three meetings related
to national defense and security.[39] These meetings discussed agendas similar to those of the 1975 meeting, but they contained more and more discussion on Vietnam. The February meeting mentioned that the transfer of
ammunition from Vietnam must be made at the border crossing, and the
Vietnamese must not be allowed to drive into Cambodia. The minutes also
recommended that:

> With regards to the border issues, the principle is to negotiate with Vietnam
> but more importantly, we must prepare our forces. If we take only political mea-
> sures and no military measures, when they [the Vietnamese] swarm us, it will be
> difficult. We must study the strengths and weakness [of the enemy] and if they
> [the Vietnamese] come, we'll hit them immediately.[40]

One might interpret this as a normal policy of self-defense that should not
be taken as an aggressive stance toward Vietnam. Nonetheless, considering the
past relations between the two countries during the civil war, such a statement
was simply too extreme for friends. The meeting on March 30, 1976, also gave
many clues to the frictions between Democratic Kampuchea and Vietnam.
Changing the history of the party was only the first step. In its final section, the
1976 report concluded with a paragraph that would sum up the mindset of the
Khmer Rouge leaders:

Regarding the security issue, the Central Committee noted: "In the country we have achieved autonomy [and self-sufficiency]. [. . .] The problems are
landmines and ambush attacks. These can be solved by evasive tactics. Going
to Vietnam: must find evasive measures. Comrade Secretary [Pol Pot] does
not need to go to Vietnam. For solidarity, arrange for the President of the state
presidium or the assembly to go."[41]

What is important in this series of meetings is the relation between
Democratic Kampuchea and the People's Republic of China. One question that
arises is whether the assistance of the People's Republic of China to Democratic
Kampuchea was the main, if not the only, reason why the Khmer Rouge dared
to attack the bigger Vietnam. The truth is much more complicated. There are
issues at two analytical levels.

Firstly, at the factual level, assistance from the People's Republic of China
did actually exist. In all of the previous three meetings, the Central Committee of the CPK mentioned in all instances about China's assistance in rebuilding the revolutionary army. The October 1975 meeting mentioned the study
conducted by China on how to help rebuild Democratic Kampuchea's army.
The most specific area of assistance in this meeting was the air force, which

China was studying in terms of how to assist with building radar stations as well as some issues related to the planes and airports.[42] In 1976, Chinese technicians arrived to help in many projects, including sea ports and arms factories.[43] Nayan Chenda and Dmitry Mosyakov noted that one of the most important projects was the construction of a large air base in Kompung Chhnang province, one that was large enough to accommodate bombers that could reach Ho Chi Minh City in only half an hour.[44] In 1977, an internal report of the Khmer Rouge military listed the following cooperation with China (here is an excerpt):

[. . .] VI. Air Force

- Training in China

    - Bomber training will complete in March 1978
    - Fighter training will complete in June 1978

- Comrade China will provide us in 1978, after training:

    - Bombers will be provided in March 1978

        - 8 bombers
        - 2 trainer planes

    - Fighters will be provided in June 1978

        - 12 fighters
        - 6 trainer planes

    - Now we lack students.

[. . .]- Remark on the prior agreement that China must provide:

- Bombers

    - 17 bombers
    - 3 trainer planes

- Fighters

    - 30 fighters
    - 6 trainer planes
            Total: 56 planes.

[. . .] Kompung Chhnang airbase can be completed in 1979.
    [. . .] Marine infantry base will be completed at the end of 1977 or early 1978
    [. . .] Anti-submarine ships might be provided late 1977 [under discussion]
[. . .].[45]

At this first analytical level, we have only established that China provided training, as well as promised to provide hi-tech equipment such as fighters, bombers and antisubmarine ships. The second analytical level, however, is the question of whether this assistance was the direct cause of the war. Based on the currently available archival documents, the alternative argument made here in this book is that the Khmer Rouge actually decided to go to war, with or without the Chinese aid. As always, the Khmer Rouge wanted to maintain their independence and autonomy.

The document above (related to the number of planes and ships) was dated September 1977, during the time of conflict between Democratic Kampuchea and Vietnam. It was true that the agreement had already been made before 1977 (such as the antisubmarine ships, which were agreed upon since February 1976), but the actual amount that was provided did not match the need of Democratic Kampuchea during a time in which the war with Vietnam was raging. In late 1977, many units of the Khmer Rouge had already been driven back from Vietnamese territory, and the Central Committee was already preparing for a purge in the East Zone. It is puzzling that the heavy equipment which might help the war efforts, especially to negate the Vietnamese air superiority, did not arrive on time. The year 1977 would have been the best year to fully respond to the Khmer Rouge proposals or even exceed those proposals. But that did not happen. Alternatively, the Khmer Rouge should have waited until they received all the equipment they needed from China before launching a war against Vietnam. That, too, did not happen.

Even the number of planes listed in the above document was "planned" only, and they were supposed to be provided not until 1978, after training had been completed. One can certainly argue that this delay was because the Khmer Rouge lacked capable pilots, and that was the reason why China did not provide all the planes. But this argument is not very plausible: if that were the case, the Khmer Rouge could have just sat it out until they received what they needed. After all, the Khmer Rouge raided Vietnamese provinces first, so they (the Khmer Rouge) had the initiative. Nothing compelled Democratic Kampuchea to hurry, except its own hatred and ideology vis-à-vis Vietnam.

Even after the war broke out, it was also puzzling as to why China did not hurry to fulfill all the needs of the Khmer Rouge, now that war had already reached its climax in late 1977. Why only 8 of the 17 requested bombers that were agreed upon, and why only 12 of the 30 requested fighters? And all of those were not to be delivered until 1978, after the war had already been raging for quite some time.

In the above report, on the first level of analysis, which is the factual level, the amount of equipment and support from China was great, indeed. But the report also mentioned additional unpleasant facts for Democratic Kampuchea. The Kompung Chhnang airbase was not operational until 1979. Today, what is left of the airbase is a large runway and incomplete bunkers that were carved into the mountain nearby. The antisubmarine ships, too, would arrive in late 1978, but then Vietnam had no submarines! The countermeasure would be useless.

How could one explain the fact that the Khmer Rouge fought with a bigger adversary without waiting for Chinese equipment?

Pol Pot's extremism and reckless policy seemed to be the answer. In fact, ever since 1975, long before the arrival of Chinese technicians, the Khmer Rouge had already attacked Vietnam in an attempt to regain Phu Quoc Island (Koh Tral). In the meeting on October 9, 1975, after listening to the reports of the members concerning the level of Chinese assistance, Pol Pot made a comment about the stance of Cambodia vis-à-vis China, which was captured by the minutes of that meeting:

> Based on the independent and self-reliance principle, Comrade Secretary [Pol Pot] believed that we will receive support, but also based on the independent and self-reliance principle. If the assistance [from China] interferes with this principle, we will not accept. If we are fully equipped we will fight, if we are not fully equipped we will fight nonetheless.[46]

Pol Pot was true to his promise: he would fight, regardless of whether or not his forces were properly equipped. And fight he did. Even China would have been concerned, very concerned and upset, if it had seen this report at the time. In essence, Pol Pot did not care about the amount of aid received from China. Regardless of the assistance, Pol Pot would still carry out his plan to fight with Vietnam. Pol Pot's ideology and overconfidence seem to be the primary cause of the war. Pol Pot came to power in almost a miraculous way, but once in power, he immediately wasted the chance to preserve it.

THE FOUR YEAR PLAN (1977–1980): 3 TONS PER HECTARE

The second policy that was stated in the 1976 decisions was to reaffirm the collectivization of private property to maximize rice production. This was second in importance only to national security. In early 1976, a Four Year Plan (1977–1980) was announced in which all private properties were to be confiscated and then used for rice production. The Khmer Rouge divided the land into two categories. Normal land was required to produce 3 tons of rice per hectare, while the best quality land was required to produce at least 4 to 7 tons per hectare.

According to the United Nations' Food and Agriculture Organization (FAO) statistics, rough rice yield was 2.03 tons per hectare on average in Asia in 1965 and for Cambodia, this was 1.07 tons per hectare on average.[47] And this yield was before the war. The Four Year Plan of Democratic Kampuchea, on the other hand, required at least 3 tons per hectare.

The only areas capable of achieving that 3-tons-per-hectare target were the areas around Tonle Sap basin as well as Battambang and Siem Reap—Oddar Meanchey (in the Southwest Zone and Siem Reap—Oddar Meanchey Region). However, Democratic Kampuchea was aware that these areas were the rice bowl of Cambodia and imposed at least a 4-tons-per-hectare target. In essence, the Khmer Rouge set a target that was three times higher than the Cambodian average before the war, and the highest requirement was twice the average of Asia as a whole. By 1975, however, most of the arable land had been ravaged by bombing and unexploded ordnance, as well as land-mines. The Khmer Rouge's bias for independence also precluded machinery from the planning (since they could not produce those machineries). All of these problems combined to produce a severe famine as early as 1975 in the Southwest Zone.

Democratic Kampuchea did not pay attention to the realities but instead focused on fulfilling its fantasy. It issued a decision to designate the "Model District," which would be chosen from among the ones that could achieve the 3-tons-per-hectare target, and that model district would be awarded a "Great-Leap-Forward" flag. The Khmer Rouge simply assumed the target would be achieved.

According to Khamboly, the Four Year Plan envisaged the allocation of rice production in four categories.[48] The first part was to feed all the people with each person theoretically receiving 312 kilograms of rice per year or 0.85 kilograms per day. The second category would be used for seeds, the third for reserve, and the fourth category was the largest one which would be used for export in exchange for ammunition, weapons, and other goods. When the yield fell short of the target, however, only the export quota was maintained and this was at the expense of the quota for individual ration. It was in this way that many people perished. Malnutrition combined with the lack of even the most basic health care killed tens of thousands, for these two reasons alone.

TERRITORIAL ADMINISTRATION: A FORMIDABLE FORM OF COUNTERINSURGENCY

In addition to these two policies (national defense and agriculture quota), the Khmer Rouge had three more policies related to the structure of their state: territorial administration, military organization, and prison system.

The Khmer Rouge oversimplified the administration system. At each level, the entity was always governed by a three-man board: a chief, a deputy chief, and an assistant. The territorial administration system before Democratic Kampuchea was composed of a *Phoum* (hamlet) which was the lowest level, comprising of a dozen families or so, depending on whether it was in the city or in the provinces. Several *Phoums* were organized into a *Khum* (equivalent to "village") and *Khums* were organized into a *Srok* (equivalent to "district"). A province was composed of many *Sroks*. A province was the highest unit in the territorial administration system. The military was also loosely based on this system, except that the military units in several provinces were organized into "Military Regions." This system is still in place today. Under Democratic Kampuchea, however, a new system was established; one that was probably designed by military minds—this comprised the Region and the Zone.

The Khmer Rouge did not allow any school to open, and the motto was "Angkar uses tree shades as classrooms and meeting places."[49] Yet, the Ministry of Education published a textbook for elementary class 2, which described its administration system in detail. The document made it very clear that the new coding system was used to hide the identity of the guerilla forces operating in those areas. The system then persisted under Democratic Kampuchea. In essence, the Khmer Rouge territorial administration was designed for military purposes and was maintained throughout its reign.

Before the war, there were 19 provinces: Stung Treng, Ratanakkiri, Mondulkiri, Kratie, Kompung Cham, Svay Rieng, Prey Veng, Kandal, Takeo, Kampot, Koh Kong, Kompung Speu, Kompung Chhnang, Kompung Thom, Preah Vihear, Siem Reap–Oddar Meanchey, Sihanouk Ville (known as Kompung Som under the Khmer Republic), Pursat, and Battambang. Phnom Penh was the capital city. Under Democratic Kampuchea, the province became "Region" and several regions combined into "Zones." Therefore, the administrative system now became *Phoum, Khum, Srok*, Region (*tambonn* in Khmer, which replaced province), and Zone (*phoum phiek* in Khmer).

Phoum, Khum, and *Srok* maintained virtually the same names as before. But regions and zones were new. To avoid confusion, I will use the English terms, starting from the lowest level: hamlet, village, district, province/region, and zone. While the highest units were zones, there were also autonomous regions under the direction of the central committee of the CPK.

Democratic Kampuchea was divided into six zones and four autonomous regions. The names of the zones were based on their compass direction in relation to the country as a whole. Instead of having a name like the provinces of the previous regime, a region under Democratic Kampuchea was normally identified by a code. A normal region under a zone was identified by a one, two, or three digit number. Only the autonomous regions under direct command of the Central Committee bore the same name as the former provinces (for example, Siem Reap–Ouddar Meanchey region). The Khmer Rouge leaders always boasted that such a system was put in place to confuse the enemy.[50] This is typical of the military mindset. Essentially, the Khmer Rouge still viewed itself as being under attack from all sides, and thought that existential threats were omnipresent.

Territorial Administration System of Democratic Kampuchea. Adjacent to the East Zone is a map of Vietnamese provinces involved in the war between 1977 and 1978. (All boundaries are not official. They are used for illustration purposes only.) (©Map by Boraden Nhem, adapted from parts of the map provided by the Documentation Center of Cambodia.)

The six zones were:

1. Northwest Zone (code 560) controlled by Nhim Ros. This Zone encompassed the former provinces of Pursat and Battambang. This Zone consisted of seven Regions: Regions 1, 2, 3, 4, 5, 6, and 7.
2. West Zone (code 401) was controlled by Tchou Chet, and included the former provinces of Koh Kong, Kompung Chhnang and part of Kompung Speu. The Zone consisted of five Regions: Regions 11, 15, 31, 32, and 37.
3. South-West Zone (code 405) was controlled by the notorious Ta Mok (whose real name was Chhit Tchoeun), and included Kampot, Takeo, and parts of Kompung Speu. There were four Regions in this Zone: Regions 13, 25, 33, and 35.

4. North Zone (code 303) was controlled by Koy Thourn. Koy Thourn's tenure was very brief and accused of moral misconduct, he was sent to work at the ministry in Phnom Penh. When he was executed in 1976, this region was transferred to Ke Pauk and then to Korng Chap. Ke Pauk received a new appointment as secretary of the Central Zone which was created in 1977. The North Zone encompassed Kompung Thom, parts of Kompung Cham, and one district in Kratie. It had three Regions: 41, 42, and 43.
5. East Zone (code 203) was controlled by Sor Phim, veteran of the KPRP. The Zone included Prey Veng, Svay Rieng, parts of Kompung Cham, one district from Kratie, and parts of Kandal. The Zone was composed of five Regions: Regions 20, 21, 22, 23, and 24.
6. North-East Zone (code 108) was controlled by Nay Saran (also executed in 1976). The Zone included Rattanakkiri, Mondulkiri, parts of Kratie, and parts of Stung Treng. It had six Regions: 101, 102, 104, 105, 107, and 505.

In addition to these six Zones, Democratic Kampuchea also had four autonomous Regions which were not subordinated to any Zone, but were directly under the control of the Central Committee: Siem Reap–Oddar Meanchey Region, Preah Vihear Region, Kratie Region, Mondulkiri Region, and Kompung Som Region. The Kratie and Mondulkiri regions were formerly under the North-East Zone. In 1977, when the country was in disarray after the failed attacks on Vietnamese provinces, the Khmer Rouge created a new Central Zone which was located at the North Zone and the North Zone was relocated to Siem Reap–Oddar Meanchey Region and Preah Vihear Region.

This was the official territorial administration system that Democratic Kampuchea devised to confuse its enemies. In later years, however, amidst the confusion resulting from the war with Vietnam, many new areas and zones were established and until this day, scholars have had difficulties tracking them all, especially when some regions and zones were created for only a very brief period without any meaningful actions. In this book, only the stable system in the early years is discussed and we will leave the details of many other changes to future research.

ADMINISTRATION OF THE COUNTRY

The evacuation of Phnom Penh on April 17, 1975, was a tragedy. At that time the countryside, which was supposed to accommodate everyone, could not cope with this sudden influx of people. Lack of housing, health facilities, as well as food (because most of the rice fields were unusable due to unexploded ordnance and lack of farming equipment), put additional pressure on the local administration. Finally, the fact that the local administrator did not have any experience in managing a community combined with the above factors to produce a disaster.

The first attempt by the Khmer Rouge to cope with the problem was to distinguish between the "Old People" or "Base/Local People" and the "New People," or "17th April People." The former were considered the owners of the country, while the latter were considered "latecomers" to the revolution. This latter group would not understand the true value of labor because they had spent years living under capitalist rule. They were "subpeople" and could only obtain the status of full-fledged citizens by way of forced labor. Not all local people were considered "Old People," however. The wealthy, those who had big houses, those who were well educated, the monks, as well as former office bearers in local authorities of the old regime were also considered "capitalists" and they too suffered the same fate as the new people.

The second attempt by administrators to cope with the problem was to root out perceived traitors and enemies. This was the first wave of the "purification purge." Any intellectuals or former officials of the Khmer Republic were first told that they were needed to assist in the reconstruction of the country. Many volunteered for this call and never returned. People who stepped over the rules laid down by the local administrator were often told that they would need to go to "reeducation camp" for their offense. They too would never come back. Apparently, the Khmer Rouge believed that the people should be deceived in order to avoid unnecessary resistance. This was done since the evacuation in 1975. At first, no one noticed this deception, and everyone was eager to go. But then people noticed that volunteers left in the afternoon, and the next morning the guards who escorted them began to divide amongst themselves various goods that could be identified as belonging to the volunteers.[51] This could mean only one thing: the volunteer would never return.

The justice system of the old regime was abolished altogether. After all, to the Khmer Rouge, what was good in a system that arrested and was responsible for the disappearance and torture of many Khmer Rouge fighters? When the old system was abolished, a new one was not established. There was no law under Democratic Kampuchea. The law rested on the will, and the mood, of the cadres. Democratic Kampuchea was governed like a country under constant and extreme martial law. The chief of the hamlet and the chief of the village had ultimate authority over the fate of its members. This was the power of life, or death by execution. Even an offense as small as stealing a potato could easily result in a person being executed.

Normally, the Khmer Rouge chose the chief of the hamlet and village from the poorest of the Old People. These people mostly could not read or write. To make matters worse, the chief was not assisted by any technicians or intellectuals, but instead, by a unit called *korng chhlorb*, which can be translated as "guerrilla unit." These units had their roots in the war before 1975 when the Khmer Rouge conducted spoiling attacks and hit-and-run tactics against the larger Khmer Republic forces. Even in peace, the Khmer Rouge still kept these units and actually used them to help the administration. Without any education, these people knew only one thing: combat. And the chief, who also had no knowledge of administration, used them as spies on the 17th April people. The *chhlorb* normally went near the houses of the 17th April people and listened throughout the night. Those who let slip any "revolutionary-incorrect words" would certainly face execution the next morning, if not that same night.

The chiefs of the hamlet and the village did not bear the title "secretary" or "party secretary." Only the chiefs of the district, the region, and the zone could have the title "party secretary." Apart from the three-man board, there was no other body that helped govern the territory. According to the memoirs of Ith Sarin, the third position after the chief and the deputy chief might consist of many members in charge of different areas (economic, social, welfare, military, etc.) and the system was still functional in 1972–73. After 1975, however, the third position consisted of one person only.[52] Apparently, the system was contracted after the purges that claimed the lives of Hou Yuon and other intellectuals in the former Special Zone and North Zone.

Therefore, the territorial administration units essentially became a miniature police state. As the main goal of this organization was to root out spies and saboteurs, the measure of effectiveness became the number of saboteurs and spies who were caught; in effect, body count became the only measure of effectiveness. It was in this way that many people were either executed or sent to various Khmer Rouge prisons, and then were later executed anyway. The administration at the region- and zone-level, which was led by a party secretary, also gave the appearance that the Khmer Rouge actually had a civilian administration. All of the party secretaries for each region and zone were also former fighters. Even though they could be called "civilian" because of their title as party secretary, that still did not hide the fact that they simply did not have enough workers to perform civilian duties.

Apart from this simplified system the Khmer Rouge also established "cooperatives," which existed even before 1975. When it took power, the Khmer Rouge implemented this system to its fullest extent. In fact, it was at the cooperative that people would work for their own subsistence, as well as for export. The cooperative was a special unit that could cover many hamlets and villages, depending on the scale of the rice fields as well as the number of workers. The chief of the cooperative determined the daily food ration for everyone under his command, and this was the only place where eating was allowed. Anyone caught eating outside of the cooperatives would be considered a traitor to the Angkar and the revolution. The offender would be arrested and killed. Thus, the cooperatives also had the authority to kill anyone they deemed unnecessary to the revolution.

THE KAMPUCHEAN REVOLUTIONARY ARMY

The local administration was very simplistic with a trio working as chief of each level. However, even though these administrations were not supported by any skilled technicians or civilians who could run a civilian administration, they were all supported by a sophisticated military structure. The armed forces of Democratic Kampuchea were designed as a multilayered system akin to that of the Soviet Union, China, and Vietnam. This was the second basic structure of Democratic Kampuchea. The armed forces were divided into three levels: the central or combatant command, the regional forces, and the militias.

 សញ្ញាជាតិ

កម្ពុជា ប្រជាធិបតេយ្យ

Coats of arms of Democratic Kampuchea. The Khmer letter on the insignia reads "Democratic Kampuchea." (©Documentation Center of Cambodia. Used by permission.)

The central or combatant command was known in Khmer as *toap srouch* (literally "sharp" troops) and was under the direct command of the general staff and the Central Committee of the CPK. Between 1970 and 1975, this formation was not yet in existence. Soldiers were recruited from the locales in which they lived and were then organized into small units. During that time, each Region was supposed to have either one regiment or a division, depending on the situation on the ground. However, some Regions could muster only a battalion with some subordinated units. Then, some parts of those units would be upgraded into operational divisions under the command of the CPK and the general staff during the final push toward Phnom Penh.

After the Khmer Rouge victory in April 1975, the Kampuchea Revolutionary Army (KRA) was established in Phnom Penh (at the Olympic Stadium) on July 22, 1975, and was presided over by Son Sen (codename Borng 89 or Elder Brother 89) who was the minister of defense and security; the event was attended by 3,000 representatives from all branches and units of the armed forces.[53] Then, the Central Committee of the CPK organized many divisions under its command, and they were stationed in and around Phnom Penh. Before the fighting with Vietnam in mid-1977, elements of these units were sent for "rice growing duties" all over the country. After the situation with Vietnam deteriorated, and during the purge in the East Zone, all units were recalled, and many divisions were sent to the border to fight with Vietnam.

In March 1977, a document of the general staff of the KRA laid out the forces under the command of the Central Committee.[54] Nine divisions were under direct command of the Central Committee. Each was identified by the three-digit number that distinguished them as troops of the Central Committee. These nine divisions were: 703, 310, 450, 170, 290, 502, 801, 920, and 164. Each division was a full division with personnel ranging from 4,000 to 6,000. Division 703 divided some of its forces for the S-21 office (see below). Division 310 had a total number of 6,096 personnel, of which 1,127 soldiers were based in Kompung Chhnang province. Division 450 also had 1,522 soldiers in Kompung Chhnang. Kompung Chhnang was important because it had a large airfield—built with the support of China—which could accommodate large bombers.[55] Mosyakov speculated that this airfield was capable of launching bombers that could reach Ho Chi Minh City in about half an hour, which later explained why the Vietnamese took a tougher stance against Democratic Kampuchea.[56]

The central command also had three independent regiments, 152, 488, and 377. The KRA general staff maintained three offices, Office 63 and Office 62 (this office controlled training facilities, the military school, and body guard units) under Borng 89 (Son Sen) and Office S-21 under Kaing Guek Eav, alias Duch (which was also under the supervision of Son Sen). Office S-21 was a security prison, the only highest level of prison under direct control of the Central Committee of the CPK. This third office was hardened by security forces taken from division 703. In total, the soldiers under direct command of the Central Committee of the CPK amounted to 61,189 as of March 1977.[57] These were the divisions Pol Pot sent to fight against Vietnam as well as to execute orders to purge the East Zone. Later, however, many cadres from these divisions were also purged and sent to S-21, including the division 703 which provided the guards for the S-21 itself.

The second layer of military power of Democratic Kampuchea was the regional level.[58] Both the Zone and the Region had their own military units. The Zone might organize a division or some brigades to carry out operations in its area of responsibility. The Region could have a regiment. The district (*srok*) also had one company of soldiers and this was the lowest level of the regional troop formations. This was the standard: a region could have one regiment or a battalion depending on the situation in that region, and several regions combined to become a zone where the standard force was one division only. Any surplus would have to be transferred to central. However, the East

Zone, by virtue of the good relations between its party secretary Sor Phim and Pol Pot, could retain two of its original three divisions.[59]

The Region's troops and the Zone's troops frequently clashed with the troops from the Central Committee even before 1975. Soldiers of division 12 (the predecessor of division 703), for example, had captured and then summarily executed soldiers of Region 23 and those of the East Zone who just wandered across the line into their area of responsibility.[60] During the brief occupation of Phnom Penh in 1975, the rivalry between the East Zone and other units also played out when the other units arrested even their fellow soldiers who barely crossed the line dividing the areas of responsibility.

The third layer of military forces in Democratic Kampuchea included the militias. The militias were also regional in character similar to the regional forces. However, the dividing line between the militia and the regional forces was the scope of the area of responsibility and combat equipment. The militias were responsible only for the security in the hamlet and the village and therefore they were very lightly armed compared to the regional forces. However, their main weapon was the knowledge of the terrain and the mobility in their environs. Between 1970 and 1975, these forces were responsible for maintaining the party structure in their locale, also security, as well as carrying out ambushes against the FANK. It was their presence that drove all local authority of the Khmer Republic out of the hamlets and villages to the provincial towns. Later, these groups also recruited soldiers in their own areas.

Under Democratic Kampuchea, the militias were known as *korng chhlorb* (meaning they were designed as guerilla units) and they assisted the chief of the village as well as the chief of the hamlet. Their main mission was to root out saboteurs by spying on every 17th April person. These were the local forces before 1975. Children of the 17th April people and other youngsters would be separated from their parents and put into the other two units before being promoted to *korng chhlorb* if necessary. The first unit was *korng kumar* (children units), which consisted of children who were not yet teenagers. The second group was *korng tcha'lart* (mobile units), which were composed of teenagers. These groups followed the cooperatives and usually did manual labor to support the cooperatives.

While these two groups were designed as military units, their main tasks were not always military in nature. Gardening, cooking, and cleaning were among many other duties that these units performed. However, when the fighting with Vietnam intensified, more and more children were used as messengers, runners, and transporters of ammunition.[61] There were no schools, and the Khmer Rouge considered the battlefield as well as manual labor as the only valid schools. Children were taught to love guns and were required to dress in military uniform during their work.

The military itself was preoccupied only with counterespionage, and because there was no other institution to run the state, the then Democratic Kampuchea functioned as a giant military base with the people acting as forced laborers, among whom lurked saboteurs and spies. To justify their existence, all organizations had to hold on to the original mission for which they had been established. To eliminate that purpose or mission meant that the organization would no longer be useful, thus subject to liquidation. As a result, any organization would try to hold on to their mission and would always assert that their mission had not been completed. The Khmer Rouge emphasized this by establishing over 100 prisons all across the country in an attempt to enforce their rule.

THE PRISON SYSTEM OF DEMOCRATIC KAMPUCHEA

The third sophisticated organization that the Khmer Rouge established was the security system. Prisons, together with the military, remained the two most sophisticated organizations that were designed based on a modern system. Unfortunately, there was nothing good associated with the security prisons. Just like the military, there were also different layers of prisons or "security offices."

The Khmer Rouge established a prison section in all levels of their territorial administration system, which was quite unprecedented. The most common prison for the Khmer Rouge before taking power in 1975 was the security office at the district level and the region level. In the liberated areas, there was no judge nor was there a justice system. Any perceived act of treason or disloyalty to the Angkar could easily land anyone in jail. The chiefs of hamlets, villages, and districts as well as the militias all had the authority to arrest people. But the prisons at the lower level were a means of keeping order only. Usually, there was no torture or killing, and many people were released after a few months of imprisonment.[62] Before 1975, these prisons mostly functioned as correctional facilities.

The security office at the district level was much more brutal. People who were arrested usually disappeared. In Region 23 for example, the district security office was responsible for the disappearance of people as well as their fellow Khmer Rouge cadres who protested against the presence of Vietnamese troops in Cambodia.[63]

The Central Committee controlled one important prison—the S-21, a maximum security prison also known as *sante barl* which, according to David Chandler, was a combination of *sante sok* (a Khmer word meaning "security") and *norkor barl* (Khmer word for "police").[64] The two words were contracted to *sante barl*. Of all the security offices under Democratic Kampuchea, none rivaled it in terms of the number of prisoners, the brutality, and the security. This requires some description at length.

The office was headed by a former schoolteacher named Kaing Guek Eav, alias Duch.[65] Kaing Guek Eav had been a math teacher under the Prince Sihanouk regime, which was then a prestigious position. He was later branded communist by the local authority, arrested and tortured. Like many other people, Eav joined the revolution and adopted the revolutionary name "Duch."

Before 1975, he had already assumed responsibility over a local security office known as Office 13 (M-13).

According to the court (ECCC) document related to the judgment on Duch's case, Office M-13 was created in July 1971 to interrogate the suspects and the enemies of the CPK.[66] M-13 had two sections. Office M-13 "A" under the command of Duch himself was where the prisoners were usually tortured and killed. Office M-13 "B" was under the command of Duch's deputy and functioned more like a correctional facility where many prisoners were later released. Duch recruited his guards and interrogators mostly from among the farmers' children and he taught them how to torture. Duch openly admitted that despite his suspicion of the accuracy of the forced confession of the prisoners, he still sent them to the Central Committee and as a result, all prisoners were executed after the interrogation.[67] From July 20, 1971 to mid-1973, Duch answered to Vorn Vet and from 1973 to January 1975, he answered to Son Sen.

After the fall of Phnom Penh, S-21 was immediately established in October 1975, even before Democratic Kampuchea was formally established (which was in 1976). "S" stood for "security" and "21" was a secret code.[68] The building of the S-21 was a former high school. The S-21 was supported by two facilities in the suburb of Phnom Penh, at Tcheung Ek and Prey Sor (S-24), which was supposed to be the correctional center. Tcheung Ek was the place where the prisoners were executed. Duch was head of the interrogation section until his promotion to the position of chief of S-21 in March 1976 when his superior was transferred to the general staff.[69]

The S-21 security office took care of three categories of people. The people jailed at S-21 consisted of those who had committed serious offenses. These could be accusations that someone was a spy, was plotting against the revolution, was the head of a spy network, and so forth. S-21 was special because it answered directly to the Central Committee of the CPK and had the authority to arrest the cadres. The security offices at the lower levels were not allowed to deal with these types of prisoners.

The interrogation techniques used in S-21 were intended to produce a result that could be dubbed "narrative confession." In this system, the prisoners were required to confess their life as a spy plotting to overthrow the revolution. There was no other choice. The prisoners must accept a priori that they were spies. Their only job was to relate such a confession. Anyone who refused to do so would be tortured until they produced a confession related to their espionage, however false that might be.

Most allegations that brought people to S-21 were almost always baseless. David Chandler noted that the prisoners were usually asked why they were arrested. When the prisoner replied that he or she did not know anything, Duch would answer that Angkar was omniscient and was not as stupid as to arrest the wrong person.[70] Duch accepted only one answer, that the prisoner was a spy. Any prisoner who refused to admit he or she was a spy would be tortured by various brutal techniques such as electrocution (the internal rule was 3 to 5 consecutive shots per wrong answer, i.e., denial), pulling out finger nails, beating, water boarding, hanging above the floor from one hand or foot, and so forth.

Duch also brutally enforced internal rule. The guard or interrogator could torture the prisoner to get the answers, but if the prisoner died during the interrogation, the interrogator would also be executed.[71] When female prisoners arrived, any guards who raped the prisoners would be executed if caught. Some of the rules were: the guards must not talk to each other during shift, they must prevent the prisoners from talking to each other, and they must not sleep on the job. Ultimately, most prisoners would be forced to write a false confession claiming responsibility for all the things they had never actually done. In each report, there was also a section on "collaborators" or "networks" where the prisoner was required to give a list of his or her alleged spy network. Prisoners could range from normal people to region secretary to zone secretary. When such high-level purges occurred, soldiers from other zones would be sent to "cleanse" that zone, and most low-level cadres were arrested on the spot and summarily executed without being sent to the S-21.

During his trial, Duch admitted that he knew at the time that most of the information contained in the confession letter was false, inaccurate or entirely fabricated, but still reported it nonetheless out of fear for his own safety if he could not catch any spies.[72] Each note would contain a section on the network, which the prisoners would be forced to confess too. The list was used to arrest more suspects who met the same fate as the ones who accused them.[73] When interviewed by the Documentation Center of Cambodia, Chum Manh, a survivor of the S-21 (because of his skill as a mechanic), prayed forgiveness from other people who he had pointed out as being part of his network in his confession since he (Chum Manh) too would have been tortured and killed had he not done such things.[74]

What is equally pertinent is the fact that S-21 created a special rule to ensure that even though the prisoners could confess about their networks, there did exist a list of the "untouchables." Normally, a confession that contained many collaborators was the most acceptable one. Yet, any accusation against any of the untouchables would receive more punishment.

In one prominent example, in the internal rules for the prisoners at S-21, the prisoners were required to follow these guidelines, among others, during the interrogation:

- Do not praise the Revolution.
- Do not hide or deny your guilt, or you will be beaten countless times.
- Do not accuse the members of the Central Committee.
- Do not use Kampuchea Krom[75] to hide your guilt.[76]

Therefore, Duch explicitly prohibited the prisoners from accusing the top leadership of the CPK. Some prisoners got smart and tried to use their acquaintance with the senior leadership to plead for forgiveness. This was explicitly prohibited and confession letters bearing those names would not be accepted. In 1978, when the purge of division 703 was in full swing, some fighters were taken to S-21. Because the security of the S-21 was hardened by the guards from division 703, some of the prisoners actually knew the guards. In one instance, the prisoner accused Comrade Huy, a guard from division 703 who was Duch's right hand man at S-21. Vannak noted that when the confession letter was sent to central, Huy's name had already been erased from that letter.[77]

During his trial, Duch claimed that central command required him to find spies because central was convinced that foreign spies had already penetrated many levels of the party and the state organization. Therefore, he claimed he had to do what he did in order to survive.[78] Once again, organizations needed to produce results in accordance with their "missions." In the case of the S-21, it was deadly.

COMMUNIST LIFE: A PARADISE THAT NEVER WAS

The Khmer Rouge claimed that a new society would be a just society and would be free for everyone. There would be no different classes, nor exploitation by the bourgeoisie, or so they claimed. But before that could happen, old remnants of society, the old superstructure, had to be demolished. It was from the ashes of the old society that the new one could be built. However, the society the Khmer Rouge created was simply another form of exploitation. The Khmer Rouge took the term "dictatorship of the proletariat" literally.

Many books have already described in detail about life under the Khmer Rouge.[79] Here I will not repeat these details, but I will attempt to reexamine some aspects and clarify some of the issues raised in earlier works. Five aspects of life under Democratic Kampuchea are therefore worth examining. Basically, the Khmer Rouge boasted that these five aspects were the distinguishing factors from other regimes in all of Cambodian history. But the Khmer Rouge failed to do what they claimed they intended to do.

First of all, the Khmer Rouge marked their rule with the creation of a sophisticated lexicon. Some authors such as Chandler speculated that these new terms were probably designed by Khieu Ponnary, wife of Pol Pot and sister of Ieng Sary's wife, who was the first female Cambodian to pass the high school diploma and who became a professor in Khmer literature.[80] Among their new terms was the form of address used by the Khmer Rouge. Members of the Khmer Rouge called each other "comrade" or in Khmer, *samak mit.* The Khmer term means "equal friend" and it was no doubt used to stress the classless society.

In reality, however, this was never observed. The Khmer Rouge did indeed call each other *samak mit,* but they also added the suffix *borng* or Khmer for "elder brother." No work by Western authors has ever examined this point. Cambodia is a partially hierarchical society in which we pay respect to older people, and the Khmer term for "brother" is translated differently in English. The English term can also be used to denote equal status while the Khmer term must either be an elder or a younger brother. The term *borng* in Khmer is translated as "elder brother" and when the Khmer Rouge called each other *samak mit borng* it meant "comrade elder," a clear sign of hierarchy. In the confession letters, as well as many reports that we will see later in this book, the term *borng* was used extensively whenever the Khmer Rouge mentioned the high-ranking party leaders. Many authors translated the term *borng* to "brother," giving a false sense that the Khmer Rouge had indeed created an equal society. They had not.

The second change the Khmer Rouge made to Cambodian society was the abolition of individual free will. Traditions and customs that the Cambodian people had been observing since time immemorial were also banned. Marriages were not allowed unless they were arranged by the party and Angkar. Based on this principle, the Khmer Rouge would simply arrange mass marriage events where the bride and the groom were determined randomly. Some women were also forced to marry the disabled fighters and many committed suicide.[81] This principle, however, applied only to the 17th April people. Conversations with many survivors of the regime actually revealed that the cadres and the base people could actually have a choice. They still went to the mass marriage event but the pair could already be determined beforehand. All they needed to do was to follow the representative of the party who was the matchmaker.

Religion (Buddhism) was also abolished. Monks were forced to become civilians and pagodas were converted to warehouses. And even the New Year ceremony was banned. However, one witness observed that this ceremony existed but only for the cadres, not the 17th April people.[82]

The third change was the destruction of the family nucleus and the establishment of a purely totalitarian state. Family members were separated and sent to different cooperatives. The Khmer Rouge taught that Angkar was the only true parent for everyone, and that biological parents meant nothing.[83] As such, children around seven or eight years old were put in *korng kumar* ("children units"), an organization that was based on the design of a military unit, although the Khmer Rouge claimed these units were designed to study politics and literature. In reality, all of them were sent to do manual labor and agricultural chores.[84] When the war with Vietnam intensified in 1978, these children units were sent to the battlefield to serve in logistics and later as fighters, and many died from this failed campaign due to a lack of training, planning, and experience.[85]

Fourth, the Khmer Rouge attempted to destroy the free market economy. The Khmer Rouge abolished money, and the central bank was blown up as a testimony to the commitment to abolish the free market. However, this process was gradual. When the liberated zones were organized around 1972, the market had already been abolished and the cooperatives became the economic center of the community. During the time in which the Khmer Rouge hid behind the GRUNK, cooperatives replaced the market; it was at the cooperative that everyone would work and then receive their goods for their daily lives. During this time, money and trade were still allowed within the cooperative.[86]

Five days after their liberation of Phnom Penh, however, the Khmer Rouge revealed its true character. On May 20, 1975, Pol Pot declared that money would be abolished within the cooperatives even though new banknotes had already been printed. The notes themselves contained many images glorifying the military forces. Many notes had pictures of soldiers working in factories and rice fields.

However, all the banknotes were never circulated. Pol Pot considered money to be the vice of the ancient regime and therefore this must be eliminated. The ideology was that money creates private property that, in turn, leads to corruption, inequality, jealousy and exploitation, producing an oppressed class and an oppressing class. The motto during Democratic Kampuchea was "No sale, No exchange, No gain, No theft, No robbery, No private property."[87] So even though the notes were already printed, they were never circulated. They would spend their lives in the cooperatives. Hu Nim protested against the abolition of money and he was later arrested and executed.[88]

While money was not available, the barter economy was the norm. With an earring, for example, one could buy a plate of dessert and this could be eaten with impunity. During the Khmer Rouge regime, eating something that was not provided by the cooperative could also be a cause for execution. Eating something obtained from bartering with the local people, however, was acceptable. The free market system, it seemed, was indeed a taboo, but it depended on who was the seller and who you were buying from.

The fifth, and related, change was the destruction of "all things imperial." In fact, jewelry was considered an imperial influence and was banned. Ironically, gold, silver, diamonds, and jewelry were the most favorite bartering tools under Democratic Kampuchea. Local people might not have a concept of what money meant, but they could still like jewelry.

Long hair, wearing a watch, listening to pre-1975 music, singing a pre-1975 song, fishing, using a fancy spoon, reading books, writing, speaking foreign languages, and so forth were only some of the things that the Khmer Rouge considered to be "imperial" and therefore fit for elimination. Anyone caught practicing these vices would be executed. As a result, singers, movie stars, and stage performers were usually the first victims as they were immediately recognizable. Next came the intellectuals. Again, these principles applied only to the 17th April people. The cadre and the local people still enjoyed the luxuries that were considered to be imperial.

The Khmer Rouge was some sort of "semi-organized failed state," something between a totalitarian state and a failed state. A totalitarian state is a state in which every aspect of life is totally transformed in an unprecedented way. A failed state, on the other hand, is simply a state that could not provide basic structures such as law and order to the general population. In the former case, a lot of people died because the government systematically repressed society and killed anyone who would not conform to their radical ideology. Nazi Germany and Stalinist Soviet Union fit this description. In the case of a failed state, people die because there is no state to protect them. Many tragedies in Africa result from this phenomenon.

On the one hand, the Khmer Rouge's security apparatus killed a lot of people. They were well organized. On the other hand, there was no law or justice system and therefore the killings also occurred in a profound and profuse way at the local level. The interviews with many witnesses revealed that most deaths at the local levels happened in the cooperatives. The *chhlorb*, the cooperatives, and other security forces usually rounded up people for no reasons at all and they were never to be seen again.

POSTSCRIPT: SOME EYEWITNESS ACCOUNTS ON THE FAILURE TO RADICALIZE LIFE

Many organizations try to reshape the lives of their members in order to create what they think is a better society. Hence, we hear, and are fascinated by, stories and myths of the organizations of assassins who have no personal feelings and unquestioned loyalty, for example, special forces and commandos who have no family members (and are thus more effective in all sorts of missions), and followers of some mysterious organizations who choose to commit suicide rather than talk. These stories are the stuff of fantasy that we often see in movies. In real life, some organizations do try to follow such myths. To repeat a famous catchphrase, one then has to destroy all character and personality of a person and then rebuild that person from zero.

The Khmer Rouge adopted this stance and sought to radicalize all aspects of life so that a perfect society could be built. The first step was to build a pure cadre who would commit to the party, have no personal feelings, be unmoved by materialism, and be willing to sacrifice everything for the state, which is the only valid parent. The Khmer Rouge, thus, chose only small children and the poorest among the local people to be soldiers and cadres. In reality, however, they failed terribly. This was because the human psyche that had been built and which evolved throughout the millennia could not simply be changed in a few years. The Khmer Rouge failed to take human history into account.

To examine all evidence to prove this point would exceed the scope of this book. It would also be necessary to provide too much detail, and many books already cover this area. Here, I will only include this small section to record what I have learned as a Cambodian. These are the stories related to me by my family, my professor, and other survivors, as well as written records of the eyewitnesses. I think that these stories are not merely anecdotes, but each story illustrates some of the recurrent themes that many people witnessed under the regime.

In this chapter, I have already discussed how the Khmer Rouge detested all things imperial. That included actors, stars, performers, and adherents to the old regime. These people became victims because some of them, such as the famed signer Sin Sisamouth whose songs are still listened to today, also sang the patriotic songs of the Khmer Republic. These victims were easily recognizable and were immediately rounded up and killed after a short period in forced labor.

My father related to me an event he encountered firsthand in the North Zone where he had lived, near the house of Koy Thourn, the party secretary of the zone before 1975. He told me: "Everyday, we all needed to go to work early in the morning and the Khmer Rouge cadre often played revolutionary songs over the speaker before work started. Then one day, we heard the song of the famed Cambodian singer Sin Sisamouth. The song was played for about half a minute before it was interrupted and then replaced by the usual revolutionary songs. Apparently, it seemed like the cadres also listened to the songs they called imperial, and then forgot to change the cassette when they turned the player on the next morning, this time through the speaker." Considering all the duress of life under the Khmer Rouge, this episode provided a rare moment of comic relief. But it is also a small example to show that Democratic Kampuchea was simply replacing one form of imperialism with another. This Khmer Rouge's form of imperialism was even worse than what the Khmer Rouge claimed it had replaced.

During the selection of their local cadres, the Khmer Rouge preferred the poorest and most illiterate among the local people. The Khmer Rouge hoped that limited exposure to the free market and capitalist system would result in these cadres becoming perfect administrators and revolutionaries. These local cadres were to be aided by children soldiers and guards units separated from their parents, who had been indoctrinated that Angkar was their only parent.

However, knowing the chief of the hamlet before the war could prove to be a lifesaver. For example, my maternal grandfather came from Takeo province, but he came to the city when he was young. He ran a *cyclo* shop (a type of rickshaw used to transport people in the 1960s) in Phnom Penh at the time. He went to his hometown in Takeo with his family after 1975 and it turned out that one of his workers then became the chief of the hamlet. Life was bearable at that time, until a few months later when random families were sent to the North-West Zone as part of the new agriculture policy (3-ton-per-hectare).

Before that forced relocation, my mother was approached one day by a female cadre who asked about my mother's nail polish. My mother had gone to a friend's wedding shortly before the fall of Phnom Penh and the nail polish was still visible a month later. The female cadre asked my mother if she still had the nail polish as "Angkar wants to take your nail polish to paint the loudspeaker!" One can simply ask how could a small bottle of nail polish be used to paint a large loudspeaker, which was about one meter in diameter? My mother thought that the female cadre actually wanted to use the nail polish for herself but was too embarrassed to ask. So the female cadre came up with a ridiculous excuse, to paint the loudspeaker. My mother explained the story and the female cadre believed her and left. At that time, to wear nail polish was considered as having "imperialist tendencies."

In another story, the child soldiers that the Khmer Rouge used extensively due to their "unquestioned belief in the revolution" also could not totally leave behind their inner childishness. When I was a second year student at a university in Phnom Penh, my professor of international relations told the class about his experience under the Khmer Rouge regime and how he survived through his skill in storytelling. His father ran a newspaper shop before the war and as a keen student, he read every article in the newspaper, especially the series of Chinese stories and folklores that were published sequentially. He remembered every detail of the landscape and everyday life of ancient China as described in those stories. Under Democratic Kampuchea, he was arrested without any reason, just like hundreds of thousands of other Cambodians.

In the prison, he was guarded by young soldiers with guns that were taller than the gunmen themselves. One night, the child guard was bored and he asked my professor if he knew any story to amuse him to pass the time. Having no other choice, my professor told all the stories that he had learned over the years when he read his father's newspaper. The guard was very excited and brought him rice the next day and told him not to work in the field but only to prepare to tell him more stories at night. It turned out that my professor never ran out of stories and he told my class that the Khmer Rouge child soldier was immersed in these stories that he told, even though the child had absolutely no idea about ancient China or Shaolin martial arts. He survived just like Scheherazade, the vizier's daughter in *The Arabian Nights*, who also survived by telling stories every night.

One day, the child guard packed up with his comrades and prepared to leave. In most cases, when a prison was deserted or when there was no possibility of keeping those prisoners locked up anymore, all prisoners would be summarily executed. However, that did not happen to my professor. The child gave a final glance to his favorite storyteller and then left without a word: the soldiers of the Kampuchea Solidarity Front for National Salvation had arrived. My professor went on to win a scholarship of the PRK and has worked since as a spokesperson of the government as well as an ambassador of the Kingdom of Cambodia. The story reveals one fundamental truth: you can take the child out of the classroom but you cannot take the classroom out of the child. Even a prison cell can be made into a makeshift classroom.

Of all the survival stories under the Khmer Rouge, perhaps none rivaled the chilling account of the survival of the late Van Nath who was an artist before the war.[89] One day he was arrested without any apparent reason and was transported, blindfolded, to S-21 where Duch interrogated him personally. The routine was like any other interrogation session. "Are you CIA or KGB or Yuon? Don't answer 'no' because Angkar is not stupid and never arrests the wrong people!" And then they tortured Vann Nath. During the first stage, they asked him to recount his background and he told Duch he was an artist, at which point, Duch was interested, and then tested him. As an artist, Vann Nath's first portrait, despite having been tortured, gave signs that he really was an artist. Because of this, Duch allowed him to rest and eat fully so that he could paint portraits for Duch. According to Vann Nath, Duch always came to inspect his works and the only portrait that Vann Nath created was none other than Pol Pot's portrait, which Duch made him paint over and over again. Less than 10 prisoners survived S-21, which was known as the "one-way prison." All of the survivors had some manual and technical skills that were useful for S-21, as mechanics, photographers, repairers of clocks, and sculptors.[90]

The survival stories at S-21 showed that Duch actually knew that the question "are you CIA or KGB?" was nonsense, and the answer had already been determined *a priori*. In most cases, prisoners were forced to confess that they were members of both the CIA and the KGB, something that would intrigue even a very able Cold War historian. Upon learning he could gain something from the prisoner, he immediately dropped the deadly question.

In sum, the Khmer Rouge sought to establish a radical society and they fielded a distinct group of cadres who might fit the type of pure society that the Khmer Rouge leaders fantasized about. However, try as they did, the Khmer Rouge still could not suppress the innate desire and personality that defines a human being. People need tools to survive in nature and children need to learn and study. Law, money, trade, religion, technical knowledge, technical know-how, subject matter experts, and intellectuals are only minor examples of the requirements for a society to function.

Old laws were abolished and when the new ones were impossible to apply, the cadres looked into their respective organizations to find purpose. When they followed the purpose of an organization that was designed for war, and then used it in the civilian sphere, "body count" and "number of spies caught" became the measure of effectiveness instead of maximizing the welfare of their members (which would be the mission of civilian state organization). Once this mission flourished, they never ceased to find new targets. At some points, they ran out of targets and began to apply the rules on their fellow colleagues.

The Khmer Rouge essentially merged the civilian administration with the military unit. And because the party secretary himself was the commander of the military unit, the Khmer Rouge did not have civilian administration in their liberated areas, despite the nominal position to the contrary. When the military, military-like, or counter-espionage organizations were put to run the country or when those organizations were designed using a military or counterespionage model, they brought with them a specific measure of effectiveness. In the 18th century, Voltaire had reportedly said that "while France is a state that has an army, Prussia is an army that has a state." What he meant was that France was a more orderly country with a functioning civilian system while the Prussian government was nothing more than an army that happened to control everything in the state. The implication here was that because the army controlled the state, foreign policy tended to be erratic and adventurous. While Voltaire's comment is subject to debate, the Khmer Rouge on the other hand was a true case of "an army that has a state," and the tragedy did not lie only in their foreign policy, especially toward Vietnam, but also with regard to their internal politics. Such was the tragedy of Democratic Kampuchea.

3

⸺⸻⸺

The Enemies Could Be
Everywhere and Everyone!

[...] at the border of Kampot province, they [the Vietnamese] have evacuated their people 3 kilometers from the border and they had written in Khmer and Vietnamese languages: "Vietnam-Cambodia, Solidarity for Thousands Years" [...]

—Report from the Southwest Zone, March 3, 1977.[1]

The only plausible clue to what was behind the murderous raid was a Khmer Rouge slogan scrawled in charcoal on a door: "*Ti nih srok young*—This is our country."

—Nayan Chanda, *Brother Enemy,* page 224, on a
visit to Ha Tieng in March 1978.

If what was reported in the above two quotes were correct, and there are reasons to believe that they were, then they can both be used to sum up the attitude and strategic approaches of the Khmer Rouge and the Vietnamese during the border war. This border war lasted for almost the entire period during which Democratic Kampuchea was in power.

In the previous chapter, I have already described the ideology and some deficiencies in the mindset of the leadership that drove a small group of radicals to turn society upside down. In this chapter, I will add three more deficiencies that defined Democratic Kampuchea, although these received inadequate attention in the standard literature. These deficiencies were: micromanagement by the Central Committee, extreme anti-Vietnamese ideology that led to a strategy attempting to annihilate a bigger adversary, and brutal operations in support of this impossible strategy. The following analysis seeks to provide and explain the details involved.

The first problem inherent in the governing style of Democratic Kampuchea was administrative inefficiency. This flaw can be discerned from the main characteristics of the reports made by the lower echelons to the Central Committee of the CPK:

- Officers who reported to the Central Committee seemed to show a lack of attention to the standard of reports. We do not know whether the reporters were not serious, were illiterate, were not trained to prepare concise reports; or perhaps the reports included a combination of all of the above. A lot of information was either presented without supporting evidence, or was lacking in clarity. As we will see later in this chapter, in most cases, the information was not vetted. The reports were comprised of completely raw information and the author did not even attempt to apply a structure to the report that could assist the reading.

In one example, many reports explicitly mentioned the partnership between "Vietnam and the CIA, bent on destroying Cambodia," an assertion that was totally absurd, especially when one takes into consideration the fact that only a few years earlier the United States had fought bitterly with the Vietnamese. This assertion reveals an absolute dysfunction in the Khmer Rouge intelligence apparatus. A small country with an almost nonexistent intelligence organization tried to fight with a large country. That was the root cause of all the destruction that followed.

- The reports were also marred by grammatical and typographical errors and sometimes even Pol Pot's name was misspelled or contracted.[2]
- The Central Committee wanted to be updated on everything that was happening. One cannot imagine how many reports were sent to Office 870, but the clues left behind by the surviving documents show that this micromanagement was implemented to the extreme. In one instance, a request to the Chinese government for a total of six plows to be used in the North Zone was reported directly to Office 870, without any involvement from, or delegation to, the ministries involved.[3] When the fighting with Vietnam intensified, even a report involving the arrest of one single person with apparently no incriminating evidence was also sent up to Office 870.[4]

The reporting procedure was also peculiar. It was not uncommon for the Central Committee to refrain from issuing an order from a distance on important matters, in preference for face-to-face briefings, even though such briefings would have been grossly inefficient. This deficiency would come back to haunt the Khmer Rouge later on, but in their early years, this exclusive centralization brought about a clash with the United States at the very end of the Vietnam War, involving the capture of the SS Mayaguez.

THE MAYAGUEZ INCIDENT

Barely a week after the failed attempt to take Phu Quoc Island, on May 12, 1975, the troops from the same Southwest Zone had provoked another incident with an American merchant vessel bound for Thailand. It was an incident that sparked what Wetterhahn called the "last battle of the Vietnam War."[5]

On the early morning of May 12, 1975, an American merchant ship, the SS Mayaguez, approached Poulo Wai Islands. The garrison sent out gunboats to intercept this ship at approximately 2:00 P.M. (3:00 A.M. EST). The ship then sent out a Mayday message that was picked up by some civilian ships near the Indonesian coast, who then alerted the U.S. Embassy in Jakarta. The Ford administration considered this incident to be a vital challenge to the reputation and resolve of the United States which had, only one month earlier, pulled out of Phnom Penh and Vietnam. The United States then vowed to take strong action if the hostages were not released.

On a side note, since 1969, the border clashes between the People's Republic of China and the Soviet Union had led to the Sino-Soviet split in 1969, and the United States had subsequently opened up communication with China. Both countries began to repair their diplomatic relations in 1973 with the establishment of the United States Liaison Office in Beijing. When the SS Mayaguez was intercepted and her crew taken hostage, the only channel the United States could use to talk to the Khmer Rouge was by way of this Liaison Office in China. At 12:00 P.M. on May 12, 1975, President Ford convened the first National Security Council meeting on the matter, and on the afternoon of the same day, Secretary of State Henry Kissinger sent a message to the head of the Chinese Liaison Office in Washington D.C., who refused to take the note.[6] Then Kissinger asked the Special Liaison Officer in Beijing, George H.W. Bush, to hand a letter to the Chinese representative (to pass on to the Khmer Rouge government).

According to Wetterhahn, this message contained an implicit threat concerning the use of force.[7] The Chinese responded that they could not establish contact with the Khmer Rouge. The Khmer Rouge took over the country for less than a month and therefore it was simply impossible to find out exactly who was involved in this incident. The United States then continued with a plan to at least win the last battle of the Vietnam War.

The Khmer Rouge, on the other hand, claimed that they had no information whatsoever that their soldiers had boarded the ship and taken the crew hostage. Ieng Sary claimed that he did not know anything, and the first time he heard about it was in the news of the American broadcasting service. The Voice of America first broadcast details of the incident at 5:00 A.M. on May 13 (6:00 P.M. EST, then on May 12). Ieng Sary described the Khmer Rouge version of the story:

After learning about the Mayaguez, we got in touch with the armed forces at the island and we called upon their leaders to come to Phnom Penh and inform us about this affair. Around 2:00 P.M. they arrived in Phnom Penh. At 5:00 P.M. we sent them back with the order to release the Mayaguez immediately because we did not want to have any difficulties with the U.S. government. While we were ordering the release of the ship, the Americans bombed Koh Tang.[8]

Instead of employing faster ways of communication (such as telephone, tele-graph, or radio relays), the Central Committee simply called the commanders and local leaders to Phnom Penh to inquire about the situation. They had already established de facto control in many areas of Cambodia even before April 1975, and therefore, it is hard to believe that they did not have any faster form of communication. The lengthy procedure involving travel was counterproductive (travelling roughly 185 kilometers or 115 miles). More-over, what if the commanders forgot some details? Would they return to the island to find out more details and then get back to the Central Committee, or would they make up a story to avoid scrutiny from the Central Committee on their inability to grasp the real situation that was taking place under their responsibility?

By virtue of relations between the United States and China after the Sino-Soviet split, conflict with the United States was not in the best interests of the Khmer Rouge. Ieng Sary admitted the following:

> We regret this affair, this problem. The deaths were unnecessary. We gave orders at Sihanouk Ville to release all Americans and American crew, yet the Ameri-cans came and bombed us, [at] Sihanouk Ville and Ream harbor, causing a lot of casualties to innocent peasants.[9]

The United States, on the other hand, was biased toward rapid response in order to avoid damage to its reputation. By the time the Khmer Rouge commanders received orders to release the hostages, the U.S. Marines were already on their way to Sihanouk Ville. The crew was released be-fore the Marines landed. However, Koh Tang (where the American spy plane had spotted the crew of the Mayaguez being brought onto the island) had already been bombed by American planes. Other facilities such as the railways ashore, and the only Cambodian oil refinery, were severely dam-aged during the incident. Firefights also broke out between the Marines and the Khmer Rouge in fortified positions on the island.

According to Becker, the whole episode cost the lives of 35 marines to save 34 members of the crew, whose release had already been ordered.[10] According to Wetterhahn, on the other hand, the casualties were only 18 KIAs for the Marines. Among them, three marines missed their exfiltration flight under the darkness of the night. The stranded marines were later found and killed by the furious Khmer Rouge.

POL POT'S ANNIHILATION STRATEGY

Napoleon's famous quote was that "God is on the side of the big battalions."[11] The rule of thumb for modern combat operation is that the attacking force needs at least a 3:1 numerical superiority to achieve a breakthrough in the face of prepared defense.[12] Israel was able to win its war with the Arab countries against the 10:1 numerical superiority enjoyed by the combined Arab forces only because the Arab countries could not work together to surround Israel.[13]

This simple fact in the art of war should not have evaded the attention of any able commander.

In 1975, a rough estimate of the size of the Cambodian population was 7.5 million.[14] This, of course, would be an overestimation of the potential pool of military recruits and military effectiveness because the majority of the population suffered from forced relocation, hunger, mass killings, purges and forced labor, as well as illiteracy among the ranks.[15] To make matters worse, people with some military experience under the FARK and the FANK were fiercely hunted down and executed, even those who were only suspects.

Vietnam, on the other hand, had a population of 48 million in 1975.[16] Despite the tensions between the North and the South, the People's Army of Vietnam (PAVN) was well organized, along with a strong political apparatus. In this comparison, the Khmer Rouge suffered an almost 8:1 inferiority in terms of numbers alone.

Both sides were equally motivated to fight and both were battle-hardened. Other things being equal, numbers should have determined victory in this case. And the odds were against the Khmer Rouge. So what motivated Pol Pot's strategy? It was not a mere hit-and-run strategy; it was an annihilation strategy against Vietnam. This book proposes two factors: Pol Pot's wishful thinking, and Vietnam's "solidarity and friendship policy" that was interpreted as a weak appeasement policy by Pol Pot.

Two things help with an understanding of what might have been in Pol Pot's mind when he decided to attack Vietnam. The first is the "Black Paper" issued in September 1978, which justified action against Vietnam as a purely defensive strategy.[17] The paper started with the assumption that Vietnam wanted to "swallow" Cambodia (and also Laos, but that was not much of a concern to the Khmer Rouge). The paper argued that the Indochina Communist Party (ICP) itself was so named because the ICP was supposed to unite the three countries in Indochina for independence, and as an extension, would unite the people and army under Vietnam, which was the biggest among the three. The paper maintained that this analysis was accurate because "Lenin, the famous head of Communist International did not name his own party the 'Communist Party of Europe.'"[18]

The paper closed with an implicit argument that whenever Cambodia or the CPK was assertive, Vietnam either backed down or failed altogether. Perhaps it was this perception that pushed the Khmer Rouge to continue the skirmishes into Vietnam, despite repeated failure, mainly because Vietnam always expressed its predisposition toward negotiation. The Khmer Rouge might therefore have interpreted the willingness to negotiate as a weakness.

Viewing Vietnam as a threat was one thing, while designing a strategy to counter that threat was entirely another matter. There are two possibilities: offensive strategy and defensive strategy.[19] Despite the defensive tone in all the documents, the Khmer Rouge's actions were certainly offensive in practice. The official documents also revealed offensive undertones.[20]

In spite of the disparity in numbers between Vietnam and Cambodia, the Khmer Rouge did not hesitate to pursue an adventurous policy. How the Khmer Rouge planned to overcome the disparity in numbers can be discerned from a state radio broadcast on May 10, 1978. In this broadcast, the Khmer Rouge propaganda service briefed the nation about national defense between April 1977 and April 1978, which should be quoted at length:

> [. . .] We are few in number, but we have to attack a larger force; therefore, we must preserve our forces to the maximum and try to kill as many of the enemy as possible. [. . .] In terms of numbers, one of us must kill 30 Vietnamese. If we can implement this slogan, we shall certainly win. [. . .] So far, we have succeeded in implementing this slogan of 1 against 30; that is to say, we lose 1 against 30 Vietnamese. [. . .]
>
> We should have 2,000,000 troops for 60,000,000 Vietnamese. However 2,000,000 troops would be more than enough to fight the Vietnamese, because Vietnam has only 50,000,000 inhabitants. [. . .] We must use one against 30. This is just the number fixed by the Party, but in concrete, deeds of some of our comrades fought 1 against 10; we shall certainly win with 1 against 10 or 1 against 5. Some of our people have fought 1 against 20, and some have even tried to fight one against 50 or 1 against 100. There was no problem; they were still victorious. [. . .][21]

The mathematics was simplistic, if not totally absurd. But not long after the above broadcast, fresh campaigns by the Khmer Rouge restarted. These campaigns were just military adventures with no clear strategic goals after the Khmer Rouge defeat in late 1977[22] (cf. Operations section below).

The situation seemed dire for Pol Pot, who still invited and entertained foreign correspondents, even after the fighting with Vietnam intensified in 1977. While the 1-against-30 slogan might not work in practice, Pol Pot still had a strong hope in his mind that he revealed to the last group of guests he allowed for interview in late 1978. The last group to interview Pol Pot was a trio including Elizabeth Becker of the *Washington Post*, Richard Dudman, another journalist, and an English lecturer named Caldwell who, Becker wrote, was a "friend" of the regime.[23]

The visit took place in December 1978, just at the time of the most intense fighting. Becker and the others were granted an exclusive interview with Pol Pot, where he (Pol Pot) lectured the journalists about how he thought Democratic Kampuchea could still win despite the great odds. According to Becker, Pol Pot hoped that Cambodia would be the battleground of the Cold War and that it would be the place where NATO and the Warsaw Pact fought it out if Vietnam dared to invade Cambodia. Pol Pot claimed that Vietnam had nothing, and to invade Cambodia, it needed to ask the Soviet Union to send troops from the Warsaw Pact to help them (the Vietnamese).[24] When that happened, communism would roll all the way down to Thailand, Malaysia, and Singapore, something the United States could not tolerate, and as a consequence, NATO would intervene.[25]

Khmer Rouge soldiers prepared for combat. Note that the soldiers were barefoot. (©Documentation Center of Cambodia. Used by permission.)

Apparently, Pol Pot was betting his future on several faulty assumptions. First, he saw that conflict with Vietnam was inevitable. Second, he thought that the Kampuchea Revolutionary Army, with constant purges and mass killing, could achieve the 1-against-30 target he had hoped for. Third, foreign troops would swoop in, out of the blue, to help his regime. Pol Pot had to pay dearly for his mistakes.

TAXONOMY KILLED: WAR, PURGES AND THE INTERNAL CLEANSING POLICY

The Khmer Rouge's decision to go to war with Vietnam can also be explained by a self-fulfilling belief about an ongoing Vietnamese conspiracy to take over Cambodia. This psychological process is known in the academic world as "confirmation bias."[26] People tend to prefer information that confirms their preexisting beliefs or personal experiences and immediately discard any contradictory information.

The Khmer Rouge believed that Vietnamese spies were within its rank. As such, it tasked the S-21 to find such enemies at all costs. The S-21 then understood that only the number of spies caught could be the measure of effectiveness. Whether they were genuine spies or not was not the point. It all became circular: because you tried to find the enemy this way, you would find only what confirmed your preexisting belief which, in turn, fueled more purges. In this section, we will look more in depth into one particular aspect of the methodology used at S-21: the taxonomy of enemies. The Khmer Rouge used taxonomy in its administrative divisions, for different types of land for rice crops, and for different types of prisoners and potential enemies. All these taxonomies involved killing.

For the Khmer Rouge, there were three types of enemies. These three types included the "internal enemies" and the "external enemies," and then within the "internal enemies" there were the people of the old regime and the enemies within the party's circle. The main problem came when Pol Pot suspected that people within his ranks were Vietnamese agents.

INTERNAL ENEMIES: MAGGOTS IN THE FLESH

For the Khmer Rouge, there were two types of internal enemies. The first type was the old remnants of the Khmer Republic. In 1975, the Khmer Rouge carried out the first wave of its cleansing policy.[27] Anyone accused of being a former FANK member, or a member of the police, would be executed or sent to the S-21 central prison. At S-21, many people were forced to confess that they were part of the FANK before 1975.

Many FANK soldiers did actually go into hiding in the ghost city after April 17, 1975, and Khmer Rouge patrols often came under fire. Since the city had been emptied of civilians, the Khmer Rouge inferred that some elements of the FANK must have dug in, even after the city was evacuated. Sometimes, the Khmer Rouge also found corpses in some houses. The cause of death was apparently hunger, since there were no wounds on the bodies.[28] All of this combined to corroborate the suspicions of the Khmer Rouge leadership, who then applied pressure on S-21 to find more plotters. Out of fear, or out of indifference, Duch and S-21 duly complied.[29]

The second wave of purification turned to the Khmer Rouge cadres as well as the veterans of the KPRP. When suspicion and arrests began to intensify, a series of events further exacerbated the situation. According to Chandler, on February 25, 1976, there was a mysterious explosion in the heart of Siem Reap (near the North Zone), while some reported seeing a plane overhead.[30] Then in early April the same year, there were a series of mysterious explosions in the heart of the empty Phnom Penh, which, for Pol Pot and his inner circle, indicated a full-blown attempt at a coup d'état, since there was no one else in the city besides the Khmer Rouge themselves.[31]

The first explosion in Siem Reap was suspected of being linked to Koy Thourn, the former secretary of the North Zone. He was formerly the party secretary in the North Zone but was transferred to a new job in Phnom Penh after the explosion.[32] He was in charge of economics and trade relations, something that Becker wrote were rigged with problems and difficulties.[33] In his confession note, Koy Thourn was forced to reveal his networks, and probably after torture, Koy Thourn gave a list of names, one of which was Hu Nim.[34]

A renowned intellectual and a friend of Hou Yuon and Khieu Samphan, Hu Nim was also arrested and sent to S-21 in May 1977. Toward the end of his life, Hu Nim could not comprehend the reason why he was arrested and made repeated pleas to Duch for him to talk to the top leadership, to no avail.[35] He was also forced to produce a confession note linking all his "networks" so that they, too, could be arrested and interrogated. Accordingly, the North Zone was soon "cleansed" of all intellectual elements. What was interesting from this event was that Hu Nim named Nhim Ros, the party secretary for the Northwest Zone, as the one who criticized the party's policy. To understand this event, we need to go back on the history of this area.

Hu Nim came from the Northwest Zone, an area known as the "rice bowl of Cambodia." We know from the previous chapter that one of the first things the CPK did was to create the taxonomy of different types of land, and demand a rice yield accordingly. The standard was the infamous "3-tons-per-hectare," with a higher expectation for the fertile land in the Northwest Zone. Historians agreed that the reason Hu Nim was arrested was because the Northwest Zone could not meet the requirement of the 3-tons-per-hectare target set by the Central Committee.[36]

Many problems plagued this area: thick, malaria-infested jungle, lack of machinery and technicians, and a sudden influx of urban population that the CPK thought could be used for farming. It is worth reminding that during the forced evacuation of the city, many people were either stuck midway in the area around Phnom Penh or went back to their hometown in the provinces. Not long after that, however, the Central Committee issued orders for another forced relocation of people from different zones to the Northwest Zone so that the Northwest Zone could use the new labor to maximize the rice production. The Zone, however, could not cope with such a sudden influx of people and a famine ensued. When all these factors combined, the "reinforcements" that the Central Committee provided to the Zone created a famine instead of higher rice yield. It began to suspect a conspiracy.

Conveniently, the S-21 continued to produce a series of confessions in which the prisoners said they were part of the "CIA-Vietnam ring," which destroyed the crops or sabotaged the machinery.[37] More importantly, in his confession, Hu Nim actually named Nhim Ros as a fierce opponent to the party policy. In his confession, Hu Nim accused Nhim Ros of explicitly criticizing the party's policy as unrealistic when the Northwest Zone was ordered to produce 4 tons per hectare, a ton more than the normal standard, despite the lack of equipment.[38] Nhim Ros was eventually arrested later in the same year along with other cadres of the Northwest Zone.[39]

Also, during that period, one particular explosion in the city was linked to a soldier from division 170, who had been recruited from the East Zone. Various confession notes traced this chain of command up to Sor Phim, the secretary of the East Zone, as an accomplice in the explosion,[40] but because of Phim's special background, he was not included in this earlier purge.

Only a handful of cadres from the East Zone suffered in this episode.[41] This purification policy destroyed the cadres of Democratic Kampuchea to a point where even the Chinese technicians who were sent to help the regime complained about the too frequent disappearances of their Cambodian counterparts.[42]

OPERATIONAL FLAWS IN THE LIGHT OF THE STRATEGY OF THE IMPOSSIBLE: FIGHTING THE EXTERNAL ENEMY THAT INTENDS TO "SWALLOW" CAMBODIA

This part of the chapter will look at one particular period in the Khmer Rouge's history: the purge of the East Zone and the war with Vietnam. It will be devoted to a campaign analysis of the border war between Democratic Kampuchea and Vietnam and the resulting purge.

With regard to the war with Vietnam between 1975 and 1978, many archives still survive to this day (mostly at the Documentation Center of Cambodia), although there is a document gap, especially concerning the campaign planning by the Central Committee, the general staff headquarter of the KRA, or the reports of such planning sent by the East Zone to the Central Committee. Personally, I believe there are two possible explanations. First, it may be the case that the documents exist in a safe somewhere, but have not yet been disclosed by their owner. Second, it could also be the case that the KRA and the Khmer Rouge in general never bothered with meticulous planning. After all, they could fight but they did not have the intellectual skills and rigor to pull off large-scale campaign planning. In this analysis, I will need to work with tactical reports first, and then work up to the operational level, only after which it is possible to make assumptions about the planning process as well as the military imperatives of any given situation. I will then compare this process to the strategic view of Pol Pot as explained early in this chapter.

1. Sideshow: War of the Scouts

Archival evidence shows that the Khmer Rouge could very well have had plans to attack Vietnam as early as 1976. It is worth recalling an important meeting that the top Khmer Rouge leaders held on defense in February 1976. The main principle that was adopted in that meeting was to negotiate and use "politics" with Vietnam. Then, when the time was ripe, the Khmer Rouge would strike.

After the 1975 raid on Phu Quoc Island (Koh Tral, in Khmer), which ended in disaster, the Khmer Rouge still continued normal relations with Vietnam but under the surface, they nurtured a secret suspicion toward the eastern neighbor. Many internal documents of the Central Committee and the Standing Committee of the CPK show that the Khmer Rouge was preoccupied with preparing countermeasures in case of conflict with Vietnam. Small clashes and skirmishes continued throughout 1976, at least based on the fact that Vietnamese prisoners started to arrive at S-21 in late 1975 and early 1976.[43]

However, both sides did not capitalize on the conflict, and it remained dormant for the entire years of 1975 and 1976. Nayan Chanda speculated that both sides did not publicize the conflict out of fear that outside powers might exploit that opportunity to intervene.[44] But one can also argue based on the archival documents that the most plausible reason for the Khmer Rouge not publicizing or capitalizing on the event was that they still felt weak in comparison to Vietnam. This can also be discerned through many reports of the internal CPK meetings. Many cadres proposed either an upgrade or additional forces for the standard units.[45] The debacle in the Phu Quoc (Koh Tral) operation might have also influenced this delaying tactic.

Vietnam, on the other hand, still could not believe its comrades had now turned on it. According to Stephen Morris, during the war before 1975, Vietnam was convinced that the conflict was initiated by local commanders without authorization from the top. The Vietnamese sometimes suspected that their own forces might have started the action first, and then asked their own forces to look into this possibility.[46] Eventually, the Vietnamese troops withdrew from the populated areas into the woods, and the Khmer Rouge remained in the villages and towns.[47]

The year of 1975 can be viewed as a year of uncertainty. This is because, after the People's Army of Vietnam captured Saigon, the North still needed to subdue all remaining forces of the Republic of Vietnam in an attempt to consolidate its power in the South. After a few months, North Vietnam progressively finalized the unification campaign and the conflict with the remnants of the Republic of Vietnam subsided. In early 1976, a delegation from the Vietnamese military visited their Cambodian counterpart. Seven officers from the military region 5 of the Vietnamese army met with eight commanders of the Northeast Zone of the KRA and both sides agreed on the following:[48]

- There was no intention on both sides to "invade each other," the confusions being the result of "navigational errors."
- Restraint from the use of force and agreement not to wander into the area currently controlled by a "friend." Liaison officers were also assigned to coordinate and to resolve the differences.

Both stressed that "the division of the area of control for both sides as stated here shall become the temporary area of control that has value until the Central Committees of both sides give official authorization."[49] Another noteworthy point in the report is the courteous use of terms such as "Vietnam," "Vietnamese," "friend," "in the spirit of solidarity, friendship" and so forth. The telegram was an internal one intended to report on the meeting to the Central Committee of the CPK, but it was unusually polite. Despite the politeness, however, the Khmer Rouge never trusted the Vietnamese and harbored deep suspicion toward the eastern neighbor when it came to border issues. In a telegram dated March 3, 1976, Comrade Ya reported the following to the Central Committee:

> [. . .] This particular border stone that I found was consistent with the 1/100,000 map, no doubt about it. Currently, they [in Khmer this was written in quite an impolite way] the 7 [military region?] establish camp 2 kilometers from there. For us, we established the front at 300 meters from this point. The Vietnamese could find neither the stone nor the location. Because we have already hidden the stone. [. . .][50]

Not long after, small skirmishes broke out. An internal report of the Khmer Rouge suggests that soldiers from division 920 of the KRA might have been involved.[51] The skirmishes were sporadic and small in scale, and did not raise international alarm. The situation can be assessed by looking at an internal report sent by Comrade Ya to the Central Committee of the CPK on March 7, 1976. The telegram detailed the Vietnamese (military region 7) protest as follows:

> [. . .] A. [The Vietnamese] raised the issue of Phor-Muy village and O'Vai where there had been clashes and bloodshed by both sides. They claimed that those locations are in their territory.
> B. [They] raised the issue that Cambodia has forcibly removed the people of Saob village.
> C. [They] raised the issue related to situation 105 [codeword] which involved fighting that lasted from the 24 of February and again on the 29 of February. They said that the Cambodian side had gone deep into the territory of [military region] 7 for 4 to 5 kilometers, we entered South of Dac Hout. [. . .][52]

The Vietnamese delegates also suggested adhering to a temporary line of control until both Parties resolved their differences. The delegates of the East Zone also offered conciliatory messages by ceding to the Vietnamese demands, as well as emphasizing the link between the two countries. In the postscript of the telegram, however, Comrade Ya noted: "If Angkar agreed, we would like to request 89 [Son Sen, general staff HQ of the KRA] to advise [division] 920 to refrain from combat activities. We have contacted 920 too but received no response, for quite some time now."[53]

The series of skirmishes continued sporadically and unabated until 1977. In early 1977, however, there was a twist to these problems: the Khmer Rouge cadres started entering the names of "enemies from within," "networks," and "Yuon enemy" into their reports. "Yuon" is a derogatory term used to describe the Vietnamese and unlike in 1975 and 1976, terms such as "Vietnam" and "friend" disappeared from the reports and were replaced by terms such as "Yuon enemies" or activities described as "their poisonous tricks."[54]

Yet, as late as 1976, on the other side, Vietnam pondered the question of whether the Khmer Rouge local commanders acted outside the limits set by the Central Committee of the CPK. Regardless, sporadic fighting occupied most of the year 1977. According to an undated report from the East Zone, summarizing the situation for the first four months of 1977, clashes (up to the platoon level) with Vietnamese forces recurred in many areas.[55] Yet, the Vietnamese still believed that the Khmer Rouge could be reasoned with, and a meeting took place on April 29, 1977, when the Vietnamese delegates lodged a protest against Democratic Kampuchea.

Sun, a Vietnamese delegate, protested to the representative of Democratic Kampuchea, the content of which can be summed up as follows:[56]

- Cambodia and Vietnam had a long and cordial relationship. The border issue is a historical issue and both sides should exercise restraint on the use of force before there is any official resolution.

- Vietnam reminded the Cambodian counterpart about past clashes including the Phu Quoc Island in early 1975. Sun mentioned that they had accepted the Cambodian explanation about a navigational error but he also suggested that the errors were being repeated again and again.

- The Vietnamese also made inquiries concerning 515 Vietnamese villagers that the Khmer Rouge had arrested, with no information provided about the fate of these people.

- At one point, the issue was raised bluntly: "During the meeting in May 1976, the Cambodian side proposed to defer the meeting because the leadership was busy in the countryside. From then on, the Vietnamese side has reminded twice about the need to have a new meeting, but the Cambodian side has not responded yet. About Condition 3 in that meeting, he [Sun] said that they [the Vietnamese] had fully respected it but the Cambodians did not respect that but also conducted activities to violate Vietnam in a systematic and serious manner."[57]

Finally, Sun insisted that Vietnam never abandoned the possibility of negotiation. The Vietnamese still clung to the history of friendship between the two parties and countries and tried to prevent fighting by negotiation. It was unclear as to what extent the Vietnamese had learnt about the decision of the Central Committee to confront Vietnam. After all, the 30-Vietnamese-to-1-Cambodian concept was also not broadcast until 1978. Conventional wisdom seemed to overlook the fact that while the Khmer Rouge implemented a step-by-step strategy, Vietnam sought to maintain the revolutionary friendship and "the history of joint struggle" to the bitter end, a strong adherence to the ICP's principles. Historians are of the consensus that the Khmer Rouge initiated the attack.[58]

With limited information, the policy of accommodation was the best that Vietnam could do. Mosyakov asserted that even during periods of tension, the Vietnamese leadership was still convinced that it was Pol Pot and Son Sen who concocted the upheaval, and they (the Vietnamese) still believed that their people, that is, Nuon Chea and Ieng Sary, would be a restraining force on the agenda of Pol Pot.[59] Little did Vietnam know that both Nuon Chea and Ieng Sary were actually part of the mechanism that recommended tougher actions vis-à-vis Vietnam.

Barely one day after filing his report, Sun's worst fear was realized. On April 30, 1977, Democratic Kampuchea launched an attack on Vietnam. According to Stephen Morris, the Khmer Rouge chose the day of the liberation of Saigon and the eventual unification of North Vietnam and South Vietnam to launch its attack on two large Vietnamese provinces, Tinh Bien and An Giang.[60]

Vietnam retaliated, including aerial bombing, in May the same year.[61] However, the responses were still sporadic. The Vietnamese still did not have a large-scale plan for dealing with the Khmer Rouge. According to a report by Region 23 in the East Zone, the second half of May 1977 saw sporadic clashes between the two sides that appeared less and less accidental.[62] This fighting took the form of harassing attacks by small groups, and harassing artillery fire on random targets.[63] In many cases, the Vietnamese usually disengaged after a brief firefight and the Khmer Rouge did not pursue. But at this stage, we also see that the Vietnamese began to commit troops up to a platoon to the engagement.

Toward the end of May 1977, Region 23 reported at least two encounters at the platoon level. The Vietnamese fought for a brief period but did not make any attempt to move in and hold ground. They either broke contact or waited on their side of the border.[64] In another incident, Khmer Rouge soldiers clashed with a platoon of Vietnamese soldiers. According to the report by the Khmer Rouge in Region 23, the encounter in Chantrea district lasted for approximately 40 minutes.[65] The report also claimed that the Vietnamese committed up to two companies after the firefight to prepare for another offensive. But no major fight broke out afterward. According to Nayan Chanda, up until this point, the Vietnamese committed only regional troops to deal with the Khmer Rouge attack.[66] This probably explains the scale of the encounters. Apparently, the Vietnamese still held on to the belief that the Khmer Rouge could still be reasoned with.

Despite the deteriorating situation, the Vietnamese still maintained a shade of hope about resolving the issue through negotiation. Yet, because the clashes were repeated again and again, the Vietnamese no longer believed the Khmer Rouge's explanation of "error in navigation" and began taking counter measures, although these measures were limited to small-scale aerial bombing,[67] and local troops were used instead of standard divisions.[68] The Vietnamese strategy was understandable: a controlled response would show the Khmer Rouge that Vietnam would not tolerate the attack, while showing at the same time that Vietnam would not exclude the possibility of negotiation.

A kind of "negotiation by correspondence" took place in June 1977. Sun, the same Vietnamese delegate, was more furious than ever. In one of these instances, the Cambodian representative reported about the Vietnamese protest:

> [. . .] This afternoon 15th June, Sun called me to raise the following issues:
> -On the 14th June 1977, from 8:00 P.M., a big unit of our troops invaded their [Vietnamese] border for approximately 40 km, from Sasir to Dun Chit, Ha Tieng.

They said our forces, supported by the 105 mm [artillery], had launched a coordinated attack on their security office and massacred and set ablaze to the houses which caused enormous destruction. (They said they had not yet compiled the data on the losses).

They said this situation was serious. Especially, it occurred after the Central Committee of the communist party and the government of Vietnam had issued a letter inviting the [communist] party and government of Cambodia to come to the meeting and resolve [the problems]. They emphasized that this is not coincidental.

[...] During the meeting, they showed a much more bellicose attitude towards us. [...][69]

Sun's protest fell on deaf ears. The representative of Democratic Kampuchea rebutted the Vietnamese use of aircraft, which was supposedly for retaliation against the Khmer Rouge. Eventually, the meeting ended up in a series of reciprocal accusations.

After this ill-fated negotiation, the fighting and clashes continued unabated, if not further intensified. Between May and August 1977, both sides continued to exchange small arms fire in small units as well as artillery on random targets. Region 20 and 21 were also affected and had seen at least two clashes at the platoon level while the clash in Region 23 escalated into the company level.[70] We also begin to see the report where division 920 of the Central Committee became involved in the clashes.[71]

While the situation continued to deteriorate, it seems that Mosyakov's thesis was still valid. He asserted that the Vietnamese leaders counted on elements within the Khmer Rouge leadership to maintain some sympathies toward the Vietnamese and that the leaders considered that the problems were perhaps caused by either small extremist elements or by local commanders who were acting independently.

On June 17, 1977, Region 23 reported that the Vietnamese troops had disseminated pamphlets, written in both Khmer and Vietnamese:

[...] Dear people, officers [and soldiers] of Cambodia,
As was the case when both sides lived together in the trenches, fighting together against the Americans in order to gain independence for both countries, now both countries must cooperate in order to build peace. Vietnam does not encroach on Cambodian territory but we also do not allow anyone to encroach on ours either! Soldiers, officers, and Cambodian people, please do not listen to the traitors who encroached on Vietnamese territory, burned down the houses, plundered and killed Vietnamese people; they have done so only to give advantage to the American Imperialist and the traitors. The nationalist Cambodian people should join with the Vietnamese people to prevent the bloody hands of the traitors in order to protect and maintain the pure purpose of solidarity between the two nations. [...][72]

The pamphlet was probably issued based on the suspicion that only the top leadership was implicated in the conflict and that the local commanders and soldiers did not know or want to get involved in a conflict with Vietnam.

Basically, the Vietnamese tried at various levels and by various means to manage the conflict. A few days later, on July 21, 1977, Sun sent another letter to the Cambodian representative. The content of Sun's protest letter can be summed up as follows:[73]

> [. . .] Since the 12th to 17th, 30 people were killed, 50 injured and many houses were burned down. This situation was serious, especially after the Vietnamese [Communist] Party wrote a letter inviting the Cambodian [Communist] Party as soon as possible. And this incident also happened after the Cambodian Party wrote a letter responding to the Vietnamese Party. [. . .] Once again, the Vietnamese side requested that [Democratic Kampuchea] Cambodia stop these acts of invasion immediately or the Cambodian side must be entirely responsible. The Vietnamese side unequivocally respected Cambodian sovereignty but will also unequivocally defend our own sovereignty and also the lives of our people. We wish to emphasize once again that the Vietnamese side still wants to meet the Cambodian side in order to stop the bloodshed [and] defend the solidarity between the two Parties [. . .][74]

After this conciliatory opening, the Khmer Rouge's telegram (which probably originated from its embassy in Hanoi) mentioned the usual reciprocal accusations between the two parties. But in the above lengthy quote, the reader can easily see that the Vietnamese deliberately repeated many things many times. The Vietnamese also started using the word "invasion," which was absent in previous letters, and also issued warnings such as "full responsibility" and an implicit retaliatory action if the incidents continued. But the Vietnamese did not forget to emphasize the "possibility of negotiation," which was repeated at least twice and was explicit in the above quote.

The Vietnamese also tried to initiate the contact at the local level.[75] Nothing good came out of the exchange of letters and protest and contacts at the lower level. Sporadic fighting with increasing commitments of troops continued. The attacks were of the "shoot first and never ask questions" kind. Force was the instrument of "first resort." The Vietnamese this time also responded in kind.

Toward the end of August the fighting intensified,[76] and on August 29, 1977, Sun, the Vietnamese representative, lodged another protest with the Cambodian representative in Vietnam. Chhean, the representative of Democratic Kampuchea, reported the protest:

> [. . .] According to reports that are still incomplete, since the beginning of August, Cambodian troops have invaded the provinces of An Giang, Kien Giang, Long An, and Tay Ninh. [. . .]
>
> On the morning of the 21st of August, a battalion launched attacks on four of the Vietnamese local units. Two posts were in [. . .]Long An province and the other two were in [. . .] Tay Ninh provinces: all are in Vietnamese territory, between 1 km and 1.5 km from the border. [. . .]
>
> This act was opposite to what the Vietnamese [Communist] Party had proposed and also opposite to what the Cambodian [Communist] Party's claim: 'Let the situation normalize.'

Thus, the Vietnamese side would like to express our protest and to insist that the Cambodian side immediately stops all these violations and to strictly adhere to the three conditions that both sides agreed in May 1976. . . otherwise [Democratic] Kampuchea must be fully responsible for all the consequences that might occur. The Vietnamese side emphasizes once again that the best course of action would be for the Parties and governments of both sides to meet soon in order to solve the problems, stop the bloodshed, and [work] towards the maintenance and improving the solidarity and friendship between both Parties and people. [. . .][77]

Once again, the Vietnamese appealed to past relations and called for a meeting to resolve the problem. At the same time, the warning was also more serious. The next part of the letter was the usual exchange of accusations. But at the end of the letter, Chhean advised the Central Committee of the CPK that in his own opinion, the Vietnamese call for negotiation was probably a ploy to defend themselves, while in actual fact, the Vietnamese were trying to invade Cambodia. He wrote: "They were very stubborn in insisting that the meeting be conducted soon even though it would not bring any result because they would appear as the one who wanted negotiation, peace, and friendship."[78] This perhaps contributed to the difficulties in reaching agreement during the meeting.

Finally, on September 24, 1977, the Khmer Rouge launched another furious— and perhaps the most brutal—attack of the war on Tay Ninh province, killing hundreds of Vietnamese civilians.[79] For some reason, the Vietnamese still offered negotiation. After receiving a letter from the ministry of foreign affairs of Democratic Kampuchea, Vietnam issued another call for negotiation:[80]

[. . .]They mentioned that our troops invaded Tay Ninh province in September 1977 and massacred around 1,000 people. Now, our troops camped 5 or 6 km deep on Vietnamese territory [. . .]. There were also invasions in Kien Giang, Gia Lai, and Kontum . . . etc. Thus, all these tensions were perpetrated by the Cambodian side, how could [you] accuse Vietnam as swallowing Cambodian territory? [. . .]

- The Vietnamese people have years of experience and clearly understand those privileges [of independence?] and do not intend to provoke any problems but they are also determined to defend their sovereignty from any violation by anyone.
- This problem, if the Cambodian side responds to the Vietnamese side appropriately, can be resolved. Always waiting for the meeting to resolve border issues, [for] long-lasting friendship.
- The Party and government of Vietnam adhere to the spirit of strengthening the solidarity and friendship with Cambodia and that no enemy could destroy. [. . .][81]

On the ground, however, the Vietnamese were less lenient this time and retaliated on a large scale. The Vietnamese seemed to have sensed that a nonresponse would be interpreted as being weak, but at the same time, the

Vietnamese felt the need to leave the channel for negotiation open. As with previous cases, the call for negotiation was ignored by the Khmer Rouge. Vietnam also used a stronger tone and the Khmer Rouge representative no longer bothered arguing or exchanging accusations as before. It seemed that everyone had come to their senses. In the archive, the letter above was also one of the last letters mentioning the possibility of negotiation. After September 1977, the border between Vietnam and Cambodia became a battleground with large-scale maneuvers, envelopments, and breakthroughs.

2. "Now Real Men Fight": Events Leading to the Collapse of Democratic Kampuchea

It was the beginning of the end for Democratic Kampuchea. The East Zone under Sor Phim was caught in the middle of this war. A loyal commander, Sor Phim fought without hesitation.[82] The divisions of the Central Committee seemed to be involved in this campaign also. It is quite likely that the central divisions were sent deep into Vietnam while the Zone troops might only be used to cover the rear.[83] The size of the forces that both sides committed to the fighting in September 1977 remains unclear because the conflict was kept secret from the outside world. Archives related to the decisions to launch the operations are also missing. We do not know if they did not survive the

So Vanna, alias Sor Phim (center, in black), and Khmer Rouge troops visiting a unit of volunteer Vietnamese communist fighters, 1973. The photo was taken shortly before the allied guerillas launched an attack on the Krabao military base in Kompung Cham province as part of the civil war against the Khmer republic government led by Marshal Lon Nol. Sor Phim later became the secretary of the CPK for the Eastern Zone of Democratic Kampuchea. He committed suicide on June 3, 1978. (© Photo and Caption, Documentation Center of Cambodia. Used by permission.)

upheaval, or if they still have not been disclosed. But the big picture can be constructed from various existing sources.[84]

The war, as the Khmer Rouge radio broadcast mentioned in late 1977, was now on a grand scale with divisions clashing against divisions. Moreover, a closer examination of the field reports by the commanders also reveals some clues as to what happened, and also gives an insight into the strategies employed by both the Khmer Rouge and Vietnam. Since we do not have the archives about the planning process or operational orders, I looked instead at the field reports and then traced these back to the strategy.

Although the Khmer Rouge's strategic objectives during this campaign was unclear, there were a few possibilities. First, the Khmer Rouge might want to take back "Kampuchea Krom" (literally, lower Cambodia), a large chunk of land in the Mekong delta that was lost to Vietnam during French rule. While this theory is very popular with many people, the Khmer Rouge leadership rarely made direct reference to it in any official document. They did, however, use it as an example to show that Vietnam wanted to "swallow" Cambodia. When they conducted their campaign, the ethnic Cambodians (they were also known as "Khmer Krom") who lived in the area were not spared. They were considered "Khmer body with Vietnamese head" because they had lived far too long under the Vietnamese rule.

Operation-wise and tactic-wise, the Khmer Rouge used their preferred method that had helped them during the war with the Khmer Republic: guerilla warfare. The Vietnamese, on the other hand, employed blitzkrieg-type maneuvers[85] that caught the Khmer Rouge by surprise.

The main area of operations, at least in the beginning, was Region 23 (Svay Rieng province), known for its Duck-Beak salient which was located roughly 30 km from Ho Chi Minh City (formerly Saigon). To help with the understanding of this geography, Region 23, or more specifically the Duck-Beak salient, can be divided into three parts. The first part was the Barvet district or the northern part of the salient, Chantrea village was at the center, and the southern part was Kompung Ror district. It seemed that the Khmer Rouge committed a lot of troops in this Region and based on the available archives, the Khmer Rouge took particular interest in pushing through to Vietnam from this area. But while many of the Khmer Rouge formations were busy deep inside Vietnam, Region 23 in the rear was attacked by the Vietnamese forces and the ill-prepared local troops faltered during the first sweep by the Vietnamese.

In late October, however, the Khmer Rouge's local troops consolidated and tried to recapture the villages in Region 23. In the initial phase (in October), the Khmer Rouge scored many victories in their operations. Responding to the artillery bombardment and harassing attacks, the Vietnamese then crossed into Cambodia to eliminate the artillery positions. The Khmer Rouge fought fiercely and even used guerilla units to attack and destroy a Vietnamese command post inside Vietnam.[86] What was noteworthy was that the Vietnamese troops were reported to have withdrawn very quickly when the Khmer Rouge attacked. The Khmer Rouge took that opportunity and used the remaining forces to pursue Vietnamese forces into Vietnam itself.

On October 27, the Khmer Rouge reported that they had recaptured many villages previously held by the Vietnamese.[87] The victory seemed unprecedented because according to the reports, the Vietnamese could hold on to those areas for roughly only one night. The troops that were sent to fight belonged to Region 23 but they showed a quick and informal planning process that allowed the Region's forces to link up and conduct joint operations with the district troops for a counteroffensive.[88]

On October 28, the Khmer Rouge continued to recapture many more villages and defeated the Vietnamese counteroffensive at the center of the Duck-Beak salient. The Khmer Rouge boasted that the Vietnamese suffered the loss of approximately a company of personnel.[89] Not long afterward, the Vietnamese launched a counteroffensive and recaptured some of the villages. One day later, the Vietnamese launched an attack on the southern part of the salient but withdrew after the Khmer Rouge put up a stiff resistance.[90] One heavy company was involved in the operation.

Toward the end of October and early November 1977, the Khmer Rouge offensive was in full swing and the Vietnamese had systematically retreated. The counteroffensive seemed to be weak in many places and the Khmer Rouge easily defeated the Vietnamese attack. The problem, however, was that the campaign seemed to be too easy. The Vietnamese, at least according to the Khmer Rouge reports, always advertised their losses through radio broadcasts. A report on November 13, for example, noted that the Vietnamese lost a total of a platoon of soldiers with a higher number injured, a tank was destroyed, and artillery pieces and command cars as well as many officers perished due to landmines.[91] Again, it was the Vietnamese who confessed by way of radio. This was not a firsthand observation by the Khmer Rouge soldiers, but the enemy's admissions.

The Vietnamese, at least based on their radio communications (which everyone knew could be intercepted by everyone), seemed to be demoralized by the losses and their attacks and counterattacks were futile. The easy campaign motivated the KRA to push further into Vietnam because the local troops could easily handle the Vietnamese attacks to the rear. In mid-November, the Khmer Rouge succeeded in advancing into Vietnam and destroyed almost everything in sight, in essence, a scorched earth tactic. Chhon, a Khmer Rouge commander, reported to Office 870:

[. . .] First direction: The morning of 17th November, north of Route 13 (Truong), [. . .]

Preliminary Results: according to report, we have burned down 94 houses and enemy bases but we do not have the total number yet about 'the enemy casualties and spoils of war' because our comrades are busy fighting.

Second direction at Truong market:

-We have cleared out the enemy at the market and east of the market, Ongko pagoda, and Pteas Bet Dey near the woods north of Trapaing Roborng. Right now, we are maintaining static defense east of Trapaing Roborng. [. . .]
Third direction:
At Chak Chras pagoda we have annihilated all enemies.
Enemies' reactions: The enemies used medium artillery and infantry to counterattack our defensive position along Route 13—but we destroyed some of their formations and they had to turn their head and ran back.[92]

The operation looked like a large-scale maneuver with three fronts. The amount of destruction reported reveals that the number might have been at least a battalion. Later reports also revealed that this action did not involve the troops of Region 23, because Region 23 was called for assistance only later in the campaign. Chhon further reported that one day later, on November 19, they succeeded in clearing up the areas of remaining resistance and described the routing as total and disorderly: "[. . .] the enemy who remained after our annihilation withdrew and ran in all directions into the woods because this area was full of woods, tributaries, and lakes [. . .]."[93]

But the Vietnamese were playing a deception game. The Khmer Rouge was lured deep into the Vietnamese territory where the supply lines would be lengthened and vulnerable to attack. Then the Vietnamese struck with a multipronged operation and attacked decisively with the support of armor. Not more than one day later, the Vietnamese achieved a breakthrough in many sectors and the Khmer Rouge formations were thrown into total confusion. The rear could not contact the front, supplies were running low, and the couriers did not return. It was total chaos.

The Vietnamese conducted a coordinated attack, typical of a modern army, on December 6, 1977, and completely stunned the KRA. A telegram from the battlefield reported the beginning of the problem when the Vietnamese conducted a three-pronged attack:

[. . .] The whole of Ta Ey village, they have already occupied. The enemy's tactics—first they used artillery and then they used the infantry to attack.
2. At the Road 13 front, the enemy attacked us through Bosmonea village and now they have occupied the Bosmonea village too.
3. At the Road 1 front, the enemy attacked us along Road 1 to the west and used tanks to suppress us, now they have entered Chiphu village.
The damage is yet to be assessed and we have transported the artilleries back to the rear and none were lost. [. . .]
As stated above, I would like to request elder brother to take immediate measures to resolve [the problems], and to order Region 23 to come and defend immediately. [. . .]
Note: The situation of the attack on us was quite dire. [. . .][94]

Chiphu village was deep behind Barvet and Chantrea, and the Khmer Rouge did not have enough troops for adequate defense. The artillery positions were also directly threatened. The retreat of the artillery pieces would undoubtedly debilitate the forward troops that had already advanced into Vietnam. Now they had no artillery cover. The Khmer Rouge knew the attack was intended to impede the movement of the forward troops, but could not do anything to stop it. This time, the Vietnamese did not easily withdraw or rout as they had done previously:

> [. . .] 1. Situation of the enemy in [Region] 23:
> -The enemy attacked us and achieved a breakthrough in many areas from Thnar Thnong, Korky Sorsam, Ta Ey, Chi Phu to Bavet. The enemy offensive was on a grand scale and destructive. The first objective was to force us out of their territory. The second objective was not to go deep into our territory, just to destroy our crops and force our people to go back with them. [. . .]
> -We are preparing our forces to counterattack, but our forces are limited. Nevertheless, if we do not counterattack, they would not leave. [. . .]
> 2. Route 22:
> On the 4th December we have cut off traffic from Route 27 and Smach and maintained total control but the next morning on the 5th December, the enemy achieved a breakthrough. [. . .][95]

The Vietnamese also attacked north of Region 23 (Svay Rieng), toward Region 21 (Kompung Cham). They specifically targeted the Khmer Rouge supply line. "At noon on the 22nd December, one enemy tank penetrated and arrived at the rice milling warehouse near the crossroad at Kondaol Chhrum [in Region 21]. Another one followed and stopped at an area near Bot Tonle, east of Kondaol Chhrum. The first one fired at our truck which was transporting rice near the rice milling warehouse [. . .]."[96]

Region 21 now also saw some action with the Vietnamese. This time, the Vietnamese troops revealed their true skills, which the Khmer Rouge had previously underestimated. On October 23, the Vietnamese advanced to the Krek rubber plantation with little to no resistance. As one Khmer Rouge commander, Comrade Phourng, noted: "Their troop movement was very quiet, without heavy gunshots, they have arrived and then destroyed. . .in the past, I have directly contacted the front, and to Borng Phim to get a hold of the situation, but now we have lost contact. . .as for my place [command post?], I have moved to Chhlong [north of Region 21] and left only 30 fighters to defend."[97] Just 15 minutes later, Phourng relayed another message. The situation was getting worse:

> For the Yuon situation on the 22nd of December 1977, they pushed forward to capture the Krek rubber plantation in its entirety. [. . .] We lost contact with the rubber plantation and factory at Memot because the courier has not yet returned [. . .]
> This Yuon force, according to [our] soldiers, consisted of many trucks and many tanks. The fighting occurred against our forces chaotically, in front and in the rear of our artillery positions, and we could not discern which side was ours and which side was the enemy's. According to my own analysis, we have lost control to a great extent, we lost communication between the troops and the command headquarters; and that was why the enemy could penetrate this deep with ease.[98]

The Vietnamese army has moved in with only armor and motorized infantry. That was the reason why they could achieve breakthrough this easily. This was a classic blitzkrieg tactic.

One day later, on December 24, the Vietnamese struck at another rubber plantation, at Memot, with at least one attack on the Khmer Rouge truck that transported rice. The attack revealed one important aspect of the Vietnamese operational plans. Memot district was located along the Cambodian-Vietnamese border, just like the Krek rubber plantation. It was not a place to the rear of the Krek plantation. Based on the available archives, this suggests that the Vietnamese strategy was not to push deep into Cambodian territory, but to attack multiple targets along the border, disrupting supplies and artillery positions. So far, the Vietnamese army had achieved these two goals. The third effect of this blitzkrieg-type operation was psychological, to throw the rear of the Khmer Rouge operation off balance, to threaten the supply lines, to eliminate fire support, and to eventually force the forward troops to withdraw from Vietnamese territory. This objective, too, was achieved by the Vietnamese operations. The Khmer Rouge report showed a total loss of control and the depletion of supplies:

> [...] [situation in Memot district] According to analysis, they wanted to open way to Region 21 from Pro Thheat-Chhlong road to the east and they have the capabilities to do this because we have a hole in the middle with no large formation of troops. The rubber plantation's militias could not fight and the big formations went to fight at the border for a long time and were now losing control and as we know, our brothers in the big formations were routed and could not yet establish communication.
>
> This situation, [we would like to] request, please Angkar, confirms this with Borng Phim because we have witnessed this situation firsthand because [we] stayed with the big formations. [...] we would like to request the solution be quick.[99]

This report reveals one pertinent point. We know from the previous report that the forward formations already lost artillery support since the first sweep by the Vietnamese. Since Krek and Memot were very near to the border, the fact that the artillery fire bases were also there, and that the big formations could not withdraw in time to help, suggest that it is likely that the big formations were not along the border but were conducting operations deep in Vietnamese territory. This extended line was the main cause of the collapse of the KRA campaign in late 1977.

The Khmer Rouge operations probably ended in late December 1977. The following report reveals yet another sobering turn of events for the KRA:

> [...] When we cut off the enemy's formations, they immediately counterattacked [to restore the line] and then continued their march [...] Our attack was fierce but the enemies were quite numerous [...] The rice for our daily consumption has completely run out. I requested Borng the other day please immediately send us the rice [...] If we lack rice, we will face seriously complicated problems.

Note: the 2 million kilograms of rice that was given before has now run out, only little is left now.[100]

Napoleon once said that the army marches on its stomach and now the Khmer Rouge had run out of rice. The quantity of rice also revealed the scale of the formations used by the Khmer Rouge. If we assume that each soldier ate on average 1 kilogram of rice per day, then a division by the KRA's standard would eat on average 5,000 kilograms per day. If we assume that the 2 million kilograms that Chhon mentioned had been given since the campaign started around September, and if the supplies ran out in December, then the total days of consumption were 100 days (a little over three months, from September to December). Thus, on average, 20,000 kilograms were consumed in one day (2 million divided by 100). This would be an equivalent of 20,000 soldiers or 4 divisions, excluding district troops and militias.

This number is certainly not impossible because when Democratic Kampuchea attacked Vietnam in February 1978, some observers estimated that around 30,000 or even 40,000 troops were committed to the campaign.[101]

With a large formation, the Khmer Rouge's underestimation of the Vietnamese experience was fatal. When the Vietnamese took the initiative, they no longer withdrew quickly as in June or July, but stood firm and counterattacked at many places. The Khmer Rouge had met its match. Vietnamese forces stayed in Cambodia for a short period of time before withdrawing with many Cambodian refugees.

In late December 1977, Democratic Kampuchea publicly announced the arms clashes with Vietnam, as well as broke off the diplomatic relations with the Socialist Republic of Vietnam. On January 6, 1978, Pol Pot boasted about the effectiveness of the KRA, or rather, the forces of the Central Committee, and declared victory when Vietnam effectively withdrew all its forces from Cambodia, albeit unilaterally.

According to Stephen Morris, the reason why Vietnam did not follow through with its campaign was that it saw no exit strategy, that is, no political solution after the military action.[102] As late as 1977, it seemed Vietnam still had not prepared to undertake anything drastic. But the campaigns in late 1977 by both sides marked a turning point in the relations between Vietnam and Democratic Kampuchea, and also a turning point in the war. When diplomatic relations between the two countries were severed following the war, there were no longer any calls for negotiation, protest, or correspondence. The predominant issue had become military in nature.

PROPAGANDA WAR

Democratic Kampuchea survived under a veil of secrecy and the whole capital city, Phnom Penh, was closed to the outside world, even from the few embassies that remained in the country after the fall of Phnom Penh in 1975. Democratic Kampuchea only maintained diplomatic relations with a handful of countries: China, North Korea, Rumania, and Vietnam. Even the Soviet Union and the United States (by virtue of its relations with China) as well as Yugoslavia and the ASEAN countries (Association of South East Asian Nations) were not recognized by Democratic Kampuchea.

Democratic Kampuchea only welcomed diplomats in its later years. The country, on the other hand, was completely off limits to journalists. However, when the war broke out with Vietnam in 1977, Pol Pot began to invite journalists into Cambodia to stage a propaganda coup.

From late 1977 onward, journalists from many different countries flooded to Cambodia and most of the time, Pol Pot himself entertained the guests. A group of Yugoslavian journalists visited the Northwest Zone (around Battambang), followed by Danish news agencies, Swedish journalists, and even American and British journalists in December 1978. The journalists saw an apparently innocent country in which the famine, killing, cleansing policy, forced evacuation, school closures, militarization of children, and aggressive policy toward neighbors were a matter of negative enemy propaganda and unfair accusations.

The journalists saw children in neat attire studying in makeshift classrooms everywhere. In the city, young students were pondering complex chemical formulae and nurses were busy treating people at the hospitals. All the pictures showed a country that was not very advanced, but a country that was full of optimism, smiles, and happiness.[103] The question that was implied was: "how could a small and innocent socialist country like Cambodia, which was very friendly, and which was incessantly building its country, attack a bigger Vietnam?" That was the desperate message the Khmer Rouge wanted to send out.

The pictures conveyed a story of hope and happiness, but beneath them were the stories of horror and darkness. The journalists were not fully aware of the horror behind this charade. Unbeknownst to them, the Khmer Rouge showed them only what they wanted the journalists to see.

Pol Pot also tried to prove Vietnam's guilt in a grisly manner, using his own colleagues. According to one Khmer Rouge commander who escaped the purge after that campaign, Pol Pot killed those who were accused of collaborating with Vietnam and then dumped their bodies along the border and used them as proof of Vietnamese invasion of Democratic Kampuchea.[104] "They shouted that 'You all now must die, you traitors and Yuon's servant' before executing the East Zone suspects."[105] This account is consistent with what Alexander Hinton described in his book: the Khmer Rouge often used euphemist justification before killing one of their own. This allowed them to reconcile their conscience and kill without remorse.[106] Killing without remorse was also the cause of mass killing because, metaphorically, the executioners could always go back to sleep without seeing innocent faces of their victims in their dreams.

The Khmer Rouge hastily tried to present itself as a civilized state instead of the great-leap-forward, revolutionary country. Bringing foreign journalists to Cambodia was part of this new tactic.

The propaganda happened in tandem with real purges. By simply looking at the reports that were coming in, one could see that the Vietnamese could easily penetrate the rear of the formations and effectively disrupt the Khmer Rouge supplies and artillery support. Once that occurred, the front formations collapsed. If a proper post-mortem analysis is conducted, one can easily see that the Vietnamese triumphed because of a brilliant strategy. In the mind of the Khmer Rouge leader, however, when the campaign ran so well and then immediately and inexplicably collapsed, this could only mean one thing: internal treachery that was perpetrated by Vietnamese sympathizers. They did not even know that sudden attack to achieve immediate breakthrough was one of the pillars of a blitzkrieg tactic.

In addition to the purge, the local units that remained in place were stripped of their weapons and in the next campaign starting in February 1978, the Central Committee used its own troops in the spearhead; the local troops and the Zone division (such as division 4 of the East Zone) were used only to cover the rear of the forward divisions.[107]

But these things did not deter the Khmer Rouge. On February 25, 1978, the Khmer Rouge, with at least 30,000 troops according to some sources,[108] had launched a brutal attack on the Vietnamese province of Tay Ninh. Now it was no longer a time for negotiation. The conflict had become an entirely military matter.

4

≈≈≈

The Last Great War

> Khieu Samphan: We [Democratic Kampuchea] have shown our understanding to let the 'Puppet' [PRK] to join the SNC.
> Prime Minister Hun Sen: I am so 'thankful' for the understanding from the 'murderers.'
>
> —Prime Minister Hun Sen's reminiscence of a
> session during the SNC meeting.[1]

THE BEGINNING OF THE END

In June 1977, the Khmer Rouge started to attack Vietnam. Internally, the purge of the East Zone was also underway. Comrade Hun Sen, a junior commander in Region 21, knew he was next on the execution list.[2] He made an excruciating decision to leave his wife who was already five months pregnant, and left Cambodia with four other people at 9:00 P.M. on June 20, 1977, to go to Vietnam to seek help.[3] This was a chaotic period when the Khmer Rouge began to launch large-scale campaigns against the Vietnamese. Back in early 1975, the Vietnamese had agreed to return all Cambodians who crossed into Vietnam illegally so that they could be relocated to Cambodia.[4] In most cases, however, those who were returned were almost certainly killed by the Khmer Rouge. In most reports, the Khmer Rouge cadre wrote "we will continue to purify them," a codeword for execution.

This fear continued to haunt Comrade Hun Sen who had prepared 12 needles to commit suicide if the Vietnamese deported him back to the Khmer Rouge.[5] The group crossed into Vietnam at 2:00 A.M. on June 21, 1977. On their way, they decided to take a break and have a meal. Upon sitting down, however, all other four people were in tears, perhaps because of the prospect of being killed when crossing the border, or of being deported after arriving in Vietnam. Comrade Hun Sen almost cried but had determined that, as a leader, his own tears would only aggravate the hopelessness.[6] In the afternoon, they arrived in the province of Song Be (in 1979, the province was split into Binh Duong and Binh Phuoc). Fortunately for them, it was a good time to arrive in Vietnam. By 1977, the Vietnamese were becoming aware of the fate of the Cambodians who were returned to Democratic Kampuchea. In this political climate, Comrade Hun Sen and his four comrades were warmly welcomed.

Comrade Hun Sen talked with many Vietnamese officers who were probably impressed with the intelligence and sharpness of this young commander. In August 1977, Comrade Hun Sen wrote various essays analyzing the situation in Democratic Kampuchea and also outlining his visions for liberating Cambodia. On September 27, just as the Khmer Rouge began their brutal campaign in Vietnam, Comrade Hun Sen met with Lt. Gen. Van Tien Dung, a member of the politburo of the Vietnamese Communist Party, who was also the chief of staff of the People's Army of Vietnam.[7] Dung was likely impressed by the writing of Comrade Hun Sen and met with him for 2 hours and 40 minutes.[8] At the end of the meeting, however, no explicit pledge for support was given but Dung praised Comrade Hun Sen and said the following: "comrade, you are very young and the future is bright ahead, so please keep secret so that they [the Khmer Rouge] will not eliminate your family, but [you] must follow the situation, continue to learn. [. . .] Wish you good health and [you should] believe in your future."[9]

From this narrative, we can see clearly that the Vietnamese had begun to consider taking a tougher stance vis-à-vis Democratic Kampuchea, but still maintained hope of negotiating with them as well, as expressed in many correspondences and protests that accompanied the fighting along the border.[10] As late as December 1977, the Vietnamese still did not offer any full-scale military support to Comrade Hun Sen, but he was allowed to return to Cambodia to search for his family when the Vietnamese achieved a breakthrough in the Memot sector. However, the Khmer Rouge had already evacuated many of the people from the areas prior to the Vietnamese breakthrough and the arrival of Comrade Hun Sen.[11] The remaining population escaped to Vietnam with Comrade Hun Sen and the Vietnamese forces. According to Prime Minister Hun Sen, that number amounted to tens of thousands (mostly from three provinces: Kompung Cham, Prey Veng, and Svay Rieng).[12]

Furthermore, according to Stephen Morris, during the attack in September 1977, the regional commanders in Vietnam invited a Hungarian journalist named Kandor Dura to visit Tay Ninh to witness and publicize the Khmer Rouge attacks.[13] But before he left Vietnam, the Vietnamese leadership decided to withhold Dura's reports and materials. Morris suggested that this was because the Vietnamese still believed that the problem could be solved by negotiation.

In late 1977, the campaign intensified, diplomatic relations between the two countries were broken, and the Vietnamese decided to return Dura's reports and materials.[14] At this point, the Vietnamese still called for negotiation, but this call took a different turn. Instead of using confidential channels, in February 1978, Vietnam made a public broadcast that the Socialist Republic of Vietnam remained predisposed toward negotiation with Democratic Kampuchea to find a peaceful resolution to the problem. Nayan Chanda claimed that a Vietnamese officer told him that Vietnam knew the Khmer Rouge would not accept the call, but Vietnam would win a propaganda coup.[15]

In sum, it seems that up until the end of 1977, Vietnam was very sincere in its call for negotiation. But when nothing more could be done and when there was no longer any diplomatic channel open for negotiation after diplomatic relations were broken in late 1977, Vietnam decided to continue the broadcast anyway for propaganda purposes.

1978: TO THE LAST MAN AND BULLET!

For the Khmer Rouge, the year 1978 was eventful. It marked a much larger offensive against Vietnam. However, the campaign in 1978 was a total disaster for Democratic Kampuchea, once again and for the final time. The campaign can be divided into two main periods at this time. During the first period, which ran from January to May 1978, the Khmer Rouge and the Vietnamese clashed in various skirmishes along the border. In the second period, which ran from June to December 1978, the Cambodian resistance and the Vietnamese army pushed into Cambodia and ended the bloody rule of Democratic Kampuchea.

Perhaps, after learning from the mistake they had made in 1977, when they used large formations deep into Vietnam only to be cut off from supplies and fire support by the Vietnamese blitzkrieg operations, the Khmer Rouge changed tactics. A large formation was still considered, but this occupied only a paragraph in the instructions that Office 870 disseminated on January 3, 1978. The bulk of the instruction was about the use of guerilla tactics:

[. . .] 2. Conduct guerilla attacks in an overwhelming manner, within and without the enemy's areas of control in order to cause attrition of the enemy's force, to make the enemy exhausted, and then take the opportunity to eliminate the living force of the enemy and sometimes cut their transportation lines, their supply lines, their reinforcements, and weapons [. . .]

One group [consisting of] 10 soldiers sought out the enemy and tried to eliminate them, resulting in 3 to 5 heads either killed or injured in one day and night. If in one sector there are 5 groups, we will be able to eliminate the enemy in one day and night from 15 to 20 heads. If we have many sectors where we send many groups to conduct guerilla attacks in the enemy's areas, in one day and night we will be able to eliminate the enemy in the hundreds of heads. [. . .] In 20 or 30 days how many will they lose? In one year how many will they lose? [. . .][16]

Once again, the Khmer Rouge relied on a simplistic calculation to fight the Vietnamese. Large formations were used, but even so, the predominant tactics and operations were still based on guerilla attacks. And because this strategy was too ambitious, that is, the total annihilation of Vietnam, it was unachievable with the attrition tactics. The campaign was a disaster, just as in 1977. The first attacks of the 1978 campaign started in mid-January. Even though large formations were used, they were divided up into smaller units to attack Vietnam. The main reason for this split was perhaps the fact that it was the only tactic the Khmer Rouge was able to perform best. They tried big units in 1977 but failed, now they went back to the small units tactics just like during the war with the Khmer Republic. Nonetheless, because the attacking units were too small, they could not do anything beyond pure destruction and implementing scorched earth tactics. An example was the situation in Region 23 and Region 24, as set out in the report of Chhon. Chhon was a commander whose name figured prominently in the 1977 campaign and it seemed he was still active in the first part of the campaign. His name disappeared from the reports around May 1978. Chhon reported the following:

> [. . .] We conducted guerilla attacks in their territory, 2 km from our border.
>   Result: we have destroyed 30 military houses and burned down a number of civilian houses. We have destroyed 2 enemy boats, killing all civilians inside. In total, we have eliminated the enemy 30 heads on the 18th January. On the same day of 18th January, we continued to fire the 107 [mm] rockets at 1:00 A.M. and into Hoc Gnu market. We do not know the full result but we saw it was on fire. [. . .][17]

The rest of the report did not mention whether or not such "successes" (i.e. killing civilians) would contribute to winning the war. It seemed that attrition and destruction were the only and implicit objectives. It was easy to declare success by attacking unarmed civilians, but it was a different matter when the enemy retaliated with battle-hardened troops.

The first wave of the campaign was conducted by local troops along with divisions from the Central Committee. Division 703 and troops of the newly created Central Zone (under the command of comrade Ke Pauk) were sent to assist the local troops in pushing back the remaining Vietnamese troops who remained on the Cambodian side of the border after the 1977 campaign. This proved to be quite an easy task because firstly, the bulk of the Vietnamese troops had already been withdrawn since December 1977. Second, the Khmer Rouge's morale was high in the face of Vietnamese presence on the land along the border.[18] Third, the operation was well supported (in terms of able commanders and logistics). Around January 1978, this offensive was generally successful in driving the remaining Vietnamese troops out of Cambodia. But then the Khmer Rouge began a new offensive into Vietnam.

The second wave (in this first period) was launched in late February by the Southwest Zone and the divisions from the Central Committee. According to one report, the second wave consisted of around 30,000 to 40,000 troops and was aimed at Tay Ninh province.[19] But the Khmer Rouge still could not think beyond their mindset of fighting for extreme strategic objectives that could not be achieved. According to a former Khmer Rouge soldier who participated in the raid, the operations consisted only of laying mines, blowing up bridges, and destroying factories in Tay Ninh.[20]

In April 1978, the People's Army of Vietnam (PAVN) responded in kind. This was a multidivisional campaign. In one sector, there may have been up to 20 tanks supporting the Vietnamese infantry, and the counterattack involved up to two regiments.[21] Unlike in 1977, the Vietnamese now used tanks in greater numbers, as well as air support.[22]

The Khmer Rouge field reports also revealed another important aspect of tactics used by the Vietnamese army. In 1977, the Vietnamese moved swiftly with armor and motorized infantry to penetrate behind the Khmer Rouge lines, avoided strong points, and induced the confusion and collapse of the main forward formations of the Khmer Rouge. In 1978, however, the Vietnamese pushed forward more slowly. Tanks supported the infantry, the infantry protected the tanks, and both rarely moved far from artillery cover. Beginning in 1978, the Khmer Rouge's reports often mentioned sighting the combination of these three elements together.[23] This combination produced slow operational tempo and was consistent with only one specific strategy: sheer attrition. This strategy would buy time for Vietnam to help organize the refugees (who had escaped the Khmer Rouge genocide) into a political organization that could govern Cambodia after the fall of Democratic Kampuchea.

NEW LIFE 1: THE KAMPUCHEAN SOLIDARITY ARMED FORCES FOR NATIONAL SALVATION

On the other side of the border, Vietnam changed its policy toward Democratic Kampuchea. In April 1978, Col. Gen. Tran Van Tra, the commander and chief political commissar of military region 7, told Comrade Hun Sen that the Vietnamese leadership had already agreed to provide support for organizing the liberation movement.[24] The rules were made clear: the Vietnamese would help only with training, arms procurement, and logistics while the Cambodians would be in charge of political leadership. Comrade Hun Sen immediately accepted this offer of assistance.[25] Accordingly, an armed force, the "Kampuchean Solidarity Armed Forces for National Salvation," was established on May 12, 1978.

The command structure was codenamed "578" (5th month of the year 78) and was under the leadership of Comrade Hun Sen with a combatant unit, "Unit 125" (day 12 of the 5th month), with 200 fighters.[26] After one month of training, half of these forces were sent to other military schools in Vietnam for further training. The remaining half was divided into "armed operations groups"[27] with each group consisting of between 10 and 15 soldiers who were sent back into Cambodia for various operations.[28] Gradually, the number of the combatant units swelled to 21 battalions, 1 all-female battalion, and 100 armed operations groups, while the headquarter units consisted of a general staff section, a political section, a logistics section, a finance section, one special forces company, one medical company, and one unit for military bands.[29] It was actually beneficial for the resistance movement to select people this way. After all, the fact that these people could traverse the dangerous terrain and cross the battle lines to escape from Cambodia into Vietnam was a clear testament of their survival skills. These skills are much needed in military operations.

Vietnam also reestablished contacts with other forces that, hitherto, had been fighting against Pol Pot. One significant resistance group was under the command of Comrade Say Phuthorng, a veteran of the KPRP, and Comrade Tea Banh. This group began resistance early on in the western part of Cambodia when, after 1975, Pol Pot began luring many revolutionaries to execution with the usual lies of "jobs in the new government," "education," "meeting," and so forth. Comrade Say Phuthorng and Comrade Tea Banh were among the few who were able to sense this treachery and went into hiding.[30]

This group often came into Cambodia to conduct hit-and-run and harassing attacks against the Khmer Rouge forces and they were necessarily forced to live a fugitive and underground life. Multiple attempts were made to reestablish contact with the Vietnamese, but to no avail. Very often, messengers perished during the perilous crossing from the western part of Cambodia along the Thai border to the eastern part of Cambodia.[31] The contact was successfully reestablished only after 18 attempts, when the war between the Khmer Rouge and Vietnam intensified in 1978.

NEW LIFE 2: THE KAMPUCHEAN SOLIDARITY FRONT FOR NATIONAL SALVATION

The creation of armed operations groups as well as constant harassment from within did not bode well for the future of Democratic Kampuchea. In the first stage of the 1978 campaign, the Zone troops (East and Southwest) were used in conjunction with the divisions of the Central Committee. The report also suggested close coordination between the Zone troops and the division as well as troops from other Zones. For example, when the Vietnamese pushed through on May 4, Comrade Pauk called for reinforcement from the East Zone's local troops while mentioning that Sor Phim had dispatched a battalion from Region 20 to help the frontline.[32]

Despite this coordination, the Vietnamese strategy of attrition started to take its toll on the Khmer Rouge units. Thousands of Khmer Rouge soldiers died in the face of Vietnamese tank attacks and in many cases, the KRA ran out of tank countermeasures.[33] Division 703, for example, lost thousands of their fighters when the Vietnamese attacked in April and May 1978.[34] But the biggest problem came from within.

Just like in 1977, when the campaign went bad, the field reports of the Khmer Rouge commanders turned inward once again. On April 8, when the car carrying Comrade Pin of division 703 hit a mine, the report immediately assumed it was the internal enemy who prepared the plot.[35] On April 26, a commander reported that "[. . .] they [the Vietnamese] know clearly [about the terrain] and that is why they dare to come. Request Angkar resolves this problem [. . .]."[36] On May 6, Comrade Pauk reported the following, "[. . .] on the 4th of May 78, their force is not big, at most one regiment but had 3 to 5 tanks, the tanks were in their territory and moved along Route 27 because they did not dare to come by Route 7. The enemy could come because we did not attack them and also maybe there were traitorous elements who led the way [. . .]."[37]

Sure enough, the Central Committee began a large-scale purge of the East Zone. In fact, the East Zone was already being targeted by the Central Committee since 1977. After the failed campaign that year, many regional troops were arrested, sent to S-21, or executed immediately.[38] Those who were allowed to remain at their posts were stripped of their weapons. In late April, when the Vietnamese attack intensified, some commanders of the Central Committee's division called for the rearmament of these regional troops but to no avail.[39]

Division 703, despite not being under the East Zone per se, bore the full brunt of this purge mainly because it was part of the campaign. Cadres and commanders of the division were sent to S-21. Comrade Nath, the chief of staff of the division, was arrested and sent to S-21. Not much later, Comrade Pin, the party secretary of the division, was either killed in action or killed by his own messenger.[40] Either way, he would have been killed because his chief of staff (Comrade Nath) listed him in his confession at S-21.[41] After that, other junior commanders were also sought out and killed after division 703 and the East Zone blamed each other for the defeat in April 1978.[42] After May 1978, soldiers in division 703 (which, at this point, might have already lost more than half of its personnel) did not have any motive to fight, and morale was nonexistent, and the leadership was in tatter.

The East Zone could not escape the inevitable. More and more commanders and cadres were called into secret meetings, only to be stripped of their weapons, rounded up and sent to S-21, or sent to be executed along the border.[43] Sor Phim began to have doubts about his security. According to Nayan Chanda (as corroborated by other eyewitness accounts) in late May, Ke Pauk called Sor Phim for a meeting.[44] Learning from what had happened to his subordinates, Sor Phim sent out messengers one after another, but none returned. Yet, he still believed that Pol Pot was innocent and that the upheaval was caused by the coup plot that had been concocted by Son Sen, the defense minister and chief of Office 89, the general staff of the KRA. On June 2, 1978, Sor Phim arrived on the outskirt of Phnom Penh, waiting to cross the Mekong River into Phnom Penh to meet up with Pol Pot, perhaps hoping to at least clear himself from suspicion.[45] But Phim was welcomed by a platoon of soldiers. He was cornered and committed suicide near a pagoda overlooking the city.[46]

The news of the death of Sor Phim reverberated throughout the East Zone. If its party secretary had already been purged by the Central Committee, then the reasoning was that no one would be safe. When division 4 and soldiers of the East Zone broke away from Democratic Kampuchea after the death of Sor Phim in June 1978, the war entered its second, and last, phase.

Division 4 and the regional troops of the East Zone then broke away, raided the arms depot and went into hiding in the jungle along the border. Division 4 was commanded by Comrade Rin, full name Heng Samrin, the future president of the state council of the People's Republic of Kampuchea (PRK). These forces hid between the KRA and the PAVN but engaged only the KRA. The Kampuchean Solidarity Armed Forces for National Salvation and the Vietnamese Volunteer Army took this opportunity to embolden the resistance forces. Many parts of the provinces of Kratie, Kompung Cham, Svay Rieng, and Prey Veng, in essence, a large part of the east coast of the Mekong River, were considered liberated since mid-1978.[47] On November 22, 1978, four of the five Cambodian resistance groups met together to draft a political program for the movement (the fifth group in Koh Kong under Comrade Say Phuthorng and Comrade Tea Banh could not join because these forces operated underground and needed to remain in hiding).[48]

The decision was made to name the political movement as the Kampuchean Solidarity Front for National Salvation, to have a name that was parallel to that of the armed wing, the Kampuchean Solidarity Armed Forces for National Salvation.[49] The movement was formally established in the Snoul district of Kratie province on December 2, 1978. The existence of this movement was broadcast on radio Hanoi on December 3.[50] On Christmas day, December 25, 1978, the Kampuchean Solidarity Front for National Salvation and the Vietnamese Volunteer Army combined for a final push into Cambodia to overthrow Democratic Kampuchea on January 7, 1979, ending the Khmer Rouge's bloody and genocidal reign that had lasted for 3 years 8 months and 20 days.

LAST MINUTE PACKING

While these actions were in full swing, Prince Sihanouk was still kept in almost solitary confinement by Pol Pot. Nonetheless, in late 1978, Prince Sihanouk noted an unusual generosity and kindness on the part of the regime.[51] His fridge was filled with fruits, cake, drinks, and other desserts; the Khmer Rouge also took particular care in imitating the taste of the typical Cambodian desserts that were prevalent during the rule of Prince Sihanouk.[52] The prince was also allowed to visit places outside the palace, which had been previously impossible. The prince was relocated to a small house not far from the palace. At dusk on January 5, 1979, Khieu Samphan came to the house and told the prince that Pol Pot had invited the prince for the evening tea.[53]

Upon arrival, Prince Sihanouk noted that Pol Pot was more courteous than ever before, lowering himself to welcome the prince, a standard Cambodian etiquette of showing respect to the king, something Pol Pot had never done before.[54] He also addressed the prince as "His Majesty." He dropped a hint about what he wanted the prince to do in return: "Comrade Khieu Samphan that Your Majesty had met before had told me that Your Majesty would be happy to represent our government at the United Nations and defend the righteous cause of our people against invasion by the Yuon, in the (political) discussions that might take place in the Security Council. . .of the United Nations. Your Majesty is a nationalist and Your Majesty has many friends in the world. Your Majesty could be of great advantage to the Cambodian people."[55] Pol Pot then briefed the prince that the Vietnamese would soon capture Phnom Penh, but reassured the prince that it would not be a problem, as the Cambodian soldiers and people would soon chase the Vietnamese out.[56]

As a finishing touch, Pol Pot and Ieng Sary who was nearby, played a "good cop bad cop routine" to ensure Prince Sihanouk's trust. Ieng Sary said that

Soldiers of the Kampuchean Solidarity Front for National Salvation were approaching the Royal Palace, January 7, 1979. (©Sar Pormean Kampuchea (SPK)–Kampuchean Press. Used by permission.)

only the prince and the prince's wife, Queen Monineath, would be allowed to board a Chinese plane out of Cambodia. Other royal relatives would stay behind in Cambodia, making them de facto hostages. But then Pol Pot interjected and said "No! [You—Ieng Sary] must arrange for everyone to go. [You] must arrange with our Chinese friends to make sure there are enough seats on the plane."[57] Pol Pot then gave the prince $20,000 as pocket money for the mission, the money that the prince returned in full after getting out of Democratic Kampuchea and the grip of Pol Pot. In retrospect, we can see that the prince had no choice but to agree. It was either take the money and leave or perish under the Khmer Rouge for noncompliance. Vietnam sent a special force detachment to rescue the prince so that the new regime could have legitimacy, but this operation failed.[58] Prince Sihanouk had already left the Royal Palace.

The prince travelled to New York and fought to retain the UN seat for Democratic Kampuchea and succeeded in urging the passing of a resolution condemning Vietnam on January 11, 1979. The Prince went on to create his own army for the resistance, the Armée National Sihanoukists (ANS), and in 1982 established the political movement, the Front Uni National pour un Cambodge Indépendant, Neutre, Pacifique, Et Coopératif (FUNCINPEC) or United National Front for an Independent, Neutral, Peaceful, and Cooperative Cambodia. The prince was determined not to be deceived a second time by Pol Pot. Now the prince was a full-fledged actor. The Last Great War had begun.

PRELUDE TO THE LAST GREAT WAR: ACTORS' REALIGNMENT

After the defeat in 1979, the Khmer Rouge retreated to the jungle-clad northern part of the country and continued to resist the Vietnamese presence. Despite past intrigues and atrocities by the Khmer Rouge, Prince Sihanouk persisted in his belief that the Vietnamese presence was the greater threat to Cambodian independence. Prince Sihanouk was willing to work with the Khmer Rouge once again, but this time, he had his own movement and army, better known by their acronyms of FUNCINPEC and ANS, respectively. It is not hard to understand Prince Sihanouk's need for independence, given that Pol Pot had treated the prince and the royal family so badly during the Khmer Rouge's reign of terror.

Other small movements also emerged, the most significant of which was the Khmer People's National Liberation Front (KPNLF) led by Son Sann, a former prime minister under Prince Sihanouk. The "Sponsors" (the United States, China, and the ASEAN countries) back then continued to oppose the Vietnamese presence and provided aid to those opposing the Vietnamese and the Phnom Penh government (PRK). The resulting conflict is known as the Third Indochinese Conflict,[59] the last great war in Southeast Asia.

Despite the prince's extreme distaste for the policies of Pol Pot, Prince Sihanouk still needed to be part of the "Democratic Kampuchea" umbrella, just the same as other resistance movements. This point was usually used by many people to wrongly blame the prince for collaborating with the Khmer

People started to return to the empty capital city, Phnom Penh, January 7, 1979. The street is Sok Hok Street (107). Today, it is a bustling commercial quarter and my favorite barber shop is located on the right. (©Sar Pormean Kampuchea (SPK)–Kampuchean Press. Used by permission.)

Rouge. In reality, Prince Sihanouk's decision to reassociate himself with the Khmer Rouge did not come immediately in 1979. The prince agreed to this alliance in 1982, only after pressure from the Sponsors. The prince's rational yet excruciating decision in this regard can be discerned from an interview with a German journalist-scholar, Peter Schier:

Peter Schier: During the 1979 interviews, you still refused any cooperation with the Khmer Rouge. However, in June 1982, you and Son Sann, the other nationalist leader, entered into the tripartite coalition government of Democratic Kampuchea together with the Khmer Rouge. What are the reasons for your change of mind on the subject of cooperating with Pol Pot and his followers?

Prince Sihanouk: First, in order to understand the evolution of my feelings and my position regarding the problem of the Vietnamese and the Khmer Rouge, one must understand above all, that in this respect, the feelings and the respect of the Khmer people have changed since 1982. [. . .]

Second, between 1979 and 1981 the Khmer people who had chosen between the Khmer Rouge danger and the coming to Cambodia of the Vietnamese army, chose Vietnamese protection against the horrors of Pol Pot. During the same period

> I, too, believed that the lesser evil of the two was the protec-
> tion accorded to my people by the Vietnamese. However, in
> my mind, this was not a question of accepting a permanent
> Vietnamese protectorate. [. . .]
>
> Third, in 1979, 1980, 1981, neither myself nor Mr. Son Sann
> wanted to enter into a coalition with the Khmer Rouge. But in
> June 1982, we had to do so after all, because our followers, that
> is, the patriotic and nationalist Khmers as a whole, who had
> decided to fight against the Vietnamese, in order to save our
> fatherland, would have received neither arms nor ammunition
> from China nor foodstuffs or any other humanitarian aid from
> friendly countries nor the support of the UNO [United Nations
> Organization], if we had remained simple 'rebels.' China and
> ASEAN gave us to understand that our two nationalist move-
> ments, our two national liberation fronts, would not have any
> future outside the lawful framework of the state of Democratic
> Kampuchea, a full member of the UNO.[60]

The United States was also instrumental in designing an anti-Vietnamese alliance because it saw the Vietnamese presence in Cambodia as a Soviet threat to Southeast Asia by extension. China saw the Vietnamese tilt toward the Soviet Union as a threat and had already carried out a limited war against Vietnam soon after the collapse of Democratic Kampuchea.[61] The ASEAN countries (who, back then, consisted of Indonesia, Malaysia, the Philippines, Singapore, and Thailand) agreed with both China and the United States about a Vietnamese threat to Southeast Asia, and by extension, communism and the Soviet influence. Thailand, which had a long border with Cambodia covered with thick jungle, acted as a transit route for supplies to the anti-Vietnamese fighters.[62] The question of the Khmer Rouge genocide had conveniently become a nonissue.

Caught in the middle of a debate about the Cambodian issue was another actor, the People's Republic of Kampuchea (PRK). No one talked about this elephant in the room and it had to prove itself militarily before it could become a recognized actor. For most of the Sponsors of the resistance groups, the PRK was irrelevant because it was only a "Vietnamese puppet."[63] Only Prince Sihanouk could see how ignoring the PRK would be problematic. The prince was very careful, at least in the above interview, to mention that the issue was the Vietnamese presence in Cambodia, not the PRK per se. Would the prince join with the PRK to govern Cambodia after the Vietnamese withdrew? The prince did not explicitly rule out that option and the emphasis was only on the Vietnamese presence.

On the other side, in many books written by Comrade Hun Sen, most notably *Ten Years of Cambodia's Journey* and *13 Decades of Cambodia's Journey,* he left a hint that while the prince worked under the umbrella of Democratic Kampuchea which retained the Cambodian seat at the United Nations, the prince's presence was quintessential in any resolution of the Cambodian conflict. While Pol Pot and his cliques were heavily accused in the two books, Comrade Hun Sen remained courteous when mentioning Prince Sihanouk.

But then, for Comrade Hun Sen and the PRK, the existence of the Khmer Rouge's political-military structure remained an issue that precluded negotiation with Prince Sihanouk. The Sponsors would also not be too happy to see a premature political solution when everything seemed to be in favor of resistance. Moreover, Comrade Hun Sen viewed the premature Vietnamese withdrawal as a fatal threat to the survival of the PRK.

The PRK demanded the neutralization of the Khmer Rouge before the Vietnamese withdrawal, while the resistance demanded the Vietnamese withdrawal without mentioning the Khmer Rouge. In 1982, Comrade Hun Sen and the PRK noted:

> We never refuse the possibility of a withdrawal of the Vietnamese troops from Cambodia, but at the same time we also must not play with the possibility of death [resulting from the return of the Khmer Rouge]. The government of the People's Republic of Kampuchea and the government of the Socialist Republic of Vietnam have agreed to declare that the Vietnamese troops would be totally withdrawn from Cambodia when all external threats are eliminated.[64]

Both sides reached an impasse. War was inevitable.

GUERILLAS AGAINST GUERILLAS

Pol Pot's Strategy

The war between the PRK (supported by the Vietnamese) and the resistance forces (supported by the Sponsors) started as early as 1979 and continued until the late 1980s. It was a strange war. It was a guerilla war in all interpretations of the term. Pol Pot used the term "people's war," which was most likely used in a classical sense.[65] In this approach, the guerillas must start in stages, mainly because they were too weak at the beginning and would be defeated in an open encounter with the government forces. As a result, the most common way for the guerillas to prevail was to attract and build popular support. That support would come either by exploiting grievances vis-à-vis the government, or creating noble causes for the movement. The popular support would be essential as it would provide food, intelligence, safe havens, and the unending supply of recruits. After several more stages, the guerillas would gain enough strength to take on large government forces and ultimately defeat them.

Che Guevara was too hasty in Bolivia when he took on the government forces at a time when he had no popular support. Accordingly, the struggle ended tragically for him.[66] Guerilla forces in China, Vietnam, and Cambodia (in the 1970s) all enjoyed immense popular support before they could overthrow their respective governments. The case involving the Khmer Rouge was peculiar, because the Khmer Rouge hijacked the prince's cause and used it to its own advantage in 1970. The intrigue was made known only in the inner party circle. The people, on the other hand, were made to believe that they were fighting for the prince while, in fact, they were fighting for the Khmer Rouge. But that still validates the rules: popular support and fighting in progressive stages are the two important characteristics of guerilla warfare.

Pol Pot ignored two important factors that might prevent him from achieving his objectives. Firstly, his movement still relied on Prince Sihanouk's participation in the Coalition Government of Democratic Kampuchea (CGDK). But because the prince already had his own movement and army, Pol Pot was not able to rely on the old tricks he used in 1970s to hijack the prince's reputation. Second, the majority of the Cambodian population was staunchly against the return of the Khmer Rouge because that return would mean certain death for them.

Nonetheless, Pol Pot's main advantage was his anti-Vietnamese ideology, which had reached its peak with the Vietnamese presence in Cambodia. The potential recruitment pool for the Khmer Rouge became those who were too young to remember or even be aware of the horrors under Democratic Kampuchea. The PRK's propaganda of a genocide perpetrated by the Khmer Rouge, on the other hand, virtually had no effect on many people of this new generation. When they grew up, what they saw was Vietnamese soldiers in Cambodia, clearly confirming Pol Pot's propaganda, and these recruits believed totally in his anti-Vietnamese ideology. Those who had lived under the Khmer Rouge regime, however, were more inclined to support the PRK.

The war with Vietnam exacted a high price from the KRA but in 1979, the Khmer Rouge was still the largest of the resistance fighting forces. While the estimates vary, the common assumption is that the Khmer Rouge retained around 30,000 soldiers, excluding the supporting forces (consisted of civilians) that lived in their sanctuaries along the Cambodian-Thai border.[67]

Organization and Operations

According to the classic methods developed by Mao[68] and Giap,[69] guerilla warfare in the first stage consisted of hit-and-run attacks to harass the government forces without ever engaging them in large-scale encounters, otherwise the guerillas would be destroyed. The second stage would come when the guerillas could organize as large units and have the capability to conduct large-scale encounters. The guerillas might try to hold on to some territories temporarily, but then retreat in the face of counterattack. This is the "strategic stalemate" phase where neither side can take the offensive. After a period of attrition, there would come a time when the government forces lost all offensive capabilities but the guerillas became capable of taking the offensive. Mao called this stage "strategic offensive," where the guerillas organize into large formations to fight openly and to hold ground permanently.[70] In all cases, popular support and strong political indoctrination are needed to strengthen the guerilla forces in these stages.

At the beginning of the struggle in Cambodia, the Khmer Rouge immediately started with large formations at the division level and by 1994, the estimate of the Royal Cambodian Armed Forces (RCAF) put the number at 27 divisions in all of Cambodia (see Appendix).[71] However, in Khmer language, these were known as *kbal korng pul* or "division head," in essence, a skeletal structure. None of these divisions ever had more than 500 personnel, except for a few special divisions. That did not prevent the Khmer Rouge from conducting significant attacks, however. According to one soldier of division 920: "We do not have a lot of active soldiers, but we had networks in many villages, when we want to conduct an attack, we call the local commanders and soldiers for a meeting and plan the attack. When the time comes, everyone coordinates their attack on a certain target and then we return to the respective villages."[72]

There were at least two exceptions where Pol Pot organized the force as true divisions. The first case was division 415, which was based at Pailin. Division 415 consisted of five regiments and 3 special force battalions with a total number between 7,000 and 8,000 soldiers, and 30,000 supporting civilians.[73] Another important division was division 785, which was used as a transportation unit but would also be used to break any sector that the normal units could not defeat. The unit was based in Siem Reap but could also move as deep as Kompung Cham province when this was required.[74]

The coordination, however, appeared to exist only at the local level. At the higher level, the command was more decentralized. The military regions were divided into three main regions.[75] The first was the area around the Tonle Sap

Guerillas against Guerillas—KPRAF district military and the railway militias conducted joint patrol along a railway track, Oudong, Kompung Speu province, circa 1988. (© Sar Pormean Kampuchea (SPK)–Kampuchean Press. Used by permission.)

basin. This was a strategic location for various reasons. Many provinces shared their borders with the Tonle Sap Lake where it might be difficult for the KPRAF to conduct joint operations. In fact, many Khmer Rouge units operated only along the border of the provinces and districts.[76] The Tonle Sap basin was also a rich source of fish for Cambodia, and the Khmer Rouge, as well as other resistance forces, could easily blend in with the population and survive on fishing or extortion from the fishermen in the area. As one soldier of the Siem Reap provincial garrison noted, the Khmer Rouge was usually active in the population centers during the dry season, but they were busier in the areas around the lake during the rainy season when the fish became more abundant.[77]

The second strategic area was located along the Cambodian-Thai border, the flesh and blood of the resistance forces. The area was covered with thick jungle and was heavily infested with malaria-carrying mosquitoes. If the situation became tense, the Khmer Rouge and other resistance forces could easily blend in with the refugees in the camps on Thai territory, which would be off limits for both the Vietnamese and the KPRAF. This area was always a gateway for all the supplies to support operations in the interior of the country. Of the five permanent sanctuaries for the Khmer Rouge, four were located in this area: Malai, Pailin, Anlong Veng, and Samlot.

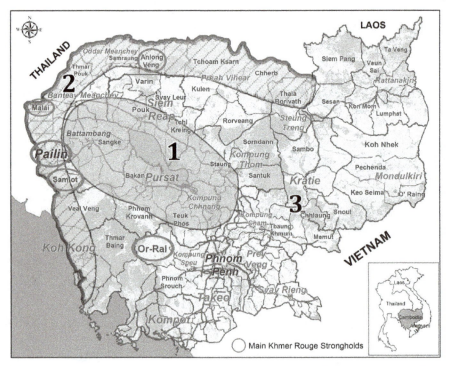

Khmer Rouge's strongholds and notable sanctuaries, after the UNTAC left in 1993. The number denotes their operational zones, not controlled areas. (Boraden Nhem)

The third military region was residual and covered the rest of Cambodia. This general area did not seem to offer any strategic value, apart from the fact that it drew the KPRAF and the Vietnamese strength away from the main areas of operations. The only exception was the Or-Ral area where, by occupying the mountain ranges including the Or-Ral summit which is the highest mountain in Cambodia, the Khmer Rouge could immediately threaten the western part of Phnom Penh. The mountains also extend into Kampot Province. Even so, this area was large and the Or-ral base was cut off from the east coast of the Mekong River with Phnom Penh, Svay Rieng, and Kompung Cham in the middle. The east coast of the river was also not suitable for large-scale operations, as the border between Cambodia and Vietnam and Laos did not offer any sanctuary comparable to the sanctuaries along the Cambodian-Thai border.

Therefore, the Khmer Rouge could come from only one direction: the west.

Operationally, the Khmer Rouge soldiers almost always attacked as guerilla groups and light infantry. Rarely did they have tank support or artillery cover. Air support was nonexistent. In fact, at the beginning and until 1998, most of the tanks used by the Khmer Rouge were captured from various withdrawals by the KPRAF and the RCAF. Lack of technicians, maintenance and spare parts further debilitated this Khmer Rouge armored support. The formation remained the same from squad up to division and front. Just like the KRA, the Khmer Rouge still did not have formal ranks. The commanders and soldiers were known only by their association to and command of a unit, but no formal rank was applied.

The tactics used by the Khmer Rouge changed little from the time they fought with the Khmer Republic, although this time, the Khmer Rouge needed to be more discrete. The Khmer Rouge always attacked in ambush mode with extensive use of antipersonnel mines, booby traps (both sides used the ancient, and dreaded, bamboo spikes), and a generous use of RPGs. Most national roads were threatened, and the railways were also constantly under attack. An ambush could be conducted in all circumstances even with a squad of only five soldiers. It was also rare for the Khmer Rouge to leave the bodies of their fallen comrades on the battlefield. A senior officer of the KPRAF noted that at most, five bodies would be left on the battlefield, and that happened only when the Khmer Rouge had no choice at all, otherwise they would fight to recover the bodies.[78] This is an indication of their high level of cohesion as a fighting force. Pol Pot decreed that the units must have clear plans and must cooperate closely during a campaign.[79] Not leaving a comrade behind would certainly boost morale and the spirit of mutual cooperation.

The Khmer Rouge also acted as true guerillas: the property of the people must not be touched and civilian lives were to be spared if possible.[80] It was only in the later period that this ideal began to break down under the pressure of the free market. Yet, the Khmer Rouge never showed any remorse for killing anyone whom they suspected had cooperated with the KPRAF. A commander of the Siem Reap provincial garrison noted that when he went into a village to clear out the Khmer Rouge, he saw nothing, and no one talked. But then a villager secretly approached him and asked if his unit was going to stay long as a prerequisite for providing information.[81] The people were known as "two-faced people" since they would cooperate with anyone just to remain safe, and that was understandable. At least in the beginning of the struggle when the Khmer Rouge received support from the Sponsors, the Khmer Rouge would compete with the KPRAF to buy rice from the farmers (usually with counterfeit money).[82] Division 785, for example, would compete with the Siem Reap provincial garrison. The PRK had a propaganda slogan: "Selling rice to the state means loving the nation." At least this was a civilized guerilla war.

Despite tactical advantages, the Khmer Rouge was faced with one problem. Unlike in the period between 1970 and 1975, the Khmer Rouge had to work with other resistance forces that did not plan to leave Cambodia as the Vietnamese troops did in 1972. They had to conduct operations by taking into account the ANS and the troops of the KPNLF. The latter two, however, were noncommunist, while the Khmer Rouge was the only communist movement. Apart from these three main forces, there were countless other smaller groups that were created mostly for smuggling and extortion in the refugee camps. Most, if not all, Khmer Rouge soldiers did not like these forces, especially those who were bent on hurting or extorting from the people.[83] Some commanders of the KPNLF, on their part, mostly consisted of former FANK soldiers of the Khmer Republic and were usually involved in heated exchanges with the Khmer Rouge leaders about the destruction of Cambodia by Democratic Kampuchea.[84] Despite the efforts of the Sponsors, the three main parties in the CGDK were not able to integrate and become a unified fighting force. Yet, they could build a modus vivendi with the understanding of at least not attacking each other. And because the Khmer Rouge controlled most of the local networks at the village level, they were the dominant group in the resistance forces.

"The Enemy Gets a Vote": The KPRAF in the Equation

An ancient dictum in strategy warns that "the enemy also has a vote." This means that no matter how flawless a plan might appear, the enemy will also react rationally to such plans. In the late 1980s, it was the KPRAF and the PRK that were the main obstacles between the Khmer Rouge and power. The KPRAF understood clearly that conventional combat was not the name of the game. Instead, the commanders always sought to disrupt the Khmer Rouge operations in a series of preemptive attacks and ambushes instead of waiting for the Khmer Rouge to attack.[85] If the Khmer Rouge conducted spoiling attacks at night, so did the KPRAF. If the Khmer Rouge cut the supplies of the KPRAF, then the KPRAF also raided the Khmer Rouge supplies depot if the depot accumulated sufficient supplies.

The organization of the KPRAF also followed the organization of socialist structure. The chief of the general staff held the title of first deputy minister of defense, which made it easier to integrate between the ministry of defense and the combatant command and the general staffs. Each unit used a dual commander system where the commander of the units had to work with the political commissar. The political commissar was considered to be a very important person because the commissar was the bearer of the party's message, and the one who monitored party discipline within the ranks, as well as determined whether the operations were in line with party policy.[86] As a result, the party had a direct line to the combat units. This structure was applied down to the company level.

Because the PRK and the Kampuchea People's Revolutionary Party (KPRP-1980s) were the result of resistance against the Khmer Rouge, the KPRAF's counterinsurgency strategy was very lenient with regard to population control. The KPRAF was given two main missions: fighting the enemy and helping protect the people from disasters and hunger.[87] The Vietnamese, in most cases, did not try to pacify the villages in the place of the KPRAF. The Vietnamese would usually attack and then man the perimeters, while the KPRAF band section went into the village to entertain and then indoctrinate the people.[88]

The second layer of the KPRAF defense was the militias system that was similar in design to the KRA militias system, but with a vastly different function. Instead of spying on the people, the KPRAF militias were very efficient defensive weapons that impeded the free movement of the Khmer Rouge to besiege the cities and provincial towns. The people were driven by their hatred and contempt for the brutality of the Khmer Rouge under Democratic Kampuchea, and fought bitterly to defend their villages.

The reputation of the militias was confirmed by former Khmer Rouge soldiers: "we went in with half a battalion but we did not know the terrain well while the militias squad knew the terrain as the palm of their hands, and with a force less than two squads, they shot at us here and there. We had to abandon the attack and were lucky to even find a way out."[89] But still, in remote villages, the KPRAF intervention forces could not arrive in case of emergency, and most of those villages were considered to be under the influence of the Khmer Rouge.[90]

The militias were further broken down into several categories: village and hamlet militias, railways militias (defending railways that passed through the villages), national road/highway militias (defending the bridges along the national highway), and fishing lot militias (defending the fishing lots around the Tonle Sap Lake).[91] In Siem Reap alone, with around 700,000 people, the militias consisted of 2,560 people in the year 2000, with the number fluctuating throughout the years. 1993 was the peak year with the militias numbering 6,303.[92]

While the militias and the provincial garrisons were in charge of the provinces, the conventional units swept into the jungle to raid all permanent sanctuaries of the resistance forces. The divisions functioned as conventional units but also allocated guerilla units to ambush the enemy and took the initiative as the commanders saw fit.

The KPRAF and the Vietnamese army divided the campaign into two main operational concepts, following the seasons in Cambodia.[93] During the dry season, major offensive campaigns would be undertaken because the artillery and armor superiority of the KPRAF could be brought to bear. The dry soil also facilitated the movement of troops and supplies. The dry season was also the only window through which the forward formations could be supplied. In the rainy season, the roads were practically unusable. Expeditions along the treacherous roads would provide too many opportunities for the Khmer Rouge to ambush the convoy.

Many of these large campaigns were mostly successful, and most border camps were destroyed. However, the resistance forces, most notably the Khmer Rouge, simply relocated to the Tonle Sap basin. This prompted many operations to chase them out, only for the Khmer Rouge to relocate along the border again.[94] In essence, it was a game of hide-and-seek on a grand scale.

WHEN THE WALL FELL DOWN. . .

The military conduct of both the Khmer Rouge and the KPRAF was somewhat evenly matched. The Khmer Rouge had no prospect at all to return to power. But at the same time, the KPRAF, which retained a more sophisticated governing structure, was not able to pacify the entire country. The Khmer Rouge would still remain a threat to peace, in essence, a military nuisance.

The war was also a product of the Cold War. Nevertheless, in the late 1980s, the Soviet Union showed signs of collapse. The war in Afghanistan was a disaster for the Soviets. The Soviet Union was also the biggest supporter of Vietnam and the war in Cambodia. It was the largest recipient of Cambodian officer students from the KPRAF. The Soviet Union was also the main source of supplies of weapons.[95] In the late 1980s, however, the Stinger missiles arrived in Afghanistan (along with other weapons and ammunitions) and largely disadvantaged the Soviet troops to the extent that they were never able to recover.[96] The Soviet economy weakened as a result, followed by the ascension to power of the progressive Mikhail Gorbachev. On July 28, 1986, Gorbachev made a historic speech at Vladivostok, outlining his new foreign policy.

The speech announced an overall reduction of Soviet troops in Mongolia, along the border with China, in Southeast Asia, and the scaling down of the military might of the Warsaw Pact.[97] But one of the agendas of Gorbachev's foreign policy in the Vladivostok speech was the withdrawal from Afghanistan, which he said could be used as the model of the withdrawal of the Vietnamese Volunteer Army from Cambodia. Accordingly, the first largest withdrawal was in November 1987 when 20,000 soldiers returned to Vietnam.[98] It is highly likely that the withdrawal was meant to facilitate the first meeting between Prince Sihanouk and Prime Minister Hun Sen, which took place at Fère-En-Tardenois, France, on December 2, 1987. On May 15, 1988, Gorbachev made the first official visit by a Soviet leader to Beijing since 1959, and during this meeting, both Gorbachev and Deng Xiaoping agreed

A Vietnamese soldier stood guard as the formation of the 2nd infantry battalion crossed the border into Vietnam as part of the withdrawal in 1988. After the total withdrawal of Vietnamese soldiers in 1989, the Khmer Rouge became an organization without purpose. (©Sar Pormean Kampuchea (SPK)–Kampuchean Press. Used by permission.)

that there should be a political solution to the Cambodian conflict for the sake of the Cambodian people and the Southeast Asian region.[99] That day (May 15, 1988) the Soviet started the large-scale withdrawal from Afghanistan, and then a few days later, Hanoi announced the withdrawal of 50,000 soldiers from Cambodia.[100]

The Vietnamese withdrawal was completed on September 25, 1989, which opened a window of opportunity for the resistance forces to take the offensive before the expected political negotiations were completed. As Prime Minister Hun Sen noted about this event, the war had now entered a new phase— "fighting on the one hand, and negotiating on the other."[101]

TOWARD THE END

The resistance forces largely failed to take advantage of the windows of opportunity opened by the Vietnamese withdrawal since that would leave the KPRAF the sole defender of the PRK. Particularly for the Khmer Rouge, several factors prevented them from taking the offensive: the collapse of the anti-Vietnamese ideology, the KPRAF's strength, the loss of support from the Sponsors, the impact of the free market economy, and ultimately the distrust that everyone had in Pol Pot. We shall examine these factors in turn.

We have already examined how the KPRAF's organizational design and tactics did not fall into the same trap as the FANK. Even though the KPRAF's conventional divisions raided the sanctuaries, only for the Khmer Rouge to be relocated elsewhere, the objective was to at least force the Khmer Rouge to keep building new sanctuaries. It was believed that if the Khmer Rouge spent more time rebuilding their sanctuaries and amassing supplies, the less time they would have in strengthening or expanding the structure of the guerilla shadow government in the villages.[102] While the war did not progress very well for the Khmer Rouge, the Vietnamese withdrawal presented two more challenges for the Khmer Rouge: the loss of external support and the collapse of anti-Vietnamese ideology.

The Khmer Rouge first learnt about the disturbing news in Malai in 1990. According to some sources, it was there near the Malai area, along the Cambodian-Thai border, that Son Sen, then Pol Pot's chief of staff, met with two representatives from the People's Republic of China on August 18, 1990, just before the Paris Peace Accord.[103]

At the end of the Cold War, China started to implement its most-revered "noninterference policy" and progressive politicians came to power in Thailand in a political transition. Both agreed that supporting the Khmer Rouge had become outdated. "Revolution" lost all its appeal after the Cold War ended. That was the implicit message conveyed by the two Chinese representatives who reportedly met Son Sen in 1990 at an office codenamed "K-18" along the Cambodian-Thai border near Malai.

At that meeting, Son Sen lauded the glorious achievements of the Khmer Rouge, including many victories over the KPRAF.[104] These claims turned out to be a gross exaggeration. Later, my interview with a former commander of Division 980 revealed another problem within the Khmer Rouge organization. Pol Pot and Son Sen did order their troops to gradually expand the controlled area by occupying all "liberated" areas. However, the low-ranking officers and field commanders knew that occupying it would be suicidal. All they could do was to raid the provincial towns and hope that a mass routing would occur. Some former commanders claimed that after the Vietnamese troops withdrew, his unit found it very difficult to fill in the ranks and they simply could not occupy any areas. All he wanted was sufficient control so that those areas could be used as bargaining chips with the government in an eventual political solution.[105]

The realities on the ground did not escape the attention of the Chinese delegates. For them, "occupation" of conquered areas was as empty as the Khmer Rouge's legitimacy itself. This time, the Chinese delegates brought a message symbolic of their new foreign policy. The delegates tried to be polite and showed their consideration of Son Sen's presentation. But they then uttered their position:

You always told us you are winning but this [office in the jungle] is what you always had since then. Soldiers are demoralized and they wanted freedom and free market [. . .] You simply can't use dictatorship for the second time [. . .] We do not intend to sell you out, but we want you to adhere to the nonviolence principles and seek a political solution to the conflict, in accordance with the goodwill of the United Nations, the goodwill of the Central Committee of the Chinese Communist Party, and the desire of the Cambodian people [. . .] The sponsors to the Cambodian civil war agreed to cease their support and negotiate for peace in 1991. The People's Republic of China must completely stop the support. Our visit here today brought this message. We think that if the peace negotiation succeeds in 1991, all Cambodian people will unprecedentedly rejoice. You should take this as priority.[106]

The news of the meeting with the Chinese delegates was ordered suppressed by Son Sen, apparently under the orders of Pol Pot. But many people who also attended the meeting were secretly rejoicing at the message brought by the delegates. Soon, the news of the meeting became a public secret among top commanders of the Khmer Rouge divisions.[107]

While China ceased all support for the Khmer Rouge, and Pol Pot more specifically, Thai leaders such as Chavalit also facilitated the discussions and the meeting between the more moderate factions of the Khmer Rouge in Malai-Pailin and the Cambodian government.[108]

That loss of external support had many debilitating consequences for the Khmer Rouge. For one, Pol Pot was forced to participate in the political process, even though everyone, including Pol Pot himself, knew that no one would accept his share of power in the future government without some retributions for his past crime. Yet, he had no better choice. Participating was not the best choice, but it was the lesser of two evils for Pol Pot.

A BRIEF TRUCE: THE UNTAC ARRIVES AND DEPARTS

Negotiations were necessary because no party by itself could successfully govern in Cambodia. Had any one party had sufficient military power, governing competence, and legitimacy, the conflict would have been settled and no United Nations peacekeeping mission would have been necessary. But that was not the case. That was the origin of the negotiations leading to the Paris Peace Accord in 1991.

As a gesture toward renouncing socialist ideology, the PRK changed its name to the State of Cambodia (SOC) just prior to the start of the peace negotiations. The Kampuchean People's Revolutionary Party was also changed to the Cambodian People's Party (CPP). Negotiations first began in France on December 2, 1987, between Prince Sihanouk and Prime Minister Hun Sen, culminating in the final accord, the Agreements on a Comprehensive Political Settlement of the Cambodia Conflict, signed in Paris on October 23, 1991. This agreement was the foundation of the UNTAC mandate for peacekeeping in Cambodia. As an interim measure, an advance mission, the United Nations Advance Mission in Cambodia (UNAMIC), was established immediately after the signing of the agreements in October 1991.[109]

Security Council Resolution 745 (1992), creating the United Nations Transitional Authority in Cambodia (UNTAC), was approved on February 28, 1992. UNTAC became operational by absorbing the personnel and resources of UNAMIC. The conflicting parties agreed to (1) cease the fighting (2) allow the UNTAC to act as the security guarantor of all parties and (3) disarm their soldiers and send them into cantonment areas monitored by the UNTAC during the transition period. The ultimate goal was to allow the UNTAC to organize a free and fair election where all four parties could participate without the outbreak of violence. A Supreme National Council (SNC), which included members from all the conflicting parties, was to act as the repository of Cambodian sovereignty. The UNTAC was led by a civilian diplomat, Yasushi Akashi, who acted as the Special Representative of the Secretary General (SRSG).

The UNTAC mission was plagued with difficulties from the start. On June 13, 1992, it was decided that 200,000 Cambodian soldiers of the different factions would be disarmed and relocated into 52 cantonment facilities.[110] By September 1992, however, the UNTAC had managed to collect only 50,000 weapons, about 42,368 of which came from the SOC.[111] As late as March 1993, only 55,000 troops had entered the cantonments and the SRSG ordered the disarmament program to be suspended, since it was failing to achieve its purpose. Most of the troops in cantonment came from the SOC, and continuation would have disadvantaged them in the negotiations and in the field. The limited success left significant arms and men available to the conflicting parties. For example, the Khmer Rouge was active in about 15 percent of the total area of Cambodia, consisting of only 7–8 percent of the population, with a strength of 10,000 to 15,000 armed men.[112]

The Khmer Rouge refused to cooperate in the process, as can be understood by its own perception of itself. Pol Pot himself must have calculated or at least suspected that the Khmer Rouge would not be welcomed in any political solution. As a result of their previous history, deep mistrust existed between the Khmer Rouge and the SOC on the one hand, and between the Khmer Rouge and the FUNCINPEC (Prince Sihanouk's movement) on the other hand.

Pol Pot's suspicion would soon be realized. On November 27, 1991, Khieu Samphan and Son Sen were attempting to inaugurate the official office of the Khmer Rouge's political party in Phnom Penh. They were attacked in their villa by hundreds, or even thousands, of people seeking retribution for the genocide committed under the Khmer Rouge regime. The mob cornered and briefly assaulted them in a room before the police (from the SOC) intervened and evacuated them to safety in an armored car. Many critical commentators suspect the SOC was behind the event,[113] although it could not have been hard to find a genuinely angry mob to attack representatives of a regime that had committed gross atrocities for over three years.

At the time, neither Prince Sihanouk nor Akashi issued any condemnation, or even heavy criticism, of the event. Given their past relationship with the Khmer Rouge, the FUNCINPEC and the SOC both had reasons to see the Khmer Rouge intimidated from participation in the election, especially when this intimidation appeared to have sprung up spontaneously in the form of an angry mob. Regardless, any parties who supported Pol Pot's participation might lose a lot of votes to those that opposed Pol Pot's entrance.

Before the mob attack, Pol Pot, the real leader of the Khmer Rouge, designed a plan called "1000 villages," providing the basis for the Khmer Rouge to consolidate control over a sizable number of the population in order to gain leverage in the postelection power sharing.[114] Such evidence strongly indicates an intention to participate in the election process. However, everyone in the Khmer Rouge would have interpreted the mob attack as a strong message from the other parties directed at excluding the Khmer Rouge from the elections. The Khmer Rouge apparently calculated that participating in the election would be impractical or unfruitful and concluded it would be better to wait until one of the other two main parties needed support. In the complex local politics of Cambodia, the Khmer Rouge was soon proven right.

For its part, the UNTAC did little to bring the Khmer Rouge on board although in terms of fairness to all signatories, it (the UNTAC) might have so chosen. Impartiality, it seems, can be violated by what you choose not to do as well as what you choose to do. This was the dilemma for peacekeeping in Cambodia. As was later evident, on the one hand, Akashi had no way of including the Khmer Rouge in the election with the consent of both the FUNCINPEC and the SOC, the two dominant factions in the peace process. Akashi thus did not include the Khmer Rouge and he contributed to the creation of a coalition government at the time. Akashi pursued what was known as the "departing train" strategy:[115] If the Khmer Rouge did not change their mind about the boycott, they would be left out of the process.

In this case, Akashi is on record as to how he interpreted the principle of impartiality when it confronted the realities of the local political context:

> One can question the legitimacy and stability of this formula, which treated the two major parties on an approximately equal basis. While this is unorthodox by universal democratic principles, we have to admit the practical wisdom of combining the 'new wind,' represented by the victorious FUNCINPEC, consisting mostly of upper and upper middle class intellectuals aspiring to the restoration of the monarchy, with the experience and power of the CPP, which is authoritarian but has 14 years of administrative experience, with much of the army and the police under its control.[116]

Impartiality would ideally call for equal treatment of all parties. However, in the Cambodian case, we find that the SRSG's departure from pure impartiality preserved, first, the conduct of the election and, second, the formulation of an acceptable form of power sharing when the election results were challenged. One can question Akashi's judgment with regard to the effects of favoring two parties over the Khmer Rouge, the risks he accepted, and even his motivations to some degree, but he essentially applied the impartiality principle correctly. Because two important actors (the SOC and the FUNCINPEC) did not want to see the Khmer Rouge included in the political process, Akashi needed to play the role of politician as opposed to lawyer with regard to the application of the Paris Peace Accord and the charter. The political resolution of conflict will invariably take priority over the sustainment of some pure idea of impartiality.

As events later illustrated, in Cambodia, the marginalization policy pursued by Akashi created a problem because it paradoxically made the Khmer Rouge more important: the Khmer Rouge military could significantly endanger the balance of power of the new coalition government by simply allying with any faction. Instead of resolving this problem, the UNTAC had simply deferred it to a later date when peacekeepers were no longer there to keep the peace.

For Akashi, the issue of the Khmer Rouge's potential boycott was a dilemma inherent in the peacekeeping mission in Cambodia. For Pol Pot and the Khmer Rouge, however, it was an inevitable disaster.

BOYCOTT!

After the attack on Son Sen and Khieu Samphan, Pol Pot called back all of the representatives of the Khmer Rouge who were sent to work with the UNTAC and the representatives of other parties in preparation for the election. Military campaigns also resumed. Then, suddenly, the Khmer Rouge conducted a fierce raid on the night of May 2 and early morning of May 3, 1993 (just before the election) on the Siem Reap provincial town, something they had never undertaken before. The Khmer Rouge made it clear that they were still a force to be reckoned with. Composed mainly of infantry and special guerilla units, the Khmer Rouge attacked the provincial town in a surprise move and tried to hold many key positions, including the airport and the power plants that provided electricity to the town.

In this surprise move, the Khmer Rouge almost overran the town. At that time, the SOC was busy rushing most of their forces, including a battalion tasked with defending the provincial town, to the battlefield in Phnom Kulen, roughly 15 km from Siem Reap.[117] Despite this apparently short distance, the road conditions were so bad that travel was very slow. When the raid occurred, only approximately 40 fighters of the SOC remained in the town.[118]

The SOC was forced to resort to guerilla tactics of its own, taking advantage of darkness (the Khmer Rouge started their raid around 3:00 A.M. in the morning). Toward dawn, the SOC reinforcements began to arrive in town. However, a small armored force and special operations units were stuck because their black uniforms were momentarily confused with the Khmer Rouge. Another SOC armor unit had its tank engines fail midway to the town. But despite these setbacks, in a matter of hours, a fierce counterattack at the Khmer Rouge field command center in the central market, combined with some psychological warfare tactics, drove the Khmer Rouge out of town.[119]

If we consider the occupation of the city as the Khmer Rouge's objective for the raid, then this was an impossible objective. Besides, the raid was conducted in a strange way: the Khmer Rouge attacked at 3:00 A.M., meaning that they were willing to hold ground. Usually, the Khmer Rouge attacked at midnight and then withdrew before first light. However, if we understand the raid as an attempt by the Khmer Rouge to send a message, this message was largely successful.

But when the dust settled, a significant problem struck deep into the Khmer Rouge organization: the loss of purpose. According to the officers of the KPRAF, the Khmer Rouge attacked in three directions, or at least according to plan.[120] The first axis came from the national road, attacking through the provincial market. The second axis came out of villages surrounding the provincial town, and the third axis came from the Tonle Sap Lake.

But then the plan fell apart. According to an officer of the KPRAF who was involved in the operation to repel the Khmer Rouge attack, the three axes failed to connect.[121] The Tonle Sap axis, in a strange twist of fate, came across a wedding reception along its way and the Khmer Rouge soldiers went in to party, uninvited.[122] The hosts were too scared to protest. This group of soldiers became drunk and arrived late into the provincial town in the morning. The market axis and the village axis were the ones that actually arrived in time, but the market axis procrastinated when they arrived at the market. Witnesses claimed the Khmer Rouge actually shot each other when they disagreed over how to divide the loot (motorcycles) from the market.[123] Only the village axis was the main thrust, but this was bottlenecked at the narrow bridges along the Steung Siem Reap, a tributary running across the town.[124]

In the end, less than 50 KPRAF soldiers and police were able to fend off the Khmer Rouge attackers—estimated to be at least 600 men—until the KPRAF reinforcements came to envelope the Khmer Rouge.[125] The Khmer Rouge did send their message, but they were also the biggest loser from the episode. The election was carried out as planned and the KPRAF had proved its strength. The attacks also exposed one inconvenient truth for the Khmer Rouge: the free market, greed, and materialism had now taken deep roots in the minds of the fighters. With no clear goal in sight, it was only natural that the soldiers would fall into this trap. To make matters worse, such materialist attachments had tragically failed an important operation that might have otherwise been a significant victory. Some said it was fate, and that time was up for the Khmer Rouge.

FROM POLITICAL GUERILLAS TO BUSINESS CARTEL: TASTE OF MONEY

Over 4 million Cambodians participated in the 1993 elections. Of the 120 seats in the legislature, the FUNCINPEC won 58 seats, the CPP 51, the KPNLF 10, and the Moulinaka party one. Because the constitution called for a two-thirds majority for a party to form a government, some scheme of power-sharing had to be reached. The negotiations that ensued, mediated by Prince Sihanouk and Akashi, resulted in a complex power-sharing system. It created a constitutional monarchy and the first country to have a dual prime ministerial system as the result of a compromise between the CPP and the FUNCINPEC. Prince Sihanouk was proclaimed the king, and Prince Norodom Ranariddh (FUNCINPEC) and Hun Sen (CPP) served as the first and second prime minister, respectively. UNTAC's mandate ended in September 1993 with the promulgation of the Constitution for the Kingdom of Cambodia and the formation of the new government. However, the various military forces tended to remain supportive of their parties as opposed to the new state.

But the boycott brought an even greater disaster for the Khmer Rouge. The anti-Vietnamese ideology that held the Khmer Rouge together as a cohesive organization was no longer relevant after the withdrawal of Vietnamese troops in 1989. With this noble cause no longer a rallying cry, the next best option would be to use existing military power to trade for some power in the newly formed, legitimate government. However, this option, too, was not feasible. Pol Pot was overly suspicious and did not really cooperate with other parties and UNTAC in the peace process. He was rejected by important players in the peace process. At the same time, the 1993 raid was a blatant rejection of the peace option. With two optimal options no longer viable, the Khmer Rouge returned to fulfill their basic need: survival. But that, too, was threatened by the loss of assistance and support from the Sponsors. The only way to survive, then, was self-help, that is, to become a business cartel.

The 1993 failed raid demonstrated that the Khmer Rouge also began to realize the value of money, something that they had never comprehended or experienced when they abolished the national currency and the free market in 1975 after taking power. The once pure communist party now began to get involved in business affairs. The areas along the Cambodian-Thai border specialized in timber trade and gemstones. Pailin was known for its rich deposit of gem stones while Samlot, Malai and Anlong Veng survived on timber trade with Thai merchants.[126]

In the Kampot area, on the other hand, the jungle could not be exploited because the province bordered with Vietnam and the area resided deep in Cambodia, far away from the Thai market. As a consequence, the guerillas in Kampot started to kidnap foreign tourists and workers for ransom. As long as the ransom was paid, the foreigners would be released. It was no longer personal or ideological, it was just business. On March 31, 1994, a US national, Melissa Himes, who was working for an NGO was kidnapped. The Cambodian government, as with other governments, followed a policy of not negotiating with the kidnappers, but the U.S. government worked out a deal to prevent an offensive so as to give enough time to allow the NGO to pay the ransom.[127] Himes was later released unharmed.

In another case, when three tourists (one Australian, one British, and one French) were kidnapped during an ambush on the train they were travelling in, the victims were killed when the negotiation for ransom broke down.[128] The Khmer Rouge demanded $150,000 for the release of the Australian hostage but the negotiation was delayed by greedy middlemen. These murders occurred, not because the Khmer Rouge hated foreigners, but only because the ransom was not paid on time. The Khmer Rouge as an organization was no longer the liberation organization that it had always proclaimed to be, but had become a full-blown criminal organization in this case.

But embezzlement and jealousy also prospered along with business. Pol Pot hated the market economy as it could "poison" the minds of the people, destroying their class consciousness. In this belief, Pol Pot was correct in many instances, but with ironic twists. Business drew the soldiers away from the fight and toward profit.

The issue that ultimately caused the biggest crack in the structure of the Khmer Rouge was the irregularity and lack of transparency with regard to funds coming from illegal trade. Many lower ranking Khmer Rouge soldiers began to despise the luxury of the top cadres when the real Khmer Rouge fighters lived in extreme poverty.[129] To paraphrase Napoleon: "Soldiers got to fight, the cadres got rich." The socialist values of equality and the classless society became all but a convoluted charade.

With business booming, cronyism and embezzlement proliferated. Noun Chea secretly admitted that:

- Wrongdoings by committee members were worsened by darker and darker criticisms.
- Praising one but criticizing another. Son Sen praised the action of Meas Muth but criticized Y Chhean in Pailin although they had been together, which created a rift between them, destroyed whatever trust they had and changed their stance.
- Appointing relatives and cronies in high-profile positions and putting no trust in others. A gap was created [between cronies and competent commanders].
- Collectivization. Factions within the Khmer Rouge confiscating equipment, including farming equipment, from other people within their factions; this caused resentment and accelerated the breakup.[130]

For Pol Pot, distrust and purges went hand in hand, and the latter would occur after the former. At this point, however, those who controlled resources controlled the Khmer Rouge. Ideology no longer mattered in the post–Cold War world. The Khmer Rouge foot soldiers no longer saw reasons to fight when there were no longer any Vietnamese in Cambodia. But now they had the future of their own children to worry about. Should they let their children continue to make booby traps to kill other Cambodians, or should they end the war and send their children to school? With the free market arriving in their area, the answer was obvious.

Brother Number One, Pol Pot, was now forced to rely on his lieutenants because he controlled areas with no potential economic interests. Pol Pot had nothing, mainly because he was forced to be on the move too frequently. In the last stage of his struggle, Pol Pot was forced to live at the mercy of Ta Mok, one of his closest lieutenants, in Anlong Veng.[131] The Khmer Rouge has become the worst kind of armed, nonstate actor. Its structure awaits disintegration. No one can stop this inevitable collapse.

5

End of an Era

WHEN A BIG TREE IS ABOUT TO FALL. . .

Cambodia has a proverb that says that when a big tree is about to fall, the nesting birds will escape out of the tree. It aptly applied to the Khmer Rouge after 1993. When Pol Pot decided to stay out of the election after a few political machinations, there was an immediate mismatch between his political strategy and his military tactics. The predominant tactic was hit-and-run. The Khmer Rouge raided towns and villages but rarely tried to hold on to the territories that they took. Up until 1991, this tactic changed little. These tactics were very effective when used to serve a limited political strategy such as bargaining but not annihilation.

The missed opportunity in the 1993 election left the Khmer Rouge as an organization without a feasible purpose. Pol Pot continued to claim that the struggle was necessary because the Vietnamese were still everywhere in the country, and even the UNTAC was collaborating with the Vietnamese.[1] This time, however, the propaganda no longer worked because there were no more Vietnamese troops in Cambodia. Moreover, Prince Sihanouk had already become king of the Kingdom of Cambodia. All foreign governments recognized the Kingdom of Cambodia, and none recognized Pol Pot. This blatant truth could not be kept from field commanders any longer. More and more of these field commanders began to question Pol Pot's leadership. They felt that they were no longer part of a liberation organization but only part of some business cartel, and they now felt that they were risking their lives for the satisfaction of the cadres who controlled all the money from border trade.

Since the beginning of the Khmer Rouge as a viable organization, everyone had been kept in line by centralization, secrecy, and deadly purges. The rule of secrecy precluded anyone from asking about purpose before carrying out an order. Centralization prevented the field commanders and mid-level cadres from having discussions with each other or conspiring to change the policy of the top leadership. Finally, purges would eliminate anyone who tried to circumvent these rules. Any rebellion or dissent would be brutally put down. Even suspicion could easily land anyone in the one-way prison, S-21. All that began to change after 1979. Pol Pot still wanted to maintain tight control over his junior commanders, but realities on the ground dictated otherwise. He was forced to allow them to take initiatives.

During the civil war from 1979 to 1989, the military bases of the guerilla forces were scattered along the northwestern side of Cambodia where the Khmer Rouge could make use of sanctuaries in Thai territory if the situation so demanded. The map on p. 114 shows the main areas occupied by the Khmer Rouge forces after the PPA. The Khmer Rouge maintained large forces and bases in or around the following areas of operations: Or-Ral in Kompung Speu province, Samlot in Battambang province, Pailin in Battambang province, Malai in Banteay Meanchey province, and Anlong Veng in Oddar Meanchey province.

The topography was more or less the same: mountain ranges and jungles. In offensive operations, the KPRAF formation usually lost its tail midway due to Khmer Rouge guerilla attacks and the front was forced to retreat from its forward position. This had always been the tactic and operational concept of the Khmer Rouge guerillas. In late 1993 and early 1994, with the combination of forces from the KPNLF and the FUNCINPEC (assimilated after the 1993 election), the newly formed RCAF attempted to carry out an operation that was supposed to conquer the Khmer Rouge rear bases. But the operation collapsed after only one month.

The main strategic goal of the Khmer Rouge was to defend their sanctuaries at all cost, and then expand to the villages surrounding them, gradually strangling the cities, and continuing on to victory as in 1975. These villages were also the defensive arms of the rear bases. According to a former member of the KPRAF's general staff in the Siem Reap provincial garrison, there were two main reasons for this strategy to work.[2] First, in order to get to those rear bases of the Khmer Rouge, all smaller villages at the front needed to be pacified. But this was a momentous task. The KPRAF simply did not have enough strength to conduct such operations in a short timeframe. Second, should the KPRAF succeed in making advances, the Khmer Rouge could simply retreat into the villages and then attack from the rear.[3] The Khmer Rouge normally raided base camps and artillery positions and conducted ambushes along the main roads. These tactics became deadly during the rainy seasons when the KPRAF could not bring its armor and air superiority to bear. During the civil war, with foreign aid flowing freely to the Khmer Rouge and other resistance movements,[4] the KPRAF found it difficult to muster enough troops to totally eliminate the Khmer Rouge.

These Khmer Rouge tactics and strategy were not without drawbacks, however. To successfully implement this operational concept, Pol Pot needed to ensure that the small units sent out to cut the rear of the KPRAF were given enough initiative so that they could operate on a timely basis without waiting for orders from senior command. It was this initiative that enabled those small units to become so deadly.

Before 1989, the initiative of the lower echelons did not threaten the Khmer Rouge chain of command, as Pol Pot always used anti-Vietnamese ideology to lift morale and ensure loyalty among the troops that operated in a semi-independent fashion under his command. Nothing could stop a soldier with a clear ideology and money cannot buy a fully committed fighter.

But still, the distance between the field commanders and the high command was indeed a problem in the context of guerilla warfare. When the independent guerilla units were isolated, they were vulnerable to propaganda and defection. These KPRAF's tactics worked better and better after the Vietnamese Volunteer Army withdrew in 1989.

Pol Pot was very well aware of this counter-tactic of the KPRAF and devised a counter-measure. In a classic dilemma, a unit is strong when it takes the initiative and knows how to innovatively respond to contingencies on the battlefield: the unit needs to retain some level of tactical independence. But after 1989, independence was something that Pol Pot feared might work against him. Such an independent unit might then think differently from its superiors, especially in the context of a guerilla war that had already lost its purpose. They become very vulnerable to the enemy's propaganda while operating deep behind enemy lines.

Pol Pot was able to reach a compromise by effectively holding the families of his field commanders as de facto hostages. Families of the units on the frontlines were usually employed for logistics and preparing booby traps. In many cases, however, these families were relocated deep in the rear on the pretext of ensuring their safety, and also because logistics bases were located at the rear.[5] Sometimes, the families worked in an area of activity controlled by other Khmer Rouge commanders. Should Pol Pot discover that anyone was about to defect, their families would suffer as a consequence. This model served Pol Pot well for years. By holding these families hostage, Pol Pot effectively ensured the loyalty of his forward units while allowing them to have a large margin of initiative. But this policy was about to meet its match and was outclassed by another, more humane approach: the Win-Win Policy (WWP) of Prime Minister Hun Sen. You can only hold people hostage for so long before they've had enough.

WIN-WIN POLICY: A KHMER SOLUTION TO A KHMER PROBLEM

The UNTAC was largely successful if measured according to its mandates. The election was held and a new legitimate government was established. The problem, however, was that peace and stability were not secured as the Khmer Rouge still roamed free in the countryside. The KPRAF, now renamed RCAF, also could not totally eliminate the Khmer Rouge. Even though the prospect of the second coming of Democratic Kampuchea was eliminated, total peace was still elusive. Attrition was too costly to continue. Since the UNTAC could not find lasting peace for Cambodia, an indigenous strategy became necessary. This came in the form of the Win-Win Policy (WWP) initiated by the then second prime minister, *Samdech*[6] Hun Sen.

There has never been an official publication of the WWP that described it in detail. However, information is publicly available in secondary publications as well as various speeches of Prime Minister Hun Sen. This section will attempt to give a general overview of this Win-Win Policy.

In its original formulation, the WWP was based on the minimization of violence and the trust-building principle of ending the war. Military superiority was needed, but only as a deterrent tool to "persuade" the other side to lay down their weapons. This was so different from total annihilation or defection. After all, the belligerents had been at war for so long that no trust existed between the two sides. Only a generous accommodation backed up by goodwill and latent military power would be able to terminate the civil war.

The basic formula, as envisioned by Prime Minister Hun Sen, was "DIFID": Divide, Isolate, Finish, Integrate, and Develop.[7] "Divide" in the first stage meant that the government would try to drive a wedge between different Khmer Rouge factions that were formed after the 1993 boycott. In fact, the decision to negotiate with Prince Sihanouk can also be counted as DIFID—mark 1.[8] The main goal of the negotiation was to isolate the Khmer Rouge by working with Prince Sihanouk. Given the past history, Prince Sihanouk would never trust the Khmer Rouge and without pressure would surely abandon the Khmer Rouge. The latter, in turn, would collapse without the help of Prince Sihanouk. Thus, negotiating with Prince Sihanouk was the first "Divide." Although the DIFID formulation appeared later, Prime Minister Hun Sen formulated the idea in his book *10 years of Cambodia's Journey*, published in 1989, where he analyzed the relations between Prince Sihanouk and the Khmer Rouge in detail and concluded that the return of Prince Sihanouk, and the prince did return, would spell the end of the Khmer Rouge.[9]

After "Divide" comes "Isolate." The communications between the Khmer Rouge's small units would be cut to make it easier to isolate individual units for dialogue. Once the organization became sufficiently weakened, the political-military organization of the Khmer Rouge would be finished. This was always a recurring theme in Prime Minister Hun Sen's conception of how the war should end. In essence, this "Finish" stage would equate with what he called "the end of the 'one country, two administrations' system."[10]

While normal war termination strategy would end at this stage, the WWP sought to continue to end all the fighting as peacefully as possible. But that goal was faced with a difficult problem: trust. Both sides had been bombarded with propaganda for years and the only place where they had met so far was on the battlefield. The Khmer Rouge field commanders had both the motive and the opportunity to join the government, but it was lack of trust that prevented a quick end to the war. How to develop trust? This was the central question that the WWP was asking. Military superiority was still necessary, yet it would need to be followed not by a forced settlement, but by a generous concession.

Rhetoric was also changed. During the 1980s, the Khmer Rouge soldiers could defect to the government side and there was a policy to help "those who have lost their way [with the Khmer Rouge]."[11]

But the WWP changed this. In the fourth stage, "Integrate," the Khmer Rouge forces would not surrender or defect, but were integrated into the government. They were not those who had lost their way, but became the ones who "decided to return to live in society."[12] The change in rhetoric also meant that they would not be discriminated against or stigmatized. After all, not everyone in the Khmer Rouge had perpetrated the crimes under Democratic Kampuchea. It was only fitting that everyone was presumed innocent until proved guilty. It was a dangerous slippery slope to stereotype everyone. The last stage, which some argue is still continuing to this day, is "Develop," meaning that after integration, the former Khmer Rouge soldiers will be assured that their livelihood will be improved.

Building trust was the basis of the WWP tactics.[13] Prime Minister Hun Sen made it known that the integration process would be accompanied by three fundamental guarantees for those who decided to break away from Pol Pot. One, their lives and security were assured, that is, there would be no arbitrary arrests. Two, the WWP allowed them to maintain their jobs and positions with only a change in uniform required, and the acceptance of one rule, and three, their ownerships of private properties would be recognized.[14]

This WWP tactic was a clever one. It was designed to guarantee that the "winners-take-all" scenario would not occur, and that life after integration would be improved. No vengeance would be allowed, and no arbitrary arrests would be tolerated. The Khmer Rouge soldiers were also allowed to keep their weapons, essentially the "right to bear arms," as long as they abided by the law of the country and became part of the armed forces or the police. Finally, private property would not be confiscated. Private property was a concept that had already run amok amongst the Khmer Rouge soldiers, and which played a very important role in contributing to the collapse of the organization.

Even with designs that had been individually tailored for them, the Khmer Rouge commanders still pondered the options, and trust was still an obstacle. What was needed was a large-scale event that could be used to prove the sincerity of the WWP and the integrity of all its promises. At this time, there was a constant stream of Khmer Rouge deserters in many areas between 1994 and 1995. These areas included Siem Reap, Oddar Meanchey, Kompung Thom, and Banteay Meanchey. In 1995, the security situation in Kampot province improved greatly, following the integration of a Khmer Rouge unit that controlled the area.

But most, if not all, RCAF commanders and people who had knowledge of the WWP process agreed that the milestone event would come in 1996 when the Khmer Rouge units under the command of Keo Pung, former guerilla Division 18 (in Or-Ral area of operations), decided to integrate with the government forces. This integration also included some other friendly forces that were active along National Road numbers 3 and 4, as well as in most parts of Kompung Speu, Kampot and Kompung Chhnang.

TOWARD THE END OF THE WAR: FIRST STOP, OR-RAL AREA OF OPERATIONS

General Situation of the Khmer Rouge before the Fall of the Or-Ral AO

As always, the Khmer Rouge was very secretive with regard to their organizational structure and never attempted to survey or to divulge the real number of their fighting forces. In some sense, this is true for all guerilla organizations. The number of fighters is never exact. According to local estimates, in 1991, the Khmer Rouge had between 25,000–27,000 combatants (most of these forces were probably assigned to support roles and transport). In April 1992 along with the arrival of the UNTAC, the total number of Khmer Rouge troops decreased to 20,000–25,000. Three years later, there were no more than 8,000–20,000 Khmer Rouge troops countrywide. Within this number, the Khmer Rouge combatants who were fundamentalist fighters did not exceed 5,000, including support and transportation forces.[15]

The Khmer Rouge was still able to use timber trade and gemstones to finance their war effort against the Cambodian government. Even though the bases and strongholds were located in the jungle-clad Cambodian-Thai border areas, life was reasonably comfortable because of the good relations with neighboring countries as well as foreign companies.

One of the six main sanctuaries was the Or-Ral area, which is a plateau located in Or-Ral district, Kompung Speu province. It is situated in the north of National Road number 4 along with road number 42, fifty-one kilometers from the center of Kompung Speu province. There are plenty of dense forests along the mountain ranges such as the Or-Ral Mountain, which is the highest mountain in Cambodia and is connected to other mountain chains. The area also directly threatened the western part of the capital city, Phnom Penh. Even Nuon Chea, the second man in the Khmer Rouge leadership, admitted that Or-Ral was a strategic area as it linked the main strongholds together.[16]

There were 10,227 people living in the area in early 1995. Khmer Rouge military forces in the RCAF's third military region (Takeo, Kampot, and the coastal provinces) included Front 715, some south-western units, 4 divisions, 1 brigade, and 14 regiments while related forces consisted of two brigades subordinated to two other fronts: Front 669 and Front 909.[17] The total number of Khmer Rouge forces in the region in 1995 was 741 personnel along with another 140 related personnel totaling 881.

RCAF Operations in the Or-Ral Area

Between January 9, 1996 and February 5, 1996, a number of Khmer Rouge commanders in the area, including Keo Pung, commander of Front 715 and Division 18, went to an "education session" at the border (or rather, these were spirit-building lessons at the sanctuary of the hardliners). After his session concluded on January 26, 1996, Keo Pung came to realize that Pol Pot had no exit strategy.[18] Everyone would participate in the struggle until they died, and only then would the war end, for them. The Khmer Rouge had known setback after setback following the withdrawal of the Vietnamese troops in 1989. The promised political solutions had never materialized, while the children of the commanders and soldiers grew up in a place where they never went to school but instead had to go out in the field to build obstacles and transport ammunition. For many foot soldiers, their future with the Khmer Rouge became bleaker by the day.

On January 28, 1996, Keo Pung returned to his unit. After the arrival, he began to order his soldiers to cease fighting or move forward, and he changed tactics from destruction to only protecting his forces and withdrawing. More importantly, he also initiated contact with officers of the RCAF who were responsible for countering his units. In the Cambodian civil war, it was not uncommon for commanders on both sides to initiate informal contact on various issues and they did not waste time in attempting to draw each other to their respective sides.

In a radio communication at 12:30 P.M. on February 3, 1996, Keo Pung contacted his local networks to request a personal meeting with a military officer of the RCAF.[19] After receiving this key piece of information, the RCAF officer immediately reported to his command station in Takeo province, the third military region, and then the information was relayed to general staff headquarters in Phnom Penh. The RCAF High Command permitted the communication by issuing a letter of guarantee sent to Keo Pung, giving the basic guarantees of the WWP.

On February 5, 1996, after receiving the order, the RCAF officer travelled to the Or-Ral area and cooperated with the military region and forces of Division 1 that were carrying out operations in the area.[20] This led to a meeting with Keo Pung. After listening to his main requests as conditions for his cooperation, the RCAF officer returned to report to his superior about some difficulties that Keo Pung faced before joining the government. The main issue was that Keo Pung's family members were held by Pol Pot in another area under the pretext that the front where Keo Pung operated was not safe, effectively keeping them as de facto hostages.

To clear up the issue, the general staff assigned a helicopter to bring Keo Pung over to Phnom Penh in February 1996 in order to give Keo Pung a chance to explain his requests and desires in person. After meeting with many senior commanders, and more importantly with Second Prime Minister Hun Sen, it was understood that Keo Pung requested the following:[21] his goal was the return of everyone, including families and civilians. At that time, Keo Pung's families were living in areas controlled by other units, Front 669. Time was of the essence.

After reviewing his requests and the prevailing situation, in order to give Keo Pung time to continue his actions, measures were implemented as follows:[22]

1. The RCAF would withdraw from the frontline in order to give Keo Pung the opportunity to submit a false report to the Khmer Rouge high command that his forces had defeated the RCAF. Then, families and other people could be brought back from other units.
2. Provide urgent food supplies to his family and supply him with enough ammunition for self-defense if the secret was leaked to the hardliners.
3. Government forces must be well prepared to cooperate in any contingencies.
4. Keo Pung needed to assign some forces for demining operations along the roads.

Also, in the areas under the control of the RCAF, soldiers would make the sounds of battle and fire shots into the air to deceive other Khmer Rouge units into thinking that he (Keo Pung) was liberating the areas previously held by the RCAF.[23]

Following these agreements, and after receiving additional orders from Second Prime Minister Hun Sen, Keo Pung returned to his area. There was a debate as to whether Keo Pung should be allowed to go back and why should he not be arrested as he was one of the most important Khmer Rouge commanders of the Or-Ral area. Second Prime Minister Hun Sen explained his decision to allow Keo Pung to return:

> What would happen if Keo Pung would not follow what had been discussed? I said 'that would not be worse or better' than previously. I mean, if Keo Pung were to not return, he actually returned though, we would lose nothing, and so would the Khmer Rouge. However, if Keo Pung was to implement what had been discussed, and he did in fact, we would gain the whole area of Or-Ral.[24]

Second Prime Minister Hun Sen represented the innovative side of the debate. He was right in calculating that the arrest would mean nothing. The Khmer Rouge could simply find another commander to replace Keo Pung. Moreover, that arrest would effectively lend Pol Pot a propaganda coup: "That was what happened when you betrayed Angkar and joined with the enemy." Such a scenario would directly defeat the core principles of the WWP.

Second Prime Minister Hun Sen saw a chance to take the entire Or-Ral area. He was once again correct that even if Keo Pung were to return to Or-Ral and never came back on the government's side, this would simply be a status quo ante bellum.[25] If the policy paid off, as it did, then the WWP would march toward ending the chronic civil war. Should the policy fail, nothing would be lost anyway. Such logical calculation was not immediately apparent, but this calculation was motivated by the principles of the WWP.

From February 1996, both parties began to take action according to the agreement they had made. On the one hand, the RCAF withdrew, while supporting Keo Pung's forces with food and ammunition. On the other hand, Keo Pung's forces began clearing mines. He also handed over a number of heavy weapons to the RCAF.[26] Keo Pung explained the importance of these decisions to his subordinates. However, the secret could not be kept for long. But by the time of the leak, their families had already been safely transported back from the border to the area under their control.

It is not surprising that other Khmer Rouge forces were alarmed by such a turn of events. Front 699 then assigned its own agents to investigate the allegations that Keo Pung had integrated with the government forces. Seeing that the time was ripe, the RCAF then took necessary actions to protect and support Keo Pung's forces. In little more than a month after the first contact, the Or-Ral area was integrated.

The fall of the Or-Ral area of operation opened a new and final chapter of the civil war in Cambodia. It gave the signal to other Khmer Rouge forces that integration with the government, on the side of Second Prime Minister Hun Sen, would be safe. These forces would not be humiliated or harmed. This was enough for other Khmer Rouge units who were fearful of Pol Pot and who were tired of war to gamble on the chance of escape from Pol Pot and ongoing hostilities.

TOWARD THE END OF THE WAR: SECOND STOP, MALAI-PAILIN

The news of the Or-Ral breakout was widely broadcasted and everyone knew that this was a turning point. The breakout triggered a process that might be dubbed "competitive defection" or more precisely, "competitive integration." In essence, this means that the one who integrated first could expect better treatment and larger spoils than the ones who integrated later. Resources were scarce but demand was not. The latecomers would certainly find that the rewards and spoils for their actions decreased over time because these rewards were diluted by more and more integrating forces. In economics, this is a simple law of diminishing returns of marginal utility: the more the forces that have already integrated the less the utility that additional forces would offer the government.

Despite the government's efforts to ensure a fair chance of entry, the process did not stop. At some level, the process benefited the government. It was only when different factions began to become jealous of each other that the divisions opened the way for violent infighting between different Khmer Rouge factions.

In the context of the weakness of the Khmer Rouge forces, the Royal Cambodian Armed Forces (RCAF) had not yet been clearly restructured and was still involved in a painstaking reform process. After the 1993 election, the KPRAF, by far the largest military formation in the battlefield, needed to be combined with other forces that were part of the political compromise, namely the Armée Nationale Khmer pour l'Indépendence (ANKI), formerly ANS, which was the military arm of the FUNCINPEC, and the troops of the KPNLF (Kampuchean People's National Liberation Front). The assimilation was undertaken systematically from the smallest unit to the top of the chain of command, although the composition of forces and the exact number were accomplished on an ad hoc basis. Such hasty assimilation was born out of political necessity at the time. The military was not the only institution touched by this compromise.

The compromise that was born out of the election in 1993 called for a system of dual prime ministers, the first being Prince Ranariddh of the FUNCINPEC, the second being Samdech Hun Sen from the CPP. The ministry of interior and the ministry of national defense were led by co-ministers. In other institutions, if the chief came from one faction, the deputy chief must come from another party. Most, if not all, government institutions followed this power-sharing rule.

Because different Khmer Rouge factions were up for grabs, any faction that could secure its allegiance first would certainly boost its position vis-à-vis the other faction. Nevertheless, the Khmer Rouge units tended to integrate with the CPP side of the government, mainly because of the WWP, which presented a clear framework for functionality. Having a clear framework for negotiation (in the form of the WWP) was also one of the main advantages that the CCP held over other factions that did not present any clear principles. The latter could not work past the trust problem.

Situation in Pailin before the Integration

The next big fish in the integration pool was Malai-Pailin. Pailin was one of the westernmost districts of Battambang, a frontier town. At the operational level, the Pailin area of operation was adjacent to Malai and Samlot. In fact, it was Samlot that was the very place of the first insurrection in the 1960s that gave birth to the Khmer Rouge. Pailin and Malai were protected by Division 415 and Division 450, respectively. During the war, Division 415 was composed of 5 regiments and 3 special battalions and all regiments and battalions operated, in combined arms or otherwise, under orders from Son Sen, who was the commander of the area of operations that consisted of Pailin, Front 250 (Samlot), and Malai.[27] Pol Pot was the supreme commander of these forces and presided over all annual and quarterly meetings.

Pailin was not a densely populated area and the town itself was controlled by the KPRAF from 1979 until 1989, although the Khmer Rouge hid in the surrounding jungle. In 1989, the Vietnamese withdrew, and this forced the KPRAF to also withdraw in order to be able to defend other more densely populated areas.[28]

The 1993 election produced a combined force under the RCAF umbrella, and initially the RCAF tried to raid many Khmer Rouge strongholds, including Pailin. On March 29, 1994, the forces of Division 415 could no longer hold off the RCAF and decided to retreat from Pailin to temporary bases north of Pailin. Then Division 415 received orders from Son Sen to continue to fight for about another month in tandem with Front 250, led by Nikan (younger brother of Son Sen) and Division 450.

Division 415 adhered to an ancient tactic of guerilla warfare, on which its whole operational concept was based. The tactics were invariably based on small groups of guerillas, operating silently, with speed and precision, without losing control and coordination with other nearby units. The small units were accorded a wide degree of initiative and retained much freedom of action. This initiative allowed the guerillas to maneuver carefully to attack a larger force with smaller forces, and to use ambush and surprise tactics to negate numerical superiority. These small groups were also skilled with the use of obstacles and improvised explosive devices (IEDs), including elaborate traps to stop the adversary. Both sides fought with brutal intensity and both repeatedly laid mines to defend their territory. IEDs were normally set on the road, beside the road, or under the logs that were used to block the road. Bamboo and metal stakes were also used in concealed pits to impede infantry movement. Pailin was recaptured by the Khmer Rouge on April 19, 1994.

The first capture of Pailin back in 1989 was considered to be a big success by Pol Pot himself. Pailin was the town that linked Samlot and Malai and formed a strong, mutually reinforcing, defensive chain adjacent to the Cambodian-Thai border. It directly threatened Battambang provincial town, in a province known as the rice bowl of Cambodia. More importantly, Pailin was known as the gemstone quarry of Cambodia, in addition to precious timber. This was the lifeblood of the Khmer Rouge after foreign aid was cut. It also offered the territory he needed for bargaining in the upcoming 1993 election.[29] The loss of Pailin in early 1994, even for less than a month, did not please Pol Pot. Just like in 1977 and 1978, criticisms followed. Divisions 415 and 450, the very units that were responsible for the recapture of Pailin, were actually the target for most of these criticisms. This time, however, the blame and accusations were also more likely to be related to the unfair distribution of profit from border trades.[30]

Along with the criticisms, Pol Pot and Son Sen also ordered the confiscation of private property under the control of Divisions 415 and 450, accusing these divisions of indulging in border trade while forgetting the struggle.[31] However, these activities were viewed by Pailin and Malai as blatant plunder undertaken by their own superiors. This double standard could be seen clearly when Pol Pot and Son Sen themselves did not refrain from those border trades. But the criticisms and pillage were considered by Malai-Pailin to be only the beginning of more sinister things to come. After all, they had lived under Democratic Kampuchea for too long to ignore the signs.

The Secret Meetings

The period between mid-1996 and the first half of 1997 was eventful and action-packed. It was a long process that led to the last great battle in the heart of Phnom Penh in July 1997 and the end of the civil war in Cambodia.

Malai and Pailin began to reach out to the government, the CCP side. The first meeting was supposedly between Defense Minister Tea Banh (of the Cambodian government, from the CPP side) and Y Chhean, the commander of division 415. This was a preliminary meeting to explore the possibility of future cooperation after contacts had been made through secret channels. The proposed meeting in early August 1996 coincided with the accusations of Son

Sen leveled against Division 415. The commander of Division 415, Y Chhean, began to receive death threats. One of the criticisms that Son Sen leveled on Pailin was the crime of "hiding the monk for Buddhist ceremonies."[32]

But when the meeting took place on August 1, 1996 in Pataya, Thailand, at the last minute, Y Chhean did not attend, but a representative, Chhun Ngib, was assigned to the meeting instead. He claimed that Y Chhean was busy dealing with the situation in Pailin because forces from Samlot and Anlong Veng were poised to attack Pailin. Despite this explanation, Defense Minister Tea Banh concluded that the change of delegates for the meeting was a test by Y Chhean to see if the meeting was safe.[33] This was the Khmer Rouge mentality, which was always suspicious of any invitation to a meeting or "education session" that normally led to execution. Yet, as a strong adherent to the WWP of Second Prime Minister Hun Sen, Defense Minister Tea Banh nonetheless received the representative as a fully fledged counterpart, and explained the WWP principle of three fundamental guarantees.

On the night of August 4, Defense Minister Tea Banh and another two assistants went to Rayorng, Thailand, where the second meeting with Y Chhean was supposed to take place. This time, Y Chhean came in person, and after the explanations and introduction, he was permitted to talk to Second Prime Minister Hun Sen by phone and received instructions with regard to the integration process.[34]

On August 5, 1996, Radio Democratic Kampuchea began to criticize the activities in Malai-Pailin. One day later, Ta Mok came to a meeting in Pailin and severely criticized divisions 415 and 450.[35] The latter rebutted by saying that they no longer supported Democratic Kampuchea. Clashes between divisions 415 and 450 and forces under Ta Mok and Son Sen broke out afterward.[36] The Malai-Pailin faction eventually captured Samlot and some key commanders, although Son Sen and Nuon Chea had already slipped out, most likely into Thailand.[37] Second Prime Minister Hun Sen intervened and ordered Pailin to release all of the captured commanders from Samlot and one of them, Nikan, was even given a position as advisor to the Ministry of National Defense.[38] The Second Prime Minister, in this episode, appeared as the wise older brother who eased the tension between the younger brothers. This perception helped him greatly as a broker of peace.

On August 8, 1996, Y Chhean reached an agreement and understanding with the leadership and the people of Pailin as well as the commanders of Division 450 in Malai under Sok Pheap. With approval from Ieng Sary, the forces in Malai-Pailin then officially dissociated themselves from Pol Pot and Son Sen.

At the same time, Ieng Sary, on behalf of the newly established Democratic National Reconciliation Movement, issued a statement in a press conference organized on August 9 declaring his irrevocable disagreement with Saloth Sar, alias Pol Pot, while reviewing the history of the party, and he attacked Pol Pot's absolutism in the party.[39] Ieng Sary also emphasized the position of the Democratic National Reconciliation Movement and requested the government to officially distribute government positions and ranks.[40]

On August 15, 1996, the forces in Pailin broadcast a response to the accusations by Pol Pot, Son Sen, and Ta Mok. Mutual accusations ensued. Finally, with authorization from Second Prime Minister Hun Sen, a face-to-face dialogue between defense ministers Tea Banh and Tir Chamrat (a co-minister of defense from the FUNCINPEC) and Ieng Sary was organized in Bangkok on September 5, 1996, with assistance from a coordination group of the Thai military.[41]

At that point, the cat was out of the bag, and the disintegration of the Khmer Rouge was in full swing. Or-Ral was not an anomaly, and was only the first of a longer process. The FUNCINPEC was keen to act. Yet, despite the need to take action, no clear strategy yet existed for the FUNCINPEC. In fact, at the meeting with Ieng Sary in Bangkok, it was the WWP—engineered by Second Prime Minister Hun Sen— that was used to reassure Ieng Sary. To make matters worse, some extreme elements within the FUNCINPEC were calling for tougher actions against the CPP.[42]

On August 15, the forces at Pailin and Malai joined up to create the Democratic National United Movement (DNUM) under Ieng Sary. On September 9, in Malai, a press conference was organized as promised, and in the presence of national and international journalists as well as other observers. Ieng Sary presided and the questions-and-answers session extended well into lunchtime. At the press conference, he publicly announced the establishment of DNUM. To fulfill the requirement of the WWP, Ieng Sary officially declared that he recognized the authority of the government and the constitution, as well as recognized the king and Buddhism as the symbols of national unity.

This was a strange move. In fact, the usual formula was this: 1. Declare the dissociation from Pol Pot, 2. Take concrete action toward integration. In the case of Or-Ral, once these forces dissociated themselves from Pol Pot, they immediately integrated with the government. Here, a new organization was established instead of integration: DNUM. Was it a political party? A social movement? Or an autonomous region?

As a result, Ieng Sary's integration was not viewed favorably by skeptics and critics. Chhang Youk, for example, opined that in retrospect, Ieng Sary's integration was only a clever attempt to use the remaining Khmer Rouge forces under his control to bargain for some power, or at least to clear himself from an eventual trial.[43] Chhang Youk also maintained that Ieng Sary even tried to block the integration of other forces that he could not control. Later developments seemed to confirm this view. Nonetheless, the WWP still tried to seek a nonviolent end to the war.

One day later, on September 15, 1996, there were meetings of the commander-cadres of divisions 415, 412, 705, 531, 320, 948, 450, 519, and 518 after which the cadres reached a peculiar decision. In this decision, they declared the establishment of a new organization of all administrative structures, military forces, and police forces in many districts including Samlot, Pailin, Komrieng, Phnom Preuk,[44] and Malai.[45] This new organization was, above all, an autonomous system because they also had "associations" and "communication boards" to liaise with foreign partners in economic, financial and social sectors.[46] In a sense, this was a twist, a thinly veiled attempt to create a new system of a "state within a state" in a context where the WWP instead envisioned a "one country, one administration" concept.

On September 24, 1996, Gen. Pol Saroeun, vice chief of staff (on the CPP side), sent a report regarding the decision in question to Defense Minister Tea Banh. After reviewing the report, which indicated complications in the promises made by the DNUM, the defense minister, with instructions from Second Prime Minister Hun Sen, instructed the commanders to change the position and integrate immediately.[47]

In a decision number 40, dated September 26, 1996, the government stressed that the integration had to go through with utmost speed and as soon as possible without waiting for all forces to come at once. Therefore, any forces that were ready for integration would be immediately integrated.[48] The government decision also required that the integrated forces that chose to be assimilated into the RCAF change into RCAF uniforms, and the ministry of national defense would determine positions and appropriate ranks. On September 30, 1996, Second Prime Minister Hun Sen, the co-supreme commander of the armed forces (Prince Norodom Ranariddh of the FUNCINPEC was the other co-supreme commander), publicly announced the decision.

But the second prime minister was not the only guest that the DNUM welcomed. On October 11, Prince Norodom Ranariddh, the First Prime Minister and in RCAF uniform, went to Pailin and participated in a Buddhist ceremony with Ieng Sary.[49] But this visit was a low-profile event with no fanfare and no symbolic ceremony was carried out. However, the visit did confirm the ambiguous position of the DNUM that many people suspected when it deviated from the usual WWP formula. With the coalition between the CPP and the FUNCINPEC about to get out of balance, the Khmer Rouge had been transformed from a persona non grata to something like a beautiful lady being courted by two men who had thrown everything they had into the competition.

Ultimately, it seemed that the CPP won in this courtship battle. On October 22, 1996, Second Prime Minister Hun Sen officially visited Pailin. A very large crowd participated in this lively and historic occasion, and a symbolic event was arranged: the former Khmer Rouge soldiers changed their dark green battle fatigues into RCAF and police uniforms. The second step of the WWP was practically implemented. It is still unclear, based on the current publicly available information, what drove Malai-Pailin to choose Second Prime Minister Hun Sen over the FUNCINPEC. But we can speculate a few possible reasons.

First of all, Second Prime Minister Hun Sen of the CPP had a sophisticated framework in the form of the WWP, which he took liberty to restate in detail during the October visit. He said "no one can take your land,"[50] the third principle of the WWP that guaranteed private property after integration. This was a comforting guarantee for every ordinary Khmer Rouge soldier. Moreover,

The then second prime minister, *Samdech* Hun Sen, greeted former Khmer Rouge soldiers who had just integrated into the government as part of his famed Win-Win Policy. The ceremony was held in Pailin, a Khmer Rouge stronghold, on October 22, 1996. (©General Nem Sowath's Collections. Used by permission.)

this promise was backed up by the Or-Ral example, where the WWP had been implemented according to the promised principles.

Second, the real intentions of Malai-Pailin notwithstanding, many other former Khmer Rouge forces were integrated into the RCAF. On October 8, 1996, in the Tonle Sap area, Ek Phnom district, 350 soldiers decided to integrate, and on October 13, 1996, in Krovanh district 2,468 soldiers decided to integrate.[51] Other areas also received many incoming soldiers. Even though Malai-Pailin might have been playing a double game at that time, these peripheral integrations (which were influenced by Malai-Pailin's decision in the first place) could have forced the hand of Malai-Pailin to choose a side. Despite the visit of Prince Ranariddh, the WWP still appeared to be the policy that attracted many people. Perhaps it looked like Malai-Pailin did not want to experience the "departing train strategy"[52] that the Khmer Rouge as a whole had bitterly experienced before the 1993 election.

Third, and finally, the Khmer Rouge forces in Malai-Pailin and Ieng Sary probably acknowledged the strength of the CPP and Second Prime Minister Hun Sen, and perhaps they thought it was better to wake up on the winning side.

While the integration was indeed a big success, an internal division within the Khmer Rouge ranks cast a shadow over the true position of DNUM. Even after the visit by Second Prime Minister Hun Sen, Pailin still despised Or-Ral, which one assistant of Ieng Sary described as "having been bought out."[53] Pailin also implied that despite integration, they still had autonomy, unlike Or-Ral which was completely integrated. .

At this point, it would be misleading to consider the Khmer Rouge to be a monolithic organization. Ever since foreign aid had been cut off, each stronghold had to rely on its own trade and therefore gained considerable autonomy vis-à-vis Pol Pot and the top leadership. Moreover, unfair distribution of revenue from these trades was the main cause of the division. Thus, there were many Khmer Rouges, many Pailins, many Malais, many Samlots, many Anlong Vengs, and so forth. While some people in Pailin considered Keo Pung to be a bad influence, many more were drawn to the CPP because of Keo Pung. It was Keo Pung who identified the potential figures for negotiation. The *Phnom Penh Post* newspaper described Keo Pung as the "point man" for the Khmer Rouge negotiation.[54] The WWP had succeeded in the "Divide" phase. The next phase, "Integration," would roll into complications when the Khmer Rouge was internally divided. But no war termination is easy. It is always sunny after the storm, but first, one must sit through the storm.

The Spoilers Strike Back

The integration of Malai-Pailin brought between 3,000 and 4,000 former Khmer Rouge soldiers into the government. Yet, just as in many cases of conflict resolution, the presence of spoilers complicated the process.[55] Many people viewed the Malai-Pailin integration as an alarming development. First of all, the FUNCINPEC, and especially some extremist elements within the party, were calling for tougher actions against the CPP. This strategy could now work because the Khmer Rouge forces were divided.

Second, the internal relations between the Khmer Rouge factions were not quite settled, especially between Pailin and Samlot. Samlot wanted to integrate with the RCAF but the effective command was still under Pailin. Previous disputes over the revenues from the timber trade were also the main cause why Samlot did not want to follow Malai-Pailin.[56]

In this situation, on November 1, 1996, high-ranking generals and officials (of the CPP) travelled to meet directly with the commanders of Front 250 in Samlot. The Khmer Rouge counterparts then told Gen. Sao Sokha of the CPP delegation that they wanted to end the war and integrate with the government, but such action would antagonize Pailin and bloodshed would ensue, as Malai-Pailin still considered Samlot to be under its command, while Samlot despised that leadership.[57]

The government delegates (CPP side) assured the commanders by restating the main principles of the WWP, but at the same time pressed for an answer. Finally, three representatives of Front 250 decided to come to Phnom Penh. The helicopter then left the area and travelled to the Battambang provincial town (government-controlled) and arrived at 2:30 A.M., whereupon they were received by Lt. Gen. Pol Saroeun, the vice chief of staff of the RCAF who was already waiting at the frontline command headquarters in the town.[58] He then escorted the three representatives to meet with Second Prime Minister Hun Sen at his private residence in Kandal province.

On November 2, 1996, Second Prime Minister Hun Sen had decided to broadcast a special speech that warned against any attempts to block the integration process by "some politicians in Phnom Penh"(most likely a reference to the FUNCINPEC).[59] The Samlot integration eventually forced the hand of Malai-Pailin. Previous forces that had broken away from the Khmer Rouge but had not yet fully integrated (even after the public event in October 1996), all now integrated, formally. Division 415 in Pailin integrated on November 6, 1996, and Division 450 in Malai on November 7, 1996.

The negotiations also took place with the Khmer Rouge from another stronghold: Anlong Veng, the sanctuary of Pol Pot and Ta Mok. On November 20, 1996, Second Prime Minister Hun Sen assigned Gen. Tea Banh and Gen. Meas Sophea (vice chief of staff, CPP) to meet with Meas Muth and other delegates who represented the remaining Khmer Rouge forces. The meeting took place in Preah Vihear province along the Cambodian-Thai border, opposite Thailand's Sisaket province.[60]

During this meeting, the Anlong Veng delegates bargained, as an exchange for integration, toward creating some systems that would amount to secessionist areas with autonomous control over the armed forces and the economic system. These delegates even demanded that the RCAF withdraw from their areas.[61] But all these demands were not acceptable to the government delegation, mainly because it was against the WWP principle which sought to end the "one country, two governments" system.

With the Khmer Rouge in Anlong Veng still adhering to their extreme views, the WWP was threatened by another setback. In early 1997, Prince Ranariddh announced that the DNUM had agreed to join his National Union Front (NUF).[62] To preempt any potentially dangerous development, on February 8, 1997, Second Prime Minister Hun Sen travelled to Malai on an official visit to encourage and speed up the integration process. However, behind the scenes, the visit was most likely aimed at obtaining a clear answer from DNUM. The visit was accompanied by reassurances about the WWP principles as well as a splendid party where soldiers from both sides were encouraged to socialize. While a bulk of the forces from Malai-Pailin supported the CPP, there were also some elements that did not want to join it. A sharp disagreement broke out between those who adhered to what had been promised during the October 22 visit and those who wanted to switch their support to the FUNCINPEC/NUF.[63]

Coincidentally, on February 10, 1997, the first armed clash between forces loyal to the CPP and those loyal to the FUNCINPEC occurred in Battambang, killing at least 50 people.[64] The clash was brief but it was a bad sign, a bad omen for the coalition government. It seemed that larger armed clashes would be inevitable, as the forces from former belligerents that were combined early on into a unified RCAF began to be divided along factional lines.

In summary, after the success of Or-Ral, it seemed that the Khmer Rouge's disintegration was far more complicated and intractable than had been previously expected. The WWP broke down the Khmer Rouge organization beyond repair. Malai-Pailin themselves disagreed with each other while they and Samlot despised each other. Anlong Veng, on its part, wanted its own autonomous region after violent accusations against Malai-Pailin. In the light of this turmoil, elements within the FUNCINPEC that wanted to break away from the coalition with the CPP started to make contact with any dissident factions. In such confusion, the search was all but easy.

DETOUR: ANLONG VENG AND SAMLOT COURTED AND BROUGHT TO PHNOM PENH!

A commander of Division 980 had been preparing his men for a special mission since dawn. It was March 1997. On that day, he was ordered to guard the perimeter of the area where a delegation from Phnom Penh (elements of the FUNCINPEC) was scheduled to arrive in Anlong Veng. This was a secret visit that was possibly designed to strike a deal with the Khmer Rouge to integrate into the government on the FUNCINPEC side.[65]

Anlong Veng was the last refuge of the Khmer Rouge's radical leadership faction (Pol Pot, Son Sen and Ta Mok), and this radical faction desperately needed an exit strategy. Contact with another faction in the coalition government was apparently their only choice. The soldiers also received explicit orders from the top command not to harm the delegates. That boosted their morale: Pol Pot had never been so accommodating toward outsiders. Maybe here is the end of the war, or so they thought.

Not long after lunch a helicopter appeared, something that looked like the Mi-17, a signature helicopter of the Royal Cambodian Air Force.[66] The soldiers noted that the helicopter followed a strange flight pattern. The helicopter circled around for a few times and then went off course from the supposed meeting place. But not long after, another helicopter came and appeared to have landed. Maybe this was it.

But suddenly, a gunshot was heard in the distance, from the direction of the landing zone, followed by another. Barely seconds after that, the deafening sound of an AK-47 was heard. The soldiers were devastated. The negotiation had failed even before it started. If the rumor was correct, one member of the delegation from Phnom Penh, who appeared to be under the influence, let loose with his gun in a misunderstanding, and the Khmer Rouge soldiers who came to receive them fired in retaliation. The exchange of gunfire escalated into the massacre of all the delegates except three crew members (a pilot, a copilot, and a flight engineer). The crew became prisoners and they only escaped later when the Khmer Rouge strongholds suffered from the government offensive.[67]

Pol Pot, Son Sen, and Ta Mok were infuriated by the incident. The delegates were supposed to be welcomed, not killed. And now, irrespective of the intentions of the Khmer Rouge, this would be assumed to be proof of unchanged behavior and continuing atrocity and intrigue by the Khmer Rouge. With external support cut off and internal resources dwindling, Pol Pot desperately needed an exit. The massacre blocked that exit. The meeting was supposed to be secret, but the massacre made it far too easy for the CPP to take note of the development. There was no need for confirmation from intelligence channels; the news was available in open sources. They had just lost the element of surprise that might have negated the CPP influence.

Now that the cat was out of the bag again, on April 21, Khieu Samphan issued the formal support of the Khmer National Solidarity Party (the name of the party created by the Khmer Rouge) toward the NUF. Such formal support only intensified the friction between the CPP and the FUNCINPEC. Many scholars came to the conclusion that this alliance was eerily reminiscent of the creation of the Coalition Government of Democratic Kampuchea (CGDK) in the past. But the alliance probably did little to surprise the CPP, which had already intercepted a copy of a "joint declaration" dated March 20, 1997, that was allegedly sent by Prince Ranariddh to Khieu Samphan and was cosigned by the two parties.[68] Khieu Samphan's announcement was only a public acknowledgment of that letter.

Now things began to escalate and quickly spiraled out of control. A series of events pushed for a showdown between the FUNCINPEC and the CPP in July 1997.

In the midst of uncertainty, and to help ease the tensions, a Bipartisan Committee for Resolving Anomaly was established in late March 1997 to control the situation after the clashes at Battambang. This bipartisan committee consisted of the co-ministers of national defense, the co-ministers of the interior, the commander in chief of the RCAF, and the high commissioner of the national police. But what was about to occur had occurred anyway.

A political-military storm occurred on May 26, 1997, when the port authority at Sihanouk Ville intercepted a container of weapons under the name of the commander of the bodyguard unit of the First Prime Minister Prince Norodom Ranariddh.[69] The cache weighed approximately 2 to 3 tons and consisted of AK-47 assault rifles, handguns, mortars, and most prominently, HEAT[70] antitank weapons. What was curious was that the container was labeled as "spare parts" belonging to the first prime minister.[71] The CPP denounced the importation as being illegal, and dishonest for a coalition partner to disguise the contents of the container, while the FUNCINPEC maintained it had full rights to import the weapons to use in the bodyguard unit.[72] The antitank weapons were perhaps aimed at negating the CPP's armor superiority.

After confiscation at the port, the weapons were transported to Pochentong airport. A standoff ensued, and a shootout almost broke out between the bodyguard unit of the FUNCINPEC and the forces of the CPP. The situation was defused only when an agreement was reached between the two forces to divide the weapons into two groups. The light weapons were taken by the FUNCINPEC and heavy weapons, such as the antitank weapons, were transferred into the RCAF arsenal.[73] The weapons import took place in tandem with the increasing presence of the new troops that some elements of the FUNCINPEC had brought in.

Despite the fact that many commanders from Samlot had met with Second Prime Minister Hun Sen, a senior commander at Samlot, Meas Muth, despised the forces from Malai-Pailin that had integrated earlier. Thus, Samlot decided not to integrate.[74] Moreover, the meeting between the delegation of the CPP and the forces at Anlong Veng in late 1996 did not produce any result, partly due to the latter's insistence on autonomous rules, which is tantamount to secession. As a consequence, forces from Samlot and Anlong Veng became the main reinforcements for the extremist elements of the FUNCINPEC.

According to a commander from Anlong Veng who defected to the CPP, his units with around 500 soldiers started to arrive in the barracks of commanders loyal to the FUNCINPEC on January 15, 1997.[75] The Bipartisan Committee reported that the total forces that were brought in amounted to 3,700 men in total.[76] As a cautionary note, after the defection of the Anlong Veng commander, this number suffered heavy attrition. Soldiers from Samlot were also reported to be seen carrying weapons publicly on the streets of Phnom Penh, as they were based at the house of a senior FUNCINPEC general.[77]

New troops from Anlong Veng and Samlot were badly managed, making it easy for the CPP to observe every move. For example, the FUNCINPEC never integrated these forces before it used them. Instead, it only declared first that it would bring them in, but this claim was met with strong opposition from the CPP. Yet, instead of defying the CPP openly, some FUNCINPEC commanders transported the Anlong Veng and Samlot troops to the capital city in secret.[78] This played into the hands of the CPP, which used the Bipartisan Committee on Resolving Anomaly to flush out these forces. The FUNCINPEC was then always on the defensive. By contacting those who were close to Pol Pot, the FUNCINPEC could easily be framed by the CPP as infringing on the legislation that outlawed the Khmer Rouge. The CPP, on the other hand, had a solid defense. When asked by a German reporter whether he was negotiating with Pol Pot, Second Prime Minister Hun Sen replied that he was not, and that his negotiation with Ieng Sary occurred only because Ieng Sary had severed all ties with Pol Pot.[79] This implied that it was against the law that the FUNCINPEC negotiated with those who had not made their position clear with regard to their ties with Pol Pot.

Because of the need for secrecy, the Anlong Veng and Samlot forces were shuffled from base to base to avoid inspection by the Bipartisan Committee. But this only heightened suspicion. The soldiers, despite being Khmer Rouge, wanted to see the nightlife in the city, but were banned by their commanders and were forced to live in almost complete confinement. Some of them defied orders and slipped out, bringing with them the secrets that they saw.[80] In other places, the troops that were stationed in the central office of the FUNCINPEC near the French Embassy caused some concern, and the embassy officially complained to the government.[81]

In other areas, those who were based in the outskirts of Phnom Penh started their own illegal business. They extorted money from the taxis, buses and cars travelling along the national Highway No. 5. On June 29, 1997, a passenger was shot dead after the Khmer Rouge soldiers failed to stop a car, and on July 1, these soldiers opened fire on their own comrades after disagreeing with each other over the division of extortion money.[82]

The next day, these soldiers took up positions along the highway, with weapon emplacements, effectively cutting off all traffic. In the afternoon, the soldiers from the Ministry of National Defense and other surrounding units clashed with these troops and reopened the highway only after routing the Khmer Rouge elements.[83]

The Snake Bites Its Own Tail: The Demise of Son Sen

While the situation deteriorated in the capital city, groups of the Khmer Rouge along the border were also thrown into confusion, pushing everyone, including the hardliners, to find an exit strategy. Then a momentous event took place: the demise of Son Sen, the feared minister of defense under Democratic Kampuchea. Even after the fall of Democratic Kampuchea, he still played a very important role in Pol Pot's general staff headquarters, and wielded considerable influence, even when each stronghold maintained a significant level of independence. Son Sen was also known for his fiery criticism of other people who were not his relatives, most notably, divisions 415 and 450 as well as other forces in Samlot and Anlong Veng.

The following is a story based on rumor, which would not stand rigorous academic scrutiny, yet this story is the major agreement about the main cause of Son Sen's death. No matter how hard I tried, I could not verify this story from exact sources, and it seems that the real story is still classified. But the rumors have a consistent and significant pattern.[84] In instances where the real story is not available, rumor and speculation are perhaps the most optimal, if not best, substitute. Here I will summarize this story from many sources about the "killing" of Son Sen and the event that led to the massacre of his entire family.

If we return to the political settlement in 1991, the Khmer Rouge appointed Khieu Samphan and Son Sen to lead the delegates to Phnom Penh to work with the UNTAC as part of the Supreme National Council. But they were then attacked by an angry mob and were forced to leave Phnom Penh. Pol Pot accused Prime Minister Hun Sen of plotting the incident. But in a meeting with other Khmer Rouge leaders held three days after his return, Son Sen is said to have asserted that "the demonstration was not of Hun Sen's doing."[85]

Not long afterward, a rumor surfaced that Son Sen was contacted by the Phnom Penh government and correspondences between Son Sen and the government authority were mysteriously found by many people who, in fact, were anonymous. No one knew the people who claimed that Son Sen was so contacted. Others said he was about to defect. But no letters were found and no contacts have been verified. There was only suspicion and rumor. But because many cadres did not like Son Sen, the rumor spread like wildfire. In Pol Pot's mind, suspicion was enough to justify a killing; killing a hundred wrongly was better than letting one enemy slip.[86] Successive breakaways in 1996 and complications in 1997 finally convinced Pol Pot of a secret plot by Son Sen.

On June 10, 1997, Son Sen and another 13 relatives, including his wife and an infant, were massacred at his home.[87] His body was also reportedly crushed by a truck after he was killed[88] (although the exact truth cannot be verified by the author). It was more likely, however, as some people claimed, that Pol Pot wanted to only arrest Son Sen for questioning. But it seemed that the guards who were sent to arrest him were the ones who had suffered most from Son Sen's fiery criticism, and they exacted their revenge. But, regardless of the truth behind these claims, the main loser was Pol Pot. When this news broke out, the bottom line became clear: Pol Pot would never change his violent behavior and living under him would bring nothing but death.

Khmer Rouge sources claimed that the situation worsened after June 9, 1997, when Pol Pot also ordered Ta Mok arrested.[89] Chaos ensued, but as the local commanders had more resources, they also had more troops and were stronger. Ta Mok retaliated by fighting back until he captured Pol Pot on June 19.

Back in the capital city, on the night of June 16, 1997, the situation worsened when the central command of the national police began to divide along factional lines. That night, Ho Sok, secretary of state of the ministry of interior, led a group of soldiers from Prince Ranariddh's residence to attack the house of Gen. Hok Lundy, a senior CPP official and chief of the national police.[90] The next morning, clues left behind told of what had transpired that night: one of the rockets failed to explode but was stuck in the outer wall of the house of Gen. Hok Lundy.[91] The split in the coalition government became more and more irrevocable and it paralleled the panic of the Khmer Rouge hardliners along the border.

If that was not bad enough, another development frightened the remaining Khmer Rouge hardliners. On June 21, 1997, both prime ministers of Cambodia (at that time, the compromise required both to agree in order to make a decision) sent a letter to the secretary general of the United Nations asking the UN to support an eventual trial of the highest Khmer Rouge leaders.[92] Two days later, the secretary general forwarded that letter to the chairman of the General Assembly and the United Nations Security Council, but no action was taken by the two bodies.[93] It seemed that Prime Minister Hun Sen was adamant in his position: no justice would be traded for political expediency.

The two UN bodies did not take any action until July 13, 1997, two weeks after the request was sent and one week after the fighting in the heart of Phnom Penh. The General Assembly then decided to send an expert group to study the feasibility of such a tribunal.[94] It was clear that even the UN personnel and leadership had no doubt as to what would soon happen in the country. With tensions rising, it was likely the UN at this time chose to sit this one out.

More importantly, the Khmer Rouge in Samlot and Anlong Veng was now more desperate than ever. The leadership was in tatters and now there was this request for a United Nations tribunal. There was no more glory, no more great leap forward, no more Pol Pot, no more revolution, and the only objective now was the urgency of survival and amnesty. The only way to go would be a last gamble with some FUNCINPEC extremist elements that were preparing for an armed confrontation with the CPP. No publicly available archive explicitly confirms this scenario in the minds of the Khmer Rouge hardliners, but the logic is compelling.

JULY 5–6, 1997: THE LAST GREAT BATTLE

It was Saturday, July 5, 1997, but I still had to go to school. This Saturday was different. Military activities seemed to escalate quite significantly and my house was shaken by the loud sound of helicopters flying above. At 3:00 P.M., deafening sounds of small arms fire, machine guns, mortar rounds, and RPGs were heard in all directions and it was so close to me that the wall shook. This was almost like the New Year fireworks, only much more deadly. I was watching national television that was broadcasting a live match of Khmer traditional boxing. Young as I was, I waited to see if there was any news about the shooting. But the match was abruptly cut and replaced by the then famous karaoke songs. Then the channel turned to static after only a few songs.

According to government reports, that day, Gen. Sao Sokha (CPP), under the framework of the Bipartisan Committee for Resolving Anomaly, went to the house of a FUNCINPEC general to check on irregular arms and personnel.[95] He was fired upon and then all troops from both sides, who were already in battle positions, opened fire across many parts of the capital city. Prior to this, only the border areas and provinces had experienced the war, but now, war had come to the capital city. If I remember correctly, there was a short pause between the first and the second, longer wave of shooting. This pause took place for about half an hour before what seemed like all hell broke loose. It looked like both sides had already prepared for such an eventuality, and after the opening rounds, both sides had paused before unleashing everything.

Many places in the city became battlegrounds: the FUNCINPEC central office near the French Embassy, Prince Ranariddh's residence (which was near the area where only 10 days earlier the chiefs of police from both sides had clashed), the 12 Building[96] (where Gen. Sao Sokha was fired upon), the headquarters of Brigade 70[97] (defender of Phnom Penh, CPP side), and the crossroad at the Royal University of Phnom Penh. Some other fronts, such as a spearhead attack against Second Prime Minister Hun Sen's residence in Kandal province, failed to materialize, most likely because the chain of command was sabotaged by the intelligence service of the second prime minister.[98] By the time the first shot was fired, Prince Ranariddh had already left Cambodia, along with scores of other high ranking FUNCINPEC civilian officials.[99] At that time, Second Prime Minister Hun Sen was also out of the country. It seemed that only the military commanders and some extremist elements stayed behind to lead the attack with the combined forces of FUNCINPEC and the Khmer Rouge from Phnom Voal (Kampot), Samlot and Anlong Veng.[100]

The event was not a coup d'état by the second prime minister as many journalists and foreign commentators have described it to be. Everyone was prepared, and both sides attacked each other on different fronts. The battle was rather a fight to settle old scores, caused in large part by the hysteria of the Khmer Rouge following dangerous political and military developments over the previous months. The goals of the Khmer Rouge momentarily aligned with those of the extremist forces in the FUNCINPEC and pushed for a showdown with the CPP. The CPP and Second Prime Minister Hun Sen were in a predicament. They needed to be on the defensive, but even in case of victory, they would be branded as coup plotters. But Second Prime Minister Hun Sen opined that fighting was a far better choice than losing, because in the latter case, the CPP would be branded as plotters of a failed coup anyway.[101]

I lived only a few hundred meters from the location of a strategic crossroad. Back then, there was only one road that was the best accessible approach to the capital city from the barrack housing the bodyguards unit of the first prime minister (near the airport). It was here that the CPP put up something like a last-stand resistance until reinforcements came in from the provinces. According to government's source, on July 5, Lt. Gen. Nhiek Bun Chhay (deputy chief of staff of the RCAF, FUNCINPEC side) moved his troops toward the capital city.[102] Many government tanks that were rushed to the defense fell victim to the HEAT antitank weapons that had been bought in only a few months back, most notably the German-designed *Armbrust*, a weapon that even a child in the city could easily recognize. It was an eerie reminiscence of the past when children in the rural areas could identify the type of aircraft based only on the sound of its approach.

My family decided that we should take precautionary measures and leave the city for now. It was not reassuring to see that the second line of defense was just behind my house. We took national highway number 2 toward Takeo province. I saw truckloads of soldiers being ferried in along the highway, no less than 10 of them (perhaps a battalion at least), during our one-and-a-half-hour ride.

There was a lull in the fighting during the night. The next morning, the FUNCINPEC and Khmer Rouge troops continued their advance into the city, but this was no use, as the government/CPP forces started to cut off their rear and effectively pushed these forces into a pincer maneuver along the road from the airport to the strategic Royal University crossroad. On the night of July 6, 1997, while we were staying in our relative's home, two men in uniform came to visit us. They were friends of our relatives. From the conversation, I thought they must have worked in the communication branch, although it appeared from their uniform that they might be in the armor branch. One of them carried a small pouch of takeaway fruit punch bought from a local store because his daughter asked for it, he told me. While I thought the war was raging, this seemed to be a normal day for him. Then he told us that the fighting had already ceased, after barely two days and one night.

The CPP and Second Prime Minister Hun Sen knew exactly what came next after victory—the accusation of a coup. The government claimed that the event was not a coup but a countermeasure taken against the presence of the hardliner Khmer Rouge. There were no arrests, no changes to the Constitution and no trials of ordinary soldiers. The government even accepted the decision of the remaining FUNCINPEC members to choose Ung Huot, the then minister of foreign affairs, to be the first prime minister. *Samdech* Hun Sen remained the second prime minister, until 1998, when the CPP won the election. In the compromise that ensued, Prince Ranariddh returned after the 1998 election and was appointed as president of the National Assembly, while *Samdech* Hun Sen became the only prime minister.

Days after the events in July 1997, the national television broadcasted a long video supposedly taken by the FUNCINPEC news crews on the battlefield, where some high-ranking officials of the FUNCINPEC can be seen clearly.[103] One proof that the CPP used to counter the accusation of a coup was a section where a high-ranking FUNCINPEC official was talking on the phone with a foreign news agency, claiming that "Hun Sen was shot dead by his own bodyguard."[104] This was most likely a disinformation campaign more akin to coup plotters. A few hours later, Second Prime Minister Hun Sen appeared on television, in his usual RCAF uniform, and announced: "I am not dead, as some people reported, and I also did not abandon my country."[105] He then offered the application of the WWP principles to the routed Khmer Rouge soldiers: ordinary soldiers would not be arrested and those who declared their allegiance to the law of the country, the Constitution, and the king would be freely integrated.

Last Breath of the Khmer Rouge

The forces that were dubbed by the CPP as "anarchist-extremist forces" were defeated in an armed clash on July 5–6, 1997. These forces had retreated and then regrouped at O'Smach, a frontier village along the Cambodian-Thai border, where they planned for a new resistance movement, just like in the past. But this goal was doomed to fail from the start due to some underlying problems: ineffective command, a fallacious cause, and the lack of unity. An RCAF offensive soon put an end to this outdated revolutionary movement. In fact, the movement already suffered from attrition within its own ranks as many soldiers deserted the camps.

The events in July 1997 were so decisive that we do not see any ambiguous positions from many groups, as per DNUM back in 1996. When we cannot guess the intention, we can only observe the action. Based on the observations, Malai-Pailin did not show any doubtful behavior and this group was greatly rewarded by the government. Even Ta Mok felt he needed to do something now that there was no hope left. On July 25, Pol Pot was put before the "people's trial" on the charge of "crimes against comrades" and was sentenced to death, but he was only put under house arrest.[106] Nevertheless, Samlot and Anlong Veng were blatantly against the government and were still resisting even after the momentous defeat in Phnom Penh in July 1997. They had crossed the Rubicon, and the die was cast.

The events in July 1997 complicated the balance of power in Samlot.[107] One of the senior commanders was Meas Muth, Ta Mok's son-in-law. In the middle of the confusion following the July 1997 conflict, Ta Mok sent some of his assistants to make contact with Meas Muth to ask him to return to him. He used the timber trade as a pretext to resume fighting, instead of accepting integration.[108] The situation simply turned upside down and Samlot was once again plunged into war.

Meas Muth defected from the government and evacuated a portion of the population through a forced march to two refugee camps along the Cambodian-Thai border. The number of people was not clear, but some estimates put the number at around 46,000.[109] Two camps were created by clearing thick jungle, although this area was infested with malaria. Commanders loyal to the Khmer Rouge were put in to guard the camps. Once again, the Cambodian people became pawns in a shortsighted political game and brinkmanship. But the refugees could not be stopped from "voting with their feet," however, and many slipped past the guards and escaped the camps.

Nonetheless, the government still continued to maintain contact and urged the Meas Muth group to reintegrate in accordance with the WWP principles. A delegation led by Defense Minister Tea Banh was then instructed by the second prime minister to meet with Meas Muth in the province of Trat, Thailand, on September 19, 1997.

The meeting became very heated when Meas Muth still clung to his narrow worldview and threw accusations against the government and other military commanders. According to an account from a participant at the meeting, the intensity of the meeting showed little sign of de-escalation when Meas Muth again and again made arguments based on his rigid ideology. Meas Muth even said at some point that he was committed to fight even if he had only one half of his body left.[110] Gen. Tea Banh, on the other hand, maintained his composure and continued to state the main principles of the WWP.

While Samlot was still outside of the WWP framework, Anlong Veng began to collapse. On April 6, 1998, rumor had it that the United States had begun negotiations with Thailand to facilitate the arrest of Pol Pot, who was then under the custody of Ta Mok.[111] From the beginning, Ta Mok wanted to keep Pol Pot alive, not because of past deeds, but only to use him as a bargaining chip, to be offered to the highest bidder in exchange for Ta Mok's own safety.[112] On April 15, 1998, the third day of the Cambodian Lunar New Year and two days short of the 28th anniversary of the Khmer Rouge's "liberation" of Phnom Penh, Pol Pot died from a heart attack at his house in Kbal Tunsoang, near Anlong Veng. Some authors, such as Philip Short, speculated that Pol Pot committed suicide as he did not want to face eventual trial by the United States or other western countries.[113] Pol Pot was cremated under a pile of old car tires near the Cambodian-Thai border (the present-day Choam border checkpoint), a fitting end for an extremely brutal dictator. He had lived long enough to witness the end of his organization.

Despite the fact that the Khmer Rouge as an organization had almost-completely collapsed, some remnants of the Khmer Rouge still used their last breath to try to gather remaining forces as much as they could for use as bargaining chips. Yet, at this point, the Cambodian government already had ample number of intelligence channels within the remaining Khmer Rouge, Anlong Veng included. In fact, it can be speculated that from July 1997 to the first half of 1998, the government simply built and strengthened its links to the mid-level forces that were less extreme than the remaining top leadership. On the May 11, 1998, the government forces (most of whom were formerly Khmer Rouge soldiers) raided and occupied the last stronghold of Ta Mok in Anlong Veng. Ta Mok, Nuon Chea, and Khieu Samphan disappeared, while smaller units continued fighting to the bitter end.

Until November 1998, the situation in Samlot was still not fully resolved, and this remained the largest and last challenge to the WWP. Secret contacts were made between local commanders and the Khmer Rouge forces. According to one account, with authorization from the top brass of the RCAF and the government, Gen. Bun Seng, the first deputy commander of RCAF military region 5, wrote letters to the commanders of Samlot, and when that did not work, he wrote other letters to the ordinary foot soldiers, making them aware of the slippery slopes that they were on.[114] According to Maj. Gen. Bun Seng, the reply letter did not respond to the original demands but instead talked about the financial scandals and the jealousy between the Khmer Rouge forces resulting from unfair distribution of profits, most notably with Malai-Pailin.[115] This was the same reason that prevented Samlot from integrating in 1996 with Malai-Pailin in the first place.

Ultimately, Anlong Veng came under the control of the government and integrated, while forces from Samlot finally decided to lay down their weapons later in 1998. It was an ironic twist of history that the root of the civil war started in Samlot and then ended in Samlot. All sides gathered at a meeting in the sacred Preah Vihear temple (in Preah Vihear province) on December 4, 1998, and all swore to cease all hostilities and fighting and prioritize national reconciliation. Ta Mok was the only one still at large, and he was arrested only in March 1999. Months earlier, on the December 26, 1998, Khieu Samphan and Nuon Chea had decided to integrate into society and were allowed to meet Prime Minister Hun Sen at his house. Prime Minister Hun Sen had been recently elected to become the only prime minister of Cambodia. Many criticized the event, saying that it was unfit for the prime minister to host such criminals. Yet, the prime minister defended this action:

[. . .]They [the critics] laid down carpets in their [Khmer Rouge leaders] receptions and granted them with diplomatic visas. [. . .] Why did I have to receive

Khieu Samphan and other leaders at my house? Let me recall that I have three messages to send out from this event:

Firstly, let's stop the fight, especially among the Khmer Rouge rank and file, except that we could not accept Ta Mok, because their leaders had surrendered.
Secondly, let the whole Cambodian people, who happened to be waiting for so long for peace, be pleased with the news that the war is over.
Thirdly, let the international community, especially those who would like to do business and invest in Cambodia, know that Cambodia is now in peace.

These three messages have been carved out carefully before we had taken the step.[116]

He also said: "How wrong could it be to just invite some people for a meal in the higher cause of national reconciliation and peace?"[117] Five years after the UNTAC departed, an indigenous solution in the form of the WWP traversed the perilous road to peace, meeting the challenges that sometimes evolved and escalated on an hourly basis. The WWP attained its ultimate objective by completely ending the political-military organization of the Khmer Rouge. The 30-year war, the Cambodian civil war, had ended.

Cambodia in total peace: the Independence Monument, Phnom Penh, 2013. (©Photo by Khut Khunworawadh. Used by permission.)

Conclusion:
End of the War That Had
Consumed a Generation

LESSONS FROM A GENERATION OF WAR, REVOLUTION, AND POLITICAL UPHEAVAL

1. A Holistic Approach to Politics

This book was designed with a specific methodology in mind. When I took up this endeavor, many of the same questions arose: how could I write a book that had apparently already been written? "Tell us something we do not already know." To simply say this book is new because it was written by a Cambodian does not count on its own as a contribution to the literature. So what is the original contribution of this book?

Before talking about this contribution, we need to look at what already exists. Currently, there are at least five types of books (four if we count only academic books) written about the Khmer Rouge. The first group is about the biography of the top leaders, especially Pol Pot. The second group includes information books about Democratic Kampuchea, most notably published by the Documentation Center of Cambodia. The third group consists of the unpublished manuscripts of mid-rank former Khmer Rouge soldiers, most of which I have access to, and which I have incorporated in this book. The fourth group comprises testimonies of individual experiences during the war, escape from Democratic Kampuchea, or chilling stories about survival. The fifth set, and the group that most people might not count but that exists anyway, consists of conspiracy theories about the Khmer Rouge. Such books are usually in Khmer and have never appeared on the international stage. They are not scientific in their methodology, and there are no reliable sources or documents to back up their claims.

In the first four groups of books, the writing is greatly simplified by their specific focus. Most of the authors are not Cambodian, and for some reason, they possess some original documents that allow them to paint a clear picture of Democratic Kampuchea and the CPK. However, while this literature is important and specific, it is still incomplete. The end of the Khmer Rouge is still open to research. For this latter period, more and more Cambodian scholars have emerged to write their own history because most original documents with regard to the end of the Khmer Rouge have become available to them. Yet, large projects, such as books that cover the entire period, are still lacking. This book intends to fill that gap.

A combination of efforts went into producing this book—using archival documents, original documents from the period between 1989 and 1998, gathering interviews to cross-check the documents, and reviewing the work done by western scholars in the period before 1979. Because I am Cambodian, not only can I speak Khmer, but I can also read between the lines as well as gain insights from the different writing styles used in the original documents. This familiarity with the language allowed me, for example, to examine more deeply the details of the war between Democratic Kampuchea and Vietnam, using archives from the Documentation Center of Cambodia. More recently, Prime Minister Hun Sen has also disclosed the origins of the organization of the KPRAF as well as the government policy that led to the collapse of the Khmer Rouge. Most of these materials are contained in speeches, and are in the Khmer language, making it easier for Cambodian scholars to interpret them. Many of these materials are incorporated in this book to paint a more complete picture of the policy that ended the Khmer Rouge.

Another contribution of this book is a new methodology to help with understanding the Khmer Rouge. Instead of looking at the specifics and the details, I look instead at the big picture. In essence, I am following a holistic approach in understanding the Khmer Rouge, meaning that I analyze the whole system rather than individual components. For example, in coming to an understanding of a decision, I analyze not only the people involved, but also the circumstances around those persons that might influence their decisions. When decisions are taken, I also look at whether these decisions have achieved their objectives as well as the external factors that might have influenced the outcome. I do include some sections that incorporate individual stories, but these are not the main elements of this book.

The holistic approach is also comprehensive. Things never happen in a vacuum and to fully understand an event, we need to look at the environment around it, in other words, both sides of the coin. To take some examples, we know from the previous literature that the Khmer Rouge was independent, but it is only after we examine the case where the Khmer Rouge attacked Vietnam before the Chinese assistance projects were completed that we understand how the Khmer Rouge valued "autonomous independence." Similarly, if we simply follow descriptions by Western journalists that the event on July 5–6, 1997 was a coup, without looking further, we risk losing sight of how difficult it was to end the Khmer Rouge. In this book, concerning that July 1997 event,

I offer a counterargument that the event was not a coup but was rather provoked by the hysteria of the remaining Khmer Rouge hardliners who saw that only an armed clash between the CPP and the FUNCINPEC in the coalition government might help them. This was because the status quo simply did not look good. The fate of the Khmer Rouge was sealed when the CPP won the July 1997 clash decisively. Only then could the war end.

The only challenge to a holistic approach is that the text will be dense, packed with details and important events. But I still choose this approach instead of the more poetic and aesthetic style of writing, where the author switches between relevant events in one paragraph and the "sage's views" in another.

2. Organization Is Everything

The book does not make a significant effort to track down all the names of the actors involved, a task that would have produced a much longer book. Only important names that will help the readers understand the story, or those that would make the events tractable, have been included. Moreover, as some documents are still classified, it is wiser to follow the evolution of the organization rather than follow the life story of the actors.

This does not mean that I did not value the study of the individuals involved, but rather that conventional literature already covers this aspect quite thoroughly. What is missing is the power of organization and how the organization affected the decisions of individuals. It is this gap that the current work is trying to bridge.

The story of the Khmer Rouge can easily be told through "the organizational lens." The KPRP had a structure, but this was later destroyed by internal treachery when Siv Heng defected. Saloth Sar (alias Pol Pot), Nuon Chea, and Ieng Sary were only able to rise up to the top leadership because they worked underground to maintain the remaining skeletal structure. Nuon Chea, for example, mentioned that the leftist movement ran newspapers and continued its activities, failure after failure.[1] It was for this reason, namely that the organization was not strong, that Pol Pot was ignored by the Soviet Embassy.[2]

But when the politics changed, these leaders, although then little known, were the ones who were in control of some working structures. Vietnam would have preferred to deal with an intact organization rather than a fragmented one, even though they had little knowledge of these new people. According to Mosyakov, this consideration was based on the need to maintain a good structure before a struggle could be successful against the Khmer Republic.[3]

Prince Sihanouk also encountered the same problem. After the 1970 coup, the prince had to deal with an organization about which he had little knowledge. Pol Pot also eased the prince's concerns and suspicions by showing off only public faces such as Hu Nim and Hou Yuon, while Khieu Samphan kept a close watch.[4] Pol Pot used the prince as a figurehead to advance his (Pol Pot's) dark agenda. The alternate organization (to Prince Sihanouk's GRUNK) was the ultrasecret CPK, the existence of which was known only to Pol Pot's inner circle.

Perhaps not coincidentally, the Khmer Rouge named their prized organization "Angkar," the Khmer word for organization. Angkar was characterized by secrecy, the mind-your-own-business mentality, total centralization, and arbitrary arrests and purges. Combined with a strong organizational structure, the Khmer Rouge was thus able to remain in power for over three years despite unimaginable atrocity. When Son Sen, who was not even a founding member of the CPK, was appointed minister of defense and chief of staff of the KRA, he was able to wield significant power, which enabled him to trim the Zone Divisions down to one for each Zone, except the East Zone. This policy met with little resistance from the Zone secretary, who might have otherwise preferred autonomy.

The fall of Democratic Kampuchea was less a story of external influence than it was the result of reckless internal policy. Vietnam tried to be patient with Democratic Kampuchea. Vietnam also knew that to intervene directly without cause would certainly result in a failed strategy. Vietnam needed to make sure that it could rely on an emerging organization strong enough to withstand the Khmer Rouge and capable of building a better society. At the same time, this emerging organization should be able to develop friendly ties with Vietnam. It was only after refugees escaped to Vietnam in great numbers that such a policy became possible.

The importance of organization once again emerged after 1979. As the interviews of Prince Sihanouk demonstrated, China, the United States, and the ASEAN argued that the resistance movements would be supported if, and only if, they worked under the umbrella of Democratic Kampuchea. To create a new organization would demand solving the question of statehood and other thorny issues that would only complicate the resistance. Unification was also important for the CGDK, or the CGDK would crumble in the face of the PRK.

After the failure to participate in the 1993 election, the organizational structure of the Khmer Rouge changed dramatically. Before 1993, in fact, between 1970 and 1993, when foreign aid flowed freely into the Khmer Rouge, all the Sponsors needed a clear organization as an agent to be supported. The junior commanders were not able to achieve sufficient stature, especially because the centralization of the Khmer Rouge worked against them. After 1993, the lack of a legitimate and strong organization pushed the Khmer Rouge to delegate authority to its strongholds so that border trades could be used to support the organization. Pol Pot still controlled the ledger, but the local commanders were the ones who prepared it. As a result, embezzlement was the norm.[5] Furthermore, realities on the battlefield also dictated tactical autonomy because Pol Pot no longer had a safe sanctuary that was permanent. A leader who is forced to run from place to place will lose sight of day-to-day activities, to the detriment of his own command, and to the benefit of local commanders.

Unfortunately for them, despite these radical changes, Pol Pot, Son Sen, and Ta Mok did not change the way they worked. They still clung to the iron-hand policy and fiery criticism with regard to their dealing with junior commanders who were experiencing more and more local authority. The painful lesson for Pol Pot and his inner circle was his inability to punish those who integrated with the government. Or-Ral broke away in early 1996 with little punishment, Kampot collapsed into many pieces, Malai-Pailin raided Samlot, and finally Ta Mok resisted and captured Pol Pot. As fate would have it, Pol Pot survived long enough to see his revolution ended this way.

3. Status Quo and Path-dependency

At the beginning of this book, we looked at the importance of the functions served by organization. Two of the main reasons why people have formed into organizations since time immemorial is that first, organizations maximize efficiency and allow the organization to produce quickly and in an orderly manner (or at least in a systematic way). Second, the organization will outlast its original purpose and its founders. Once created, all organizations strive to survive. Only in a few smaller cases (such as birthday party committees, or even up to peacekeeping missions) will the organization be dismantled after its purpose has been fulfilled. In most cases of political and military organizations, however, the organization will outlast anything that created it. This was also true of the Khmer Rouge.

Communism ended in 1989 and foreign aid was cut shortly afterward. Yet, the Khmer Rouge still survived even without a viable ideology. Even when strongholds began to fall one after another, splinter forces still fought in Anlong Veng and Samlot. One argument as to why the leaders there could still muster some forces to fight could be that all of the Khmer Rouge in these areas—including the ordinary soldiers—were hardliners and non-negotiable extremists.

But this is an oversimplification, as one cannot simply argue that over a thousand people were extremists at the same time. A more correct explanation would be that for these ordinary soldiers, amidst the confusion in 1997–98, the only safe approach was to stick with the "devil you know" instead of accepting uncertainty. The WWP was successful because it tried to offer a clear framework for integration, reducing uncertainty for the ordinary soldiers. Once these people integrated, then the hardliners would not be able to stand alone. Samlot and Anlong Veng saw some fighting in 1998, but this did not include battles of annihilation, only more mundane military operations to block dangerous military developments (such as the establishment of refugee camps).

Thus, status quo and path-dependency are the two elements that keep an organization functioning, even in the face of heavy attrition from external factors. In the case of the Khmer Rouge, even without external aid the Khmer Rouge thrived on local natural resources, and if these became depleted, then another option became kidnapping and extortion by creating illegal toll booths. For extortion, the Khmer Rouge did not require extensive resources—only a uniform, a gun and a road. Then travelers would be deterred enough to pay their way through. That is why so many small groups of troublemakers and spoilers became an obstacle to total peace in the country.

The WWP played a role in preventing this problem. The policy sets out clear objectives and procedures. Promises were kept and good deeds were rewarded. Such a policy of accommodation also drew many people in a context where the illegal trading of the Khmer Rouge benefited only the top cadres. Without this policy of accommodation, soldiers would have preferred to stay with the devil they knew.

4.   Road to Destruction, Road to Power

While this book is about the rise and fall of the Khmer Rouge as an organization, it also gives a hint about the rise and fall of other regimes such as the *Sangkum Reastr Niyum* of Prince Sihanouk, and the Khmer Republic under Lon Nol. The leader who had the most difficult time was probably Prince Sihanouk, whose neutrality policy was undermined by the conflicts between the left and the right in his own government. When the left and the right tried to outmaneuver each other, the people were the ones who suffered. To make matters worse, both tried to make false reports to the prince that it was not the people who rebelled, but rather, those who were politically motivated. While the prince was attempting to resolve these issues, the 1970 coup effectively ended any remedial action.

The rise to power of Lon Nol and the Khmer Republic has been well documented in Ros Chantrabot's book, *La République Khmère*, as this author was also one of the important figures during that period. The book also refers to another type of political movement not discussed here, which is the student and teachers' movement. Chantrabot implied that the ones who controlled such student movements and youth associations that proliferated into many different factions would control the political system. The reason is simple. Such movements were usually used to run demonstrations and write petitions in order to destabilize any government that was opposed, or to back the government that was supported. But then one can also argue that it was not the collapse of these movements that spelled the end of the Khmer Republic. Instead, it was the collapse of the Chenla operations that spelled the end for the Khmer Republic. When the Khmer Rouge entered into Phnom Penh, these movements could do nothing to stop the inevitable. Protest and association movements can create problems in society or pave the way for military intervention, or, if used properly, can also contribute to the strengthening and development of a country. But in times of war and instability, when uncertainty reigns and loyalty questionable, these movement always tend to disintegrate and divisive, and the military is still the final arbiter of the fate of a political regime.

The Khmer Rouge, on the other hand, was able to seize power only after hijacking the reputation of Prince Sihanouk. After 1970, the Khmer Rouge no longer relied on protest movements but escalated straight to armed struggle. This was Pol Pot's conception even before 1970.[6] When they took power, the Khmer Rouge strictly controlled the military. Yet, the Khmer Rouge still collapsed. The main reason for this was the Khmer Rouge's decision to go to war with the larger Vietnam. Vietnam was reluctant to go to war with Democratic Kampuchea, because a war with Pol Pot required Vietnam to have an exit strategy that was not in existence at the end of 1977. As a result, Vietnam still maintained the hope that former veterans of the KPRP, such as Nuon Chea and Sor Phim, might still harbor some sympathy toward Vietnam, and this link could be used to defuse tension. As late as 1979, Vietnam still retained the hope that Nuon Chea would return, and following the in absentia trial of Khmer Rouge leaders in 1979, only Pol Pot and Ieng Sary were condemned by the People's Tribunal of the newly established PRK, while Nuon Chea was not mentioned.[7]

The second reason for regime destruction is the nature of the use of propaganda. But propaganda was not specific to the Khmer Rouge. The Khmer Republic was also enmeshed in a series of propaganda campaigns of its own. The Khmer Rouge suffered from a more serious problem, and this was the fatal belief in its own propaganda. It is common for regimes to use propaganda, and propaganda has to be optimistic. But it was a big mistake to unreasonably believe in one's own propaganda and to design policy based on its faulty assumptions. The Khmer Rouge claimed that they had defeated the United States military, the most powerful military force in all of human history.[8] Thus, comparatively, war with Vietnam would be insignificant. A simplistic formula was employed: as long as one Khmer Rouge soldier could kill 30 Vietnamese, the war would be easily won. When things went wrong, there could be only one reason: internal treachery. Deadly purges followed.

In sum, for regime destruction, the problem was not the fact that they used propaganda, but it was the fact that they sincerely believed in their own propaganda, rejecting realities and contrary, yet valid, evidence. They settled for comforting lies in lieu of disturbing truth. It was said that in ancient Greece, the messenger who brought bad news was executed. In fact, this was what happened under Democratic Kampuchea and for Pol Pot it was worse. Comrade Chhon (codename) relayed the most accurate information possible from the battlefield. This was not complete, but most of his report was accurate and the picture was not good for the Khmer Rouge. Yet, from 1978, Comrade Chhon's name no longer figured in these reports. In contrast, others followed the way of propaganda, and reported only success. Whenever there was a failure, they implied that it must have been the enemy who had "burrowed" inside the ranks. They all survived.

The Khmer Republic fared no better. The main reason why the Khmer Republic did not fight in the latest stage of the war was its exhaustion in the war as well as a sincere belief that the Khmer Rouge would bring Prince Sihanouk back to power and peace would be ensured. The Khmer Rouge did not bring Prince Sihanouk back to power. Many Khmer Republic officials also clung to a series of comforting propagandas and the politicians were out-maneuvering each other, in a context where war was raging all around.

Overall, political regimes of the Westphalian type are resilient. It takes a great amount of effort to overthrow a regime, short of direct and overwhelming external intervention. In most cases, the status quo will prevail. Under the reign of Prince Sihanouk, the system had been quite resilient, but the Khmer Rouge took advantage of the existence of some corrupt local officials to turn the people's grievances into a war. Without this guerilla activity, and without the 1970 coup, Prince Sihanouk might have had enough time to resolve all of the problems. But time was running out for the prince, and the war was raging all around Cambodia, as the United States had positioned over half a million troops in neighboring South Vietnam. Therefore, a combination of many factors and upheavals, and finally a coup d'état in 1970, conspired to overthrow the regime.

Under the Khmer Republic, and despite internal disagreements, the regime had been resilient, despite even the self-interest of politicians. And even amidst the war that had already consumed over two-thirds of the country, the FANK could still muster enough force to carry out the Chenla I and Chenla II operations. It was the collapse of the Chenla II operation that led to the loss of initiative on the part of the Khmer Republic. Various attempts to recover offensive capabilities were blocked, and eventually, the FANK strategically assumed a defensive posture after 1972.[9] To make matters worse, youth protests, student movements, teacher movements, and internal machinations proliferated as politicians sought to outmaneuver each other.[10] Instead of using the youth to defend the regime, the politicians used them to turn on each other at a time when the Khmer Rouge was literally staring down the capital city from the other bank of the river.

The worst thing for the Khmer Republic and the Khmer Rouge was that they both presented somewhat similar problems: the regime started to believe in its own propaganda and rejected realities. Ultimately, the military is still the final arbiter for change of the status quo. But if the military was already under the influence of the propaganda, then they will be likely to launch military adventure (the Khmer Rouge) or to decline essential combat (the Khmer Republic) that ultimately doomed the regime itself.

5. Military Organization and Operations

In order for human society to function properly, many infrastructures and superstructures are needed to keep everything in place and to avoid chaos. Such a well-organized society can also advance technologically and become efficient if it has all the necessary supporting structures in place, such as police, justice, education, government, economic institutions, and so forth. States that do not have these structures usually bear the label "failed states." In contrast, the military organization surprisingly requires little supporting structure and can use the limited resources at its disposal to become deadly.

Logistics, technical assets, ammunition, ideology, chain of command, initiative, creativity, training in tactics, realistic strategy, and committed fighters are some of the most important assets for a military organization to be able to function with an acceptable level of efficiency and effectiveness. Most of these components are already inherent in the system; they depend on the personnel within, not on any structure outside of the system. Everything is within the unit itself, except technical assets, ammunition, and logistics. Even so, many military organizations try to procure these assets from indigenous sources. And even in cases where such assets are scarce, creativity and tactics can still result in a military organization with deadly effectiveness. In all of the history of warfare, guerilla tactics have been precisely designed to be used in cases where the matériel was scarce. This is a tactic of sustained action in the face of scarcity.

The best example was the Khmer Rouge after 1979. The Khmer Rouge knew that their strongholds were constantly being raided by the KPRAF and accordingly, the Khmer Rouge had a shortage of committed fighters. As a result, they adopted a guerilla strategy and hid their fighters in plain sight, distributing them throughout shadow networks in remote villages. Tactically, when weapons were scarce, bamboo stakes were used as traps in concealed pits. This weapon was primitive, but it had a strong psychological effect on those who were facing it, as the stakes were efficient and effective in impeding infantry movement. Moreover, bamboo stakes are virtually free because one can find them everywhere in the jungle.

In addition, artillery shells were converted into bombs, and even a discarded battery could be rigged to explode. Mines were laid to not only harm the victim, but also to harm the deminers who tried to remove them. The Khmer Rouge valued these tactics and applied them in minute detail. When foreign support was cut after 1993, the Khmer Rouge was still able to operate as a force to be reckoned with. The breakdown of the Khmer Rouge was not due to the inefficiency of their military tactics; it was because the top leadership was too involved with the sprawling trade along the border and internal competition, leading to violent infighting.

Even with the subsequent loss of purpose and the infighting as well as break-aways by many groups, smaller units continued to fight and presented a danger to peace until 1998. One of the main reasons why this fighting continued was that some of these units were still unified enough to retain combat capacity. Certainly, the Khmer Rouge would not be able to return to power, but diversi-fied units still remained as a constant threat to total peace in the country. This is the main reason why many civil wars fail to end permanently, unless there is a brutal annihilation strategy.

This is a pertinent point for war termination strategy. When the military is well-organized, it will be able to complete many missions, large or small. But when the military is broken down by the enemy into smaller units, there are many tactics available that allow fighting to still continue. Most civil wars continue not because the guerillas are strong, but because they fight as small units, thus they are too numerous to be totally eliminated. It is the natural con-sequence for such military organizations using guerilla tactics to be able to survive, but this is not in the interest of peace.

The WWP partly met this challenge when it focused on the termination of the Khmer Rouge's political-military organization and then integrated the former soldiers, rather than trying to break down the organization into smaller units and then trying to eliminate these units one by one. In other words, the classic "divide-and-conquer" strategy would only produce more and more guerillas with no centralized structure. In such a case, war termination would have involved military action against every single group of guerillas, something that would have been on a scale too large to be efficient, if not impossible to achieve altogether.

The second pertinent point about the military organization of the Khmer Rouge was the unclear distinction between guerilla and conventional units. While the guerilla tactics helped the Khmer Rouge to retain fighting capacity and disturb the peace, guerilla tactics were not able to help the Khmer Rouge win their wars against Vietnam in the 1970s. In fact, guerilla tactics are best used in support of the main formations, but such guerilla tactics are not an end in themselves. In 1977 and 1978, the Khmer Rouge sought to use guerilla tactics to annihilate Vietnam. But these tactics failed tragically. Since the units were essentially guerilla units with little training in large-scale coordination and combined arms, the division was not a synergy but instead an amalgamation of guerilla units operating under the umbrella of the division. These units did not simply *use* guerilla tactics, they *were* the guerillas.

Thus, when the KRA attacked Tay Ninh in 1977, the tactics were purely guerilla, based on what former soldiers of division 703 described: cutting traffic on the road, laying mines, blowing up bridges, scorched earth, and burning buildings.[11] Moreover, when the Vietnamese army raided the rear artillery positions of the Khmer Rouge in 1977, the officer in charge quickly withdrew the artillery pieces without undertaking any remedial action to sustain the support of the forward units.

This was certainly a blunder, but one can understand it through the lens of guerilla warfare. In such war, the small units must be independent so that they can turn small numbers into an advantage in speed, precision, and efficiency. However, Pol Pot tried to transplant this old operational concept into a new campaign that was different from previous wars. Any war requires some guerilla tactics, but to base a war of annihilation against a bigger adversary entirely on guerilla tactics was a strategic mismatch. As a result, the whole campaign collapsed tragically. This point leads directly to the next.

6. Return of Clausewitz

Pol Pot's strategic concept was instrumental in understanding the war with Vietnam as well as his direction of the Khmer Rouge organization later in his career. Yet this is a point that has never been analyzed within the template of the famed strategist, Clausewitz. As has been implicit in various parts of this book, the major military issue with Pol Pot was the repeated mismatch between his strategy and tactics. This started to occur at the time he took power and the mismatch had, ever since, been slowly eating away the strength of his organization.

The German theorist, Carl von Clausewitz, was born during the Napoleonic era when states had begun to organize themselves into large-scale armies to fight each other. This was no longer war between kings or warlords, it was war between nation-states. Entire nations were mobilized and fought against each other. Clausewitz wrote that in such instances, reciprocal escalation would lead to what he called "absolute war," war that approaches the extreme, a war of annihilation and total destruction of a nation-state.[12] What many commentators on Clausewitz usually miss, however, is that Clausewitz considered "absolute war" only as a philosophical construct, and he also identified "real war" which was limited in nature. This is because such war is often dictated by rational political imperatives, which, in turn, tend to be limited. For Clausewitz, war was merely a continuation of policy by other means.[13]

In all of human history, some wars have approached the theoretical limit of absolute war, most notably, World War I and World War II. Yet, even in such cases, people began to show signs of exhaustion, and ordinary soldiers would desert en masse if they had the chance.[14] Pol Pot's strategy presented a peculiar case of Clausewitz's theory: Pol Pot's strategy was dictated by policy, but this policy itself was extreme. Pol Pot chose a war of annihilation. However, this was not a means to an end, but an end in itself. Pol Pot considered Vietnam to be an existential threat; Vietnam was a threat only because of its location next door to Cambodia. But as World War I and World War II showed, a war of annihilation would require total mobilization of the entire society, and the society with the largest population pool, industrial might, and economic power would win that bloody war of attrition. Democratic Kampuchea had no such assets when it went to war with Vietnam in 1977. Thus, Pol Pot's strategy was doomed to fail even before it started.

This brings us to the second lesson derived from Clausewitz's theory. Those who view Clausewitz's theory as normative often appreciate Clausewitz for his very definition and description of strategy. Simply put, strategy, for Clausewitz, is the use of battles to win the war.[15] A less cryptic way to understand this is the template used to teach strategy classes at the U.S. Army War College, which is known as the "Ends-Ways-Means" methodology, credited to Arthur Lykke.[16] This strategy is designed around the means available, as well as how these means can best be used to achieve the set objectives. For example, is the strategy used to pursue this war feasible? If so, then at what cost? Is society ready to accept that cost? These questions need to be answered before a war can be successfully conducted and strategic objectives fulfilled.

Pol Pot did nothing of this sort. He simply set objectives and then went to war. When the means could not keep up with his expectations, he (and some of his propagandists) blamed the shortfall on hidden enemies, a misconception that led to further disaster.

Amidst the confusion when the UNTAC arrived in 1991, holding some territories and using its threat to peace as a bargaining chip was the only feasible strategy the Khmer Rouge could use, given its dwindling resources and the collapse of morale after campaigns that were met with setback after setback. Despite this stark reality, Pol Pot still maintained his annihilation strategy and went to great lengths to explain to his subordinates that there was only one existential threat (i.e. Vietnam) that justified his rule. To make matters worse, path-dependency kicked in and the brutal past of the Khmer Rouge came back to haunt Pol Pot. No one wanted him in the political compromise in 1991, and during the 1993 election.

As a result, the rank and file lost all trust in Pol Pot and considered him more of a liability than an inspiring figure. Pol Pot did not realize this, and continued to cling to his strategy before attempting to assert his iron-hand authority that had all but eroded. It was a fitting end for a brutal dictator to be arrested by his most trusted bodyguard, Ta Mok, after killing his own, most loyal lieutenant, Son Sen. The revolution had turned on itself and had finally run its course.

7. Peacekeeping and Peace Process

The Cambodian conflict exposed many dilemmas inherent in peacekeeping operations. Here, I focus on only two fundamental and related problems: the issues of impartiality and spoilers.

First of all, one of the questions that tend to haunt all SRSG is this: what should be the overarching concepts that guide the SRSG actions? The official documents of the UN stress "impartiality" as a primary guiding principle, leading to the idea that "fairness" is one of the central issues. If this is the case, then the SRSG is more like a *judge* than a *political representative* of the UN. According to this edict, all parties to the peace process must be treated fairly by the peacekeeper. In practice, some peacekeeping missions so closely adhered to this principle that it bordered on neutrality, that is, not doing anything at all besides strictly keeping the peace. The best example is the case of the inaction of UN troops (U.S.-led multinational forces) in Haiti as the former Haitian soldiers beat up the local people who came out to cheer the arrival of those UN troops.[17] Akashi is strangely silent on the role of impartiality in peacekeeping operations.[18]

As one of the conflicting parties to the Paris peace agreement, as well as being a signatory, the Khmer Rouge, according to that abstract notion of fairness, was theoretically entitled to impartial treatment from the SRSG and other peacekeepers. Yet, as a result of its previous history, deep mistrust existed between the Khmer Rouge and the SOC/CPP on the one hand, and between the Khmer Rouge and the FUNCINPEC (Prince Sihanouk's movement) on the other. Prime Minister Hun Sen was adamant: "One cannot make concessions so much as to allow the Khmer Rouge to be able to inflict new unimaginable atrocities on the Cambodian people."[19] Given the past history of atrocities, it was simply inconceivable that the Khmer Rouge would be accepted by the other two main parties and the general populace.

And this was the dilemma. Should Akashi adhere to impartiality by insisting on Khmer Rouge's participation regardless of changing local politics and international opposition (to the Khmer Rouge's participation), thereby decreasing the chance of reaching a near-term comprehensive agreement? Or should Akashi accept that conditions had changed, and then waive impartially to pursue an agreement with the other parties, assuming that the Khmer Rouge issue (which was an underlying cause of conflict) would be otherwise resolved by the new government?

As shown in the previous chapters, as a realist SRSG, Akashi chose the latter. This book argues that while it was not a perfect policy, Akashi made a good choice by bringing the CPP and Prince Sihanouk together. This was partly the basis of peace in Cambodia. But while isolating the Khmer Rouge was a sensible choice, the UNTAC leaving Cambodia before fully resolving the Khmer Rouge issue led to another related problem in the peacekeeping operation: spoilers.

A second and related issue is the handling of spoilers. This directly affected the SRSG as a judge vs. politician issue. At the time of the attack on Son Sen and Khieu Samphan in 1991, neither Prince Sihanouk nor Akashi issued any condemnation, or even heavy criticism, of the event. Prime Minister Hun Sen of the SOC intervened personally to calm down the mob, but did not issue a condemnation. Given their past relationship with the Khmer Rouge, Prince Sihanouk and the SOC both did not have any pertinent reasons to protect the Khmer Rouge. The UNTAC followed suit. For its part, the UNTAC did little to bring the Khmer Rouge into negotiations, although in terms of fairness to all signatories, it (the UNTAC) might have so chosen. Impartiality, it seems, can be violated by what you choose to do as well as what you choose not to do. From this point onward, the Khmer Rouge was traveling down a slippery slope until it boycotted the election on its own accord.

In Cambodia, the marginalization policy pursued by Akashi, that is, the so-called "departing train,"[20] created a problem because it paradoxically made the Khmer Rouge more important: the Khmer Rouge military could significantly endanger the balance of power of the new coalition government by simply aligning with any faction. Instead of resolving the problem, the departing train policy simply deferred it to a later date when peacekeepers were no longer there to keep the peace, thus avoiding blame.

By boycotting the election, the Khmer Rouge might have calculated, then quite correctly, that the new government would be a coalition government with less than cordial internal relations. If that was the case, then the Khmer Rouge would become more powerful than ever because any party with the Khmer Rouge on its side would immediately upset the delicate balance in the coalition government. At that time, the two parties (CPP and the FUNCINPEC) would sooner or later find themselves in a situation of fragile balance. At a time when the CPP controlled most of the military and the civilian administration, the coalition government called for a system of "co-leadership." This system also trickled down to the lower levels of provincial military formations. And sure enough, the hardliner Khmer Rouge became one of the main causes contributing to the events in July 1997. But because many journalists and commentators wrongly called that event a "coup" without taking a holistic view, the link between that event and the Khmer Rouge, as well as the UNTAC's premature departure, became lost in time. This book studies that event and its ramifications in detail, in the hope that a new debate can arise that will reconsider the UNTAC success in the light of the events that followed.

Chance could also have become a factor, and Cambodia could have entered another decade of conflict. In fact, it was the decisive victory in 1997 that ended the Khmer Rouge's hope that it could take power by force. The CPP's victory in 1997 also effectively cut off the support of ordinary soldiers from the hardliners.

So what is the final assessment of this book concerning Akashi's work and the UNTAC? Concerning the underlying causes of the conflict, Akashi can be credited with having contributed to success, even if not directly achieving success, especially because of the fact that he was willing to place more emphasis on solving the problem rather than adhering to some abstract notion of impartiality in the face of political realities. Ultimately, the UN intervention and his leadership, even if a mixed bag, resulted in a government that was legitimate and acceptable to both the Cambodian people and the international community. But to get to this point, the mandate had to be somehow bent until it almost broke.

Ideally, the UNTAC should have done the following to achieve total peace: first, choose to ignore the Khmer Rouge (since the CPP and the FUNCINPEC did not agree to let the Khmer Rouge participate), second, organize an election that was acceptable to the major players (except the Khmer Rouge), and third, choose to resolve the Khmer Rouge issue. But that would have been "ideal," and to achieve such an ideal, the mission would have had to be longer, costing more money, and the UNTAC should have been ready to bear the potential loss of personnel, especially in the third phase. But there was no way the UNTAC mandate could have allowed it to solve the Khmer Rouge issue.

This was the dilemma—the SRSG could neither forget the importance of the principle of impartiality nor ignore the realities of the political context. The SRSG could not have chosen the third option: to continue the mission to deal with the Khmer Rouge. That was not written in the mandate, and there was no way it could have been part of the mandate. Therefore, the most rational option for Akashi (albeit not the perfect one) was to ignore the Khmer Rouge and achieve a short peace. This led to the event in July 1997, and continued until the WWP finally nipped the civil war in the bud in late 1998. Yet, the UNTAC was out by 1993 and the link with the event in 1997 was lost. In Cambodia, an indigenous policy, the WWP, was urgently needed to achieve total peace.

I admit that no one would agree that political considerations should be written into the mandate, such as, "the SRSG should be the politician and should ignore impartiality as it sees fit," nor do I think it is best to allow bias. Error of judgment is inherent to all human beings, and to allow bias is to invite disaster. Yet, political considerations are precisely what are needed in many cases to end a war. Such is the dilemma that the SRSG and peacekeeping missions will continue to face. This book argues that peacekeeping missions are very important because they generate an environment of trust for the actors involved to come in and participate in a nonviolent competition for power. Yet, the very limited nature of the mandate means that the peacekeeping mission will not be enough on its own. One also needs goodwill from all the local parties, the agreement of the local parties to a modus vivendi, and finally, an indigenous war termination strategy. In the case of Cambodia, the war termination strategy was the WWP of Prime Minister Hun Sen. Holistically, peace cannot be solely imported from abroad; it has to be nurtured locally, in whole or in part.

8.   Society and War

The war had consumed Cambodia for almost 30 years. What was left behind was a country in tatters, although the nation and its people had survived. But the war took its toll in many other ways on Cambodian society. The first consequence was the militarization of society. For example, the Khmer Rouge was notable for using child soldiers. The Khmer Rouge considered this group of soldiers to be the most loyal to the cause, as child soldiers had not been exposed to the vices of capitalist society. Children were used as spies, couriers, guerillas units, and transporters of ammunition. These children became expert in all types of weaponry and mines.

The second, related problem was the abundance of weapons, ammunition, and explosives in Cambodia. Mines of all types had been used since the 1960s and continued to be used until 1998. Most of the time, mines were laid in large clusters and without proper mapping. Soldiers often stepped on their own mines. "When we advanced, we laid mines to defend our positions. When we needed to retreat after our rear supply lines were cut by the Khmer Rouge, we laid mines to cover our track as well as at the new front. The Khmer Rouge did the same thing," a former soldier of the KPRAF reminisced.[21] When one cannot defend a certain trail or position, it is standard practice to lay mines in high density just to "kill" the terrain. The Khmer Rouge practiced the same tactics.

Improvised explosive devices (IEDs) were placed on the roads and even today, farmers fall victim to these silent killers or dig up unexploded ordnance (UXO) with their plows. The United States was the largest contributor of UXO in Cambodia during the secret air war of the 1960s and 1970s. According to Taylor Owen and Ben Kiernan, the total bomb load dropped in Cambodia was estimated to be over 2.5 million tons between 1965 and 1973, from the U.S. Air Force alone.[22] This is an average of 15 tons per square kilometer. According to a report from the Cambodian Mine Action Center (CMAC), the demining efforts from 1992 to 2011 recovered a total of 455,970 antipersonnel mines, 9,012 antitank mines, 1,292 IEDs still intact, 1,722,044 pieces of UXO, and 5,531 abandoned explosive ordnance (AXO), leading to a total of 2,193,849 lethal pieces.[23] This is an average of 1 lethal remnant of war for every 7 Cambodian people. The CMAC is still involved fulltime in its clearance work, and uncovers more and more of these silent killers.

Small arms were also an issue for Cambodia. An estimate by the EU-ASAC (EU Small Arms and Light Weapons Assistance to the Kingdom of Cambodia) put the number of small arms in circulation at 462,500 in 1991.[24] However, this number tends to be an underestimation of the real total, as many weapons were still in secret stashes at the time, and there were those that were newly imported before the showdown in July 1997. The Royal Cambodian Government has been working with many donor states to make sure that the weapons are under legal control. According to the EU-ASAC estimate using the 1991 number, 82 percent was taken under government control, of which 142,871 weapons were destroyed in symbolic events known as the "Flame of Peace." The same report estimates that the consequent scarcity of guns caused the price of assault rifles to rise 440 percent on the black market as a result of this successful government policy.[25] It is ironic that in war, money was spent on guns and ammunition while in peace, money was spent on destroying them.

After the war ended, another immediate consequence was the search for justice. Khmer Rouge hardliners and senior leadership were often fearful for their past actions, yet they use the confusion to keep their soldiers in line and continued to fight. The WWP met this challenge by guaranteeing that no one would be arrested arbitrarily. Only the most senior leaders would be tried for past crimes and even this senior leadership would only be tried by a court that is internationally recognized. After lengthy negotiations between the UN and the Royal Cambodian Government, a special, "hybrid court" was finally agreed upon by both sides in 2003 and the Extraordinary Chamber in the Court of Cambodia (ECCC) was established.[26] The WWP ensured that there would be peace and justice at the same time but from then on, justice took on a life of its own.

The tribunal is special in that it is composed of both national and international judges, prosecutors, and defense counsels. But while the Cambodian judges outnumber their international counterparts in all chambers of the tribunal, a judgment can only be passed if and only if there is consent from at least one international judge. The tribunal can only prosecute two categories of alleged perpetrators, namely the senior leaders of Democratic Kampuchea and those who are believed to be most responsible for grave violations of national and international law.[27] The jurisdiction is also temporally limited, only alleged crimes committed between April 17, 1975 and January 6, 1979 would be considered by the tribunal.[28]

Among the senior Khmer Rouge leaders who were detained, Ta Mok died in custody in 2006 before being tried. In 2010, Kaing Guek Eav, alias Duch, the head of S-21, was sentenced to 35 years in prison, although the term was modified to remedy for past detentions.[29] As of July 2012, Ieng Sary, Ieng Thirith, Nuon Chea, and Khieu Samphan were under trial. Finally, it is hoped that justice will be served.

Another positive thing to emerge from the war is how the Cambodian government is dealing with the problems resulting from the civil war. After the war, the Cambodian demining corps was no doubt one of the best in the world. In fact, this is not a surprise, since the soldiers who were once laying mines are now experts in mines removal. An institution was established (under a national committee) in 2005, the National Center for Peacekeeping Forces, Mines, and ERW Clearance (NPMEC), in addition to the CMAC and other demining NGOs such as the Halo Trust. But the NPMEC has a particular role: to train peacekeepers and deminers to serve in operations abroad, exclusively under the UN umbrella.

As of April 2012, a total of 839 Cambodian soldiers had completed UN peacekeeping missions while 222 are currently on mission in various parts of the world, including as observers, peacekeepers, military police, Hospital level 2 Company, and demining experts.[30] Cambodia has been transformed from a country plagued by civil war into one with complete peace; it has also become a troop-contributing country to the UN peacekeeping efforts.

All these policies, including demining, peacekeeping, small arms management and contributions to the UN peacekeeping efforts might have escaped the attention of some observers, but for Cambodia and those with intimate knowledge of the WWP, these activities are important because "development" is the last stage of the WWP.

The final consequence of the civil war on Cambodian society was the relationship between the leaders and the people. While the general populace is usually thought to be disorganized and politically myopic (i.e., not adequately concerned about the political machinations of the day), the importance of their perception regarding their leaders cannot be denied. For most of Cambodia's modern history, Prince Sihanouk was greatly revered by the Cambodian people, and historians have agreed that the revolts in Samlot and other places in the 1960s were not directed toward the prince, but only against corrupt local officials. These officials worked under the protective umbrella of the prince's administration, yet abused this protection for their own gain. Prince Sihanouk himself had never been rejected by his people throughout the history of the civil war and after.

Pol Pot, on the other hand, believed that secrecy and sophisticated lies and propaganda were the basis of power. For a time, this served him well, because people had a tendency to be absorbed by the status quo (i.e., they were influenced by path-dependency). Many people fell into this trap. Sor Phim, for example, believed in the sincerity of Pol Pot until the end of his life. Pol Pot was also notorious for how badly he handled his subordinates. People could be killed for even the slightest suspicion or problem. For example, we have seen that early on, even the Chinese technicians sent to help the Khmer Rouge construction projects were furious with the constant changes of Cambodian assistants—changeovers forced by purges and executions.

But treachery has its limit. As Khieu Samphan himself is claimed to have said, "No matter how hard the wolf prays, the lamb will still not trust it."[31] This is an ironic description of Pol Pot. Even in cases where he might have been sincere, no one believed him. The most compelling examples included the killing of Son Sen and the massacre of the FUNCINPEC liaison crews in Anlong Veng. People failed to rebel against Pol Pot's lies and treachery only because they did not have the capability to resist. And when they got the capabilities, they did resist. The first outbreak of rebellion against Pol Pot was the Kampuchea Solidarity Front for National Salvation.

After 1993, the local commanders of the remaining Khmer Rouge forces began to experience autonomy. This was when foreign aid was cut, and the Khmer Rouge had to resort to border trades. Not only did they despise Pol Pot, but they then had the independence and capabilities to act on their convictions. Pol Pot was forced to move from place to place during the last stages of his life, and was eventually captured by Ta Mok, his most trusted bodyguard during the resistance era. One can only lie so much.

Finally, the case of the Cambodian civil war revealed another aspect that has not been examined in detail by previous scholars: the WWP. This policy is inseparable from its architect, Prime Minister Hun Sen. To study one without the other would be incomplete. The WWP owed its success to at least three factors: the personality of the architect (Prime Minister Hun Sen), the strength of the CPP, the PRK, and the SOC, and finally, a synchronized approach by the former KPRAF officers who implemented the WWP. The strength of the CPP, the PRK, and the SOC has been examined at various points in this book, and the deeds of the former KPRAF officers have been mentioned only in a few places. This is because of the secrecy surrounding the full accounts, which should be the subject of future research.

To conclude this book, I will point to one reason for the success of the WWP, which is the strategic thinking of Prime Minister Hun Sen. This issue has been discussed in detail in a biography of the prime minister authored by Harish and Julia Mehta, entitled *Hun Sen: Strongman of Cambodia*. But this book was completed before the total end of the Khmer Rouge, as well as before the declassification of documents about the WWP.

When devising the WWP, Prime Minister Hun Sen understood that trust in it would be the issue. Thus, at the very first meeting with the first Khmer Rouge commander from the strategic Or-Ral area to be integrated, the prime minister gave clear assurances and proposed a policy that was the exact opposite of Pol Pot's.

We do not yet have the details of the discussions of this meeting, but Keo Pung said after the meeting that he felt "to stay with Pol Pot means that everyone will be killed eventually [by continuous war or purges] but to integrate with Prime Minister Hun Sen can either mean life or death."[32] In Keo Pung's calculation, while the choice of integrating with the prime minister offered a 50–50 chance of being killed or staying alive, this was still a better choice than the devil he knew. Pol Pot would certainly have pushed the war further until everyone died. Here, too, reputation played a role. Pol Pot was brutal, as everyone knew and had experienced firsthand. Prime Minister Hun Sen, alternatively, was accused of being a puppet of Vietnam by Pol Pot, but when Keo Pung and other Khmer Rouge commanders arrived in the capital city, they did not see any Vietnamese soldiers. The Vietnamese soldiers had been withdrawn since 1989. Prime Minister Hun Sen had completely outmaneuvered Pol Pot in a propaganda coup.

The second reason for success was Prime Minister Hun Sen's daring acceptance of calculated risks. He is someone who is not afraid to take risks, but is not reckless in his actions. Any sensible decision maker would observe that such a balance is very delicate and is hard to achieve. The best example of this was his explanation of his decision to go to Pailin on October 22, 1996, the first ever visit of a former enemy into the heart of the Khmer Rouge stronghold:

> With regard to the win-win policy, my mother and my aunt, both of whom have already passed away, asked me behind closed doors why I decided to go to the enemy region. I told them that if the worst happened, only I and perhaps a hundred other people going with me would die, but if I lived, I would be able to bring peace back to the whole country. Let's imagine if I had not gone to Malai, Phnom Proeuk, Kamrieng and Samlot. Would those people have placed their trust in the win-win policy?[33]

Trust is the keyword here. But some authors such as Benny Widyono, who also accompanied the then second prime minister during that trip, recorded that around 200–300 crack troops of the elite 911 paratrooper regiment also accompanied the then second prime minister. One can also speculate that Second Prime Minister Hun Sen must have also had some underground network in place there. Nevertheless, if the worst had happened (many other important ministers of the CPP also accompanied the second prime minister), it would be hard to believe that the crack commando troops would have been able to successfully fight their way out of a Khmer Rouge stronghold that was manned by equally battle-hardened Khmer Rouge troops. Yet, Second Prime Minister Hun Sen still made the decision to go. It is most likely that the commandos were deployed only to protect the second prime minister from any spoilers who might want to disrupt the peace process.

In the 1980s, the ASEAN did not recognize the PRK and Prime Minister Hun Sen. But when his WWP finally put an end to what the Cambodian people called "the chronic civil war" and achieved total peace in late 1998, Cambodia joined the ASEAN soon after. Three years later, in 2002, Prime Minister Hun Sen of the Kingdom of Cambodia held the rotating chairmanship of the ASEAN Summit in Phnom Penh. For the first time in almost 30 years, thanks to the WWP of Prime Minister Hun Sen, peace finally prevailed.

In 2008, I was attending the University of Delaware. I was studying for my master's degree in economics and was about to continue on to a PhD in political science and international relations. During Happy Hour at the former department, we socialized with our professors. One of my professors came up to congratulate me on my graduation and then asked me, "You're from Cambodia? You know, I always wanted to visit Cambodia. Can you tell me if it is safe? I mean, do Cambodian people hate Americans?" I was stunned by this question, why do we hate Americans? I then realized it was a fair question given past history, but this was all behind us. I explained to him about the WWP and how safe it is to visit Cambodia and see the iconic Angkor Wat, the symbol that unites all Cambodians. In fact, every regime since the birth of a sovereign Cambodia in modern times (in 1953), Democratic Kampuchea included, has featured the Angkor Wat as its symbol of national unity. Every regime has represented the temple on its flag, although the shape or color might change. To let people know what transpired in Cambodia over the last 30 years is one of the main reasons why I started the projects that culminate in this book.

A year later, another of my former professors from the economics department did actually travel to Cambodia. When I met him back in the United States, he told me about how pleasant his stay had been. And then he said: "We went to Siem Reap and heard that had been a hot battlefield in the past so if not walking on asphalt road, I didn't dare walk out near the trees, I only walked on the roots of trees because you can't see landmines!" I thought to myself, well, if he had visited Cambodia in the 1980s and 1990s, everyone would have praised him for his sensible and safe walking methodology. But to walk the same way in Cambodia today would look extremely strange. Mines have been cleared from populated areas. Nevertheless, I laughed with him. An era was coming to an end and a new one had arisen.

Appendix:
Khmer Rouge Military Power after the 1993 Election

No.	Unit[1]	Name of commander	Regiments (Numeric designation)	Number of troops	Number of guerrilla	Total	Area of Activities
			Military Region 3				
1	DIV 18	Pung and Sreng	21-41-42-44	250	400	650	HourngSomnom-Or'Ral-TPung-Kompong Speu
2	DIV 785	Teng and Veoun	520-530-540-560	300	300	300	OmpovTeok-KompongChnang-Mokompoul-Kandal
3	DIV 19	Sim-Touch-San	85-88-89	200	400	600	TeokPorsSamakyMeanchy-KompongChnang
4	DIV 305	Sorn and Mon	12-14-15-16-17-18	120	300	420	KorngPisey-Paset-KompongSpeu
5	DIV 405	Bit-Bert-Mao	303-72-75-62-16	150	400	550	Phnom Vorl-TakernKoh Sra-Kompot
6	Independent Battalion 27	Bo		100	100	200	SrekOmpeul–Koh Kong province
7	Independent Battalion 107	Em		100	100	200	TmorSor-TmorParng–Koh Kong Province
			Military Region 5				
1	DIV 5	Chheoun-Chheang-Thouk	14-15-16-17	250	400	650	Road 65 Leach Talo–Pur Sat province
2	DIV 36	Parn-Sngon-Ratt-Mao	21-22-23	250	300	550	MorngSvayDounKeo–Border of Pur Sat Battambong
3	DIV 171	Met-Tith-Peou	83-84-85-86	300	300	600	ChomlorngKouy Phnom Vear Chap KoursKroLor–Battambong

4	DIV 705	Cheart-Kong Seoun	416-707-370-186	350	500	BaSreKompongPouy–East of Battambong
5	DIV 948	SreySopemn-Sok	408-903	300	750	Taponn Song Kel–East of Battambong
6	DIV 415	Chhean-Veoun	41-42-43	450	810	Along road number 10 SpeouSnengSampoeu–Battambong
7	DIV 404	Mao Chan	403-405	200	550	Along road number 10 Phnom Veay Chap–Battambong
8	DIV 305	Paiy–Rorm Nor Nhorn	901-905-909-709	350	750	Road 58 Ta KorngKompongPouy Bovil–Battambong
9	DIV 450	Pearp–Moun–Koun	106-107-108-109-185	400	800	Bovil–Om Perl–Prang Derm–Road 68B–Battambong
10	DIV 519	Prom Sou–Sou Hong	501-504-505	300	700	TmorPouk–Phnom Srok–East of Sisophorn
11	DIV 518	LorngTearm–Dorl Sa Reoun	502-503-507	130	530	East of Sisophorn–KroLanh–Phnom Srok–BanteayMeanchey
Military Region 4						
1	DIV 912	Peap–Heng	50-51-52-55-57	350	650	Varin–Angkor Chum–Siem Reap
2	DIV 980	Teum–Pav	91-92-93-94-95	350	750	Say Ler–SoutNikom–Chi Kreng–Siem Reap
3	DIV 616	Nhor Ron	14-15-16	200	500	KroYa–Sa Kream–Storng–Kompong Thom
4	DIV 612	Heoun–Chean	61-62-63	200	500	Cham San–Ku Leng–PreahVihear

(Continued)

179

No.	Unit[1]	Name of commander	Regiments (Numeric designation)	Number of troops	Number of guerrilla	Total	Area of Activities
5	DIV 919	Cheun	18-19	150	200	350	Border of PreahVihear–Siem Reap–Cham San
6	DIV 607			200	300	500	Road 12–SornDanh–Kompong Thom
7	DIV 802	Chhun–Deoun	54-55-57-58-59	300	100	400	Bara–East of SornDanh–Kompong Thom
Military Region 2							
1	DIV 801	Keo–Sot	84-85-86-88	50	200	250	KohSotinh–OraingOev–TboungMkom–Kompong Cham
2	DIV 920	Kanh–Seoung–EkBoret	91-92-93-94-96-97-98	200	300	500	Memot–Tsourl–Kompong Cham border of Kratia
3	DIV 417	Chum–Veoun	71-72-73-74-75	170	300	470	Prey Chor–Baray–ChomkaLer–Kompong Cham
Military Region 1							
1	DIV 709	Korn–Tem	65-66-67	200	300	500	SteungTraeng–MondolKiri
2	Independent Battalion 105	Ron		150	100	250	MondolKiri–KohNhaek
Total			102	7,020	9,010	16,030	

Major-General Dom Hak, Annual report of Khmer Rouge activities from November 25, 1993 to October 25, 1994, December 22, 1994.

Source: Reproduced with permission from Nem Sowath, *Civil War Termination in Cambodia.*

[1] It is to be noted that the Khmer Rouge's "Division" was understrength and the number is not commensurate with standard divisions. It was either used as a propaganda tool to inflate the number or as a skeletal structure in anticipation of future recruits.

Notes

PREFACE

1. In fact, many suggest that the letter "S" in "SOP" is actually "Standing," meaning each situation will have its own SOP and there is no single "Standard" that can apply to many different situations.

2. For a good introduction of organizational theory, one can check Graham Allison's famous article on the Cuban Missile Crisis ("Conceptual Models and the Cuban Missiles Crisis," *The American Political Science Review* 63, no. 3 (Sept. 1969): 689–718), especially the section on "organizational process" on page 698. Some terms are not the same as used here but the general tenets of the theory are the same. Also see, Barry Posen, *The Sources of Military Doctrine: France, Britain, and Germany between the World Wars*. Ithaca: Cornell University Press, 1986.

3. On this matter, the readers might be interested to read two classic pieces: Barry Posen's *The Sources of Military Doctrine* and Jack Snyder's *The Ideology of the Offensive: Military Decision Making and the Disaster of 1914*. Vol. 2. Ithaca: Cornell University Press, 1989.

4. Stephen Peter Rosen, *Winning the Next War: Innovation and the Modern Military*. Ithaca: Cornell University Press, 1994.

5. Blight, James G., and Janet M. Lang. *The Fog of War: Lessons from the Life of Robert S. Mcnamara*. Lanham: Rowman & Littlefield, 2005.

6. The "National Liberation Front" (NLF) was the anti-American resistance movement indigenous in South Vietnam. However, it was well known by its alternative name, Viet Cong. Unlike the Khmer Rouge which was originally a neutral term, the term "Viet Cong" was, from the outset, a derogatory term employed by Ngo Dinh Diem to sully the communist movement. The term was either contracted from Việt Nam Cộng-sản (Vietnamese Communists) or Việt gian cộng sản (Communist Traitor to Vietnam). A parallel term, the People's Army of Vietnam (PAVN) or Vietnamese People's Army (VPA), was also much more known by its alternative name, the North Vietnamese Army (NVA).

Most Western journalists are normally the ones who propagate the use of the wrong terms. In this book, I would be using the historically correct name, the NLF and the PAVN or VPA.

7. Andrew Krepinevich, *The Army and Vietnam*. Baltimore: Johns Hopkins University Press, 1988.

8. However, John Nagl (*Learning to Eat Soup with a Knife*) argued instead that the British won mainly because the organization can easily learn to adapt to new situations.

9. Barry Posen, *The Sources of Military Doctrine*.

10. In some versions, the name was written as "Kampuchea United Front for National Salvation." The Khmer term "samaky" is more correctly translated as "solidarity." However, the two terms have negligible difference in Khmer.

11. "What is Khmer Rouge," *Searching for the Truth*, No. 6, June 2000.

12. Ibid.

13. Ibid.

CHAPTER 1

1. Dmitry Mosyakov, *Khmer Rouge and the Vietnamese Communists: A History of Their Relations as Told in the Soviet Archives*. Translated by DC-Cam, 2000.

2. "Black Paper: The 'Indochina Federation Strategy' of Ho Chi Minh's Indochina Communist Party," Office of propaganda and information, Ministry of Foreign Affairs, Democratic Kampuchea, *Search for the Truth*, No. 9, September 2000.

3. Ben Kiernan, *How Pol Pot Came to Power: Colonialism, Nationalism, and Communism in Cambodia, 1930–1975*. New Haven: Yale University Press, 2004.

4. Ibid.

5. Ibid.

6. Ibid.

7. Ben Kiernan, *How Pol Pot Came to Power*.

8. Peter Paret, ed., *Makers of Modern Strategy from Machiavelli to the Nuclear Age*. Princeton: Princeton University Press, 2008.

9. Dmitry Mosyakov, *Khmer Rouge and the Vietnamese Communists: A History of Their Relations as Told in the Soviet Archives*. Translated by Documentation Center of Cambodia. New Haven: Yale Ctr For International Area St, 2000.

10. Ibid.

11. Nayan Chanda, *Brother Enemy: The War after the War*. New York: Collier Books, 1988.

12. Dmitry Mosyakov, *Khmer Rouge and the Vietnamese Communists*.

13. Ibid.

14. Ibid.

15. Ibid.

16. David Chandler, *Pol Pot: Brother Number One: A Political Biography of Pol Pot*. Boulder: Westview Press, 1999.

17. Nayan Chanda, *Brother Enemy*, p. 42.

18. Kenton J Clymer, "The Perils of Neutrality," *Searching for the Truth*, No. 3, March 2000, DC-Cam, pp. 22–23.

19. Ibid., Nayan Chanda, *Brother Enemy*, and Meyer, *Derrière le sourire Khmer*. Paris: Plon, 1971.

20. Nayan Chanda, *Brother Enemy*.

21. Ibid.

22. Kenton J Clymer, "The Perils of Neutrality."

23. Ibid.

24. David Chandler, "Revising the Past in Democratic Kampuchea," *Pacific Affairs*, 1983. Mosyakov, on the other hand, concurred on the new charter but did not mention the name.

25. Dmitry Mosyakov, *Khmer Rouge and the Vietnamese Communists.*

26. Interviews with Nuon Chea in 2005, presented as Annex in Diep Sophal, *Cambodia's Tragedy* (Khmer language).

27. Dmitry Mosyakov, *Khmer Rouge and the Vietnamese Communists.*

28. David Chandler, "Revising the Past in Democratic Kampuchea," and Timothy Carney (editor), *Communist Party Power in Cambodia: Documents and Discussion.* Vol. 106. Ithaca: Cornell University Southeast Asia Program, 1977.

29. Dy Khamboly, *A History of Democratic Kampuchea (1975–1979).* Documentation Center of Cambodia, 2007.

30. David Chandler, *Voices from S-21: Terror and History in Pol Pot's Secret Prison.* Berkeley: University of California Press, 2000.

31. Dmitry Mosyakov, *Khmer Rouge and the Vietnamese Communists.*

32. Peter Paret, ed., *Makers of Modern Strategy.*

33. David Kilcullen, *The Accidental Guerilla: Fighting Small Wars in the Midst of a Big One.* New York: Oxford University Press, 2009.

34. Nem Sowath, *The Tea Banh Story: Revolution in a Distant Village.* Phnom Penh: Reaho Publishing, 2007.

35. David Chandler, *Pol Pot, Brother Number One.*

36. Ibid.

37. Vandy Kaonn, *History of Cambodia (1863–1992).* Phnom Penh: Unknown publisher, 2008.

38. Ben Kiernan, *How Pol Pot Came to Power.*

39. Charles Meyer, *Derrière le sourire Khmère.*

40. Marie Alexandrine Martin, *Le Mal Cambodgien.* Mesnil-sur-l'Estrée. Phnom Penh: Société Nouvelle Firmin-Didot-Hachette, 1989.

41. Ibid.

42. When I use the term "soldiers" I would like to caution that it was probably not the Forces Armées Royales Khmères (FARK) who ordered such actions but only a small segment that was sent there that abused the power and betrayed the uniform of the FARK. Similarly, only a few local authorities were corrupt, but those were enough to cause trouble.

43. Charles Meyer, *Derrière le sourire Khmer.*

44. Marie Alexandrine Martin, *Le Mal Cambodgien.*

45. Vandy Kaonn, *History of Cambodia.*

46. Charles Meyer, *Derrière le Sourire Khmer.*

47. Ben Kiernan, *How Pol Pot Came to Power.*

48. Charles Meyer, *Derrière le Sourire Khmer.*

49. Marie Alexandrine Martin, *Le Mal Cambodgien.*

50. Vandy Kaonn, *History of Cambodia.*

51. Charles Meyer, *Derrière le Sourire Khmer,* and Marie Alexandrine Martin, *Le Mal Cambodgien.*

52. Charles Meyer, *Derrière le Sourire Khmer,* and Ben Kiernan, *How Pol Pot Came to Power.*

53. Ibid.; David Chandler, *Pol Pot, Brother Number One.*

54. Vandy Kaonn, *History of Cambodia*, and Marie Alexandrine Martin, *Le Mal Cambodgien*.

55. Charles Meyer, *Derrière le Sourire Khmer*.

56. In Sutsakhan, Sak. *Khmer Republic at War and the Final Collapse*. Washington, DC: U.S. Army Center of Military History, 1980, the operation was dubbed "Operation TEST VC/NVA." Its main objective was to test the strength of the NLF/VPA in the area, and if necessary, to seek to destroy them.

57. Interviews, PP-C-DD-041111.

58. Charles Meyer, *Derrière le Sourire Khmer*.

59. Ibid.

60. Dmitry Mosyakov, *Khmer Rouge and the Vietnamese Communists*.

61. Ibid.

62. See for example, Mark Moyar, *Pheonix and the Birds of Prey: The CIA's Secret Campaign to Destroy the Viet Cong*. Annapolis: Naval Institute Press, 1997 and Robert M. Gillespie, *Black Ops Vietnam: The Operational History of MACVSOG*. Annapolis: U.S. Naval Institute Press, 2011.

63. Dmitry Mosyakov, *Khmer Rouge and the Vietnamese Communists*.

64. David Chandler, *Pol Pot, Brother Number One*.

65. Ibid.

66. Dmitry Mosyakov, *Khmer Rouge and the Vietnamese Communists*.

67. David Chandler, *Pol Pot, Brother Number One*.

68. Ibid.

69. Ibid.

70. Ibid.

71. Interviews with Nuon Chea in 2005, presented as Annex in Diep Sophal, *Cambodia's Tragedy*.

72. Interviews, PP-C-DD-041111.

73. Sak Sutsakhan, *The Khmer Republic and Its Final Collapse*.

74. According to Mosyakov, the veterans of the KPRP mentioned that Pol Pot probably changed the name of the KPRP to CPK in 1963. But in 1977, Pol Pot publicly declared that the official date for the founding of the CPK was September 30, 1960.

75. A face-to-face meeting between Prince Sihanouk and the general population to address their grievances.

76. Chantrabot, Ros. *La République Khmère*. Paris: Editions L'Harmattan, 1993.

77. Ibid.

78. Ibid.

79. Interviews, PP-C-DD-041111.

80. Ros Chantrabot, *La République Khmère*.

81. Ibid.

82. Prince Norodom Sihanouk, *My War with the CIA: The Memoirs of Prince Norodom Sihanouk*. New York: Pantheon Books, 1973.

83. Ros Chantrabot, *La République Khmère*.

84. Ibid.

85. Interviews, PP-C-DD-041111.

86. Charles Meyer, *Derrière le Sourire Khmer*.

87. Interviews, PP-C-DD-041111.

88. Ros Chantrabot, *La République Khmère*.

89. William Shawcross, *Sideshow: Kissinger, Nixon and the Destruction of Cambodia*. New York: Simon and Schuster, 1979.

90. Prince Norodom Sihanouk, *My War with the CIA*, p. 62.

91. He was appointed prime minister after Lon Nol resigned due to the troubles in Samlot. Lon Nol succeeded him less than a year later.

92. Nayan Chanda, *Brother Enemy*.

93. "King-Father," a variant of how the people addressed Prince Sihanouk.

94. Interviews, AV-O-KR-DV920–070711.

95. Henri Locard, *Pol Pot's Little Red Book: The Saying of Angkar*. Chiang Mai: Silkworm Books, 2004.

96. In English: Khmer National Armed Forces.

97. Marie Alexandrine Martin, *Le Mal Cambodgien*.

98. See for example the case in Koh Kong province, in Nem Sowath, *The Tea Banh Story*.

99. Ros Chantrabot, *La République Khmère*.

100. Interviews, PP-C-DD-221211.

101. David Burns Sigler, *Vietnam Battle Chronology: US Army and Marine Corps Combat Operations, 1965–1973*. Jefferson: McFarland & Co Inc Pub, 1992.

102. Sak Sutsakhan, *The Khmer Republic and Its Final Collapse*.

103. Interviews, PP-C-DD-221211.

104. Sak Sutsakhan, *The Khmer Republic and Its Final Collapse*.

105. Ibid.

106. Interviews, PP-C-DD-041111.

107. Sak Sutsakhan, *The Khmer Republic and Its Final Collapse*.

108. Ros Chantrabot, *La République Khmère*.

109. Interviews, PP-C-DD-041111.

110. Sak Sutsakhan, *The Khmer Republic and Its Final Collapse*.

111. Interviews, PP-C-DD-041111.

112. Sak Sutsakhan, *The Khmer Republic and Its Final Collapse*.

113. Ibid.

114. Interviews, PP-C-DD-041111.

115. David Chandler, *Pol Pot, Brother Number One*.

116. Interviews, PP-C-DD-041111.

117. Ibid.

118. Ros Chantrabot, *La République Khmère*.

119. Robert Pape, *Bombing to Win: Air Power and the Coercion in War*. Ithaca: Cornell University Press, 1996.

120. Vo Nguyen Giap, "People's War, People's Army." DTIC Document, 1962.

121. Ben Kiernan, *How Pol Pot Came to Power*.

122. Interviews, TK-KR-S-070712. Also see Nem Sowath, *The Tea Banh Story*

123. Nem Sowath, *Revolution in a Distant Village*.

124. Interviews, TK-KR-S-070712.

125. Ibid.

126. Interviews, TK-KR-S-070712, AV-KR-DV920–270811, and PP-KR-R20-S-150712.

127. Say Bory, *Droit Administratif Général*. Phnom Penh: Lotus Publishing, 2000.

128. *Searching for the Truth*, No. 33, September 2003. The full text was published in 1973 entitled (in Khmer) "Lamenting the Khmer Soul." Carney and Becker both provide an overview of the text. However, I saw a slightly different interpretation of that text.

129. Larry Addington, *Patterns of War since the Eighteen Century*. Bloomington: Indiana University Press, 1994.

130. Timothy Colton, *Commissars, Commanders, and Civilian Authority: The Structure of Soviet Military Politics*. Vol. 79. Cambridge, MA: Harvard University Press, 1979.

131. Ibid.

132. Elizabeth Becker, *When the War Was Over: Cambodia and the Khmer Rouge Revolution*. New York: Public Affairs, 1998.

133. Huy Vannak, *The Khmer Rouge Division 703: From Victory to Self-destruction*. Translated by Rich Arant. Edited by Cougill Wynne. Phnom Penh: Documentation Center of Cambodia, 2003.

134. Ibid.

135. For a complete description, see John Keegan, *Intelligence in War*. New York: Vintage Digital, 2010.

136. Interviews, PP-C-DD-111109.

CHAPTER 2

1. The official name was "Kampuchean Revolutionary Army" (Korng Toap Pakdeiwath Kampuchea). The confessor made a mistake, please do not confuse with the armed forces of the Phnom Penh government after 1979, the Kampuchean People's Revolutionary Armed Forces (KPRAF).

2. Quoted from Huy Vannak, *From Victory to Self-destruction*. Like many other prisoners who confessed at S-21, comrade Teanh did not survive despite his plea.

3. Nayan Chanda, *Brother Enemy*.

4. Ros Chantrabot, *La République Khmère*.

5. Quote from *Le Monde* in Ros Chantrabot, *La République Khmère*.

6. Ros Chantrabot, *La République Khmère*.

7. David Chandler, *Pol Pot, Brother Number One*.

8. "Phnom Penh Liberation," *Searching for the Truth*, No. 4, April 2000.

9. Charles Meyer, *Derrière le Sourire Khmer*.

10. Ros Chantrabot, *La République Khmère*.

11. Ponchaud, François. *Cambodge Année Zéro*. Paris: Julliard, 1977; and Philip Short, *Pol Pot, Anatomy of a Nightmare*. New York: Holt Paperbacks, 2006.

12. Ros Chantrabot, *La République Khmère*.

13. David Chandler, *Pol Pot, Brother Number One*.

14. "Phnom Penh Liberation," *Searching for the Truth*.

15. Ibid.

16. Ibid.

17. François Ponchaud, *Cambodge année zero*.

18. "Phnom Penh Liberation," *Searching for the Truth*.

19. Dy Khamboly, *History of Democratic Kampuchea*.

20. Ibid.

21. Marie Alexandrine Martin, *Le Mal Cambodgien*.

22. Dy Khamboly, *History of Democratic Kampuchea*.

23. "Constitution of Democratic Kampuchea," DC-Cam collection.

24. Normally, a constitution does not mention a political party. But in the communist regime, the party is unique in that it is the only party and most constitutions mention it.

25. Dy Khamboly, *History of Democratic Kampuchea*.

26. Marie Alexandrine Martin, *Le Mal Cambodgien*.

27. Dy Khamboly, *History of Democratic Kampuchea*.

28. Nayan Chanda, *Brother Enemy*, p. 39.

29. Prince Norodom Sihanouk, *Norodom Sihanouk, Prisonnier des Khmers Rouges.*

30. Nayan Chanda, *Brother Enemy,* p. 43.

31. "Decisions of the Central Committee," by Chuong Sophearith, *Searching for the Truth,* no. 26, February 2002.

32. "Chum Manh: a Survivor of the S-21," by Som Sorya, *Searching for the Truth,* no. 22, October 2001.

33. "Decisions of the Central Committee," *Searching for the Truth.*

34. David Chandler, *Voices from S-21.* One veteran of the KPRP, Keo Meas, was arrested and sent to be tortured at S-21. In the confession note, he was forced to admit that the Workers' Party of Kampuchea was created to oppose and undermine the CPK.

35. "Decisions of the Central Committee," *Searching for the Truth.*

36. Sok Vannak (DC-Cam), "Koh Tral under the Khmer Rouge Regime," *Rasmey Kampuchea Daily,* August 26, 2012.

37. Ibid.

38. "The Standing Committee Meeting, 9 October, 1975," *Searching for the Truth.*

39. Chuong Sophearith, "Standing Committee Meetings on Defense," *Searching for the Truth,* no. 23, November 2001.

40. Ibid.

41. "Decisions of the Central Committee," *Searching for the Truth.*

42. "The Standing Committee Meeting, 9 October, 1975," *Searching for the Truth.*

43. "Standing Committee Meetings on Defense," *Searching for the Truth.*

44. Nayan Chanda, *Brother Enemy,* and Dmitry Mosyakov, *Khmer Rouge and the Vietnamese Communists.*

45. "Report about the situation of military assistance from Comrade China," September 27, 1977, File: D01858, DC-Cam.

46. "The Standing Committee Meeting, 9 October, 1975," *Searching for the Truth.*

47. International Rice Research Institute, *Rice Statistics.* http://www.irri.org/index.php?option=com_k2&view=itemlist&layout=category&task=category&id=744&Itemid=100346&lang=en

48. Dy Khamboly, *History of Democratic Kampuchea.*

49. Ibid.

50. David Chandler, *Voices from S-21.*

51. Conversation with Lt. Gen. Nem Sowath, November 18, 2011.

52. David Chandler, *Pol Pot, Brother Number One.*

53. Huy Vannak, *From Victory to Self-destruction.*

54. "Statistics of Total Forces," File: L00065, DC-Cam.

55. Nayan Chanda, *Brother Enemy.*

56. Dmitry Mosyakov, *Khmer Rouge and the Vietnamese Communists.*

57. "Statistics of total forces," File: L00065, DC-Cam.

58. The total number of regional troops and militias is not clear because the documents are incomplete. Moreover, after sensing an impending purge, some units in the East Zone were upgraded beyond the standard allowance and we could not trace the correct number. Only the total number of troops under Central is clear.

59. Elizabeth Becker, *When the War Was Over.*

60. Huy Vannak, *From Victory to Self-destruction.*

61. Ibid.; and Dy Khamboly, *A History of Democratic Kampuchea.*

62. Dy Khamboly, *A History of Democratic Kampuchea.*

63. Huy Vannak, *From Victory to Self-destruction.*

64. David Chandler, *Voices from S-21.*

65. Much of what we know about this notorious chief of S-21 comes from two sources. The first one is Nic Dunlop's book, *The Lost Executioner,* where he tracked down Duch and then interviewed him. It was Dunlop who found out who Duch really was after the fall of Democratic Kampuchea. Duch was later indicted by the Extraordinary Chamber in the Court of Cambodia (ECCC), also known as the Khmer Rouge tribunal. The second source of information about Duch as well as the functioning of the S-21 is David Chandler's *Voices from S-21,* focused on the functioning of the prison.

66. Trial Chamber Judgement, *Case 001, Kaing Guek Eav, alias Duch.*

67. Ibid.

68. David Chandler, *Brother Number One.*

69. Trial Chamber Judgement, *Case 001, Kaing Guek Eav, alias Duch.*

70. David Chandler, *Voices from S-21.* For firsthand accounts, see "Chum Manh: A Survivor of the S-21," by Som Sorya, *Searching for the Truth,* no. 22, October 2001 and Vann Nath, *A Cambodian Prison Portrait: One Year in the Khmer Rouge's S-21.* Bangkok: White Lotus, 1998.

71. Dy Khamboly, *A History of Democratic Kampuchea.*

72. Trial Chamber Judgement, *Case 001, Kaing Guek Eav, alias Duch.*

73. Ibid.

74. "Chum Manh: A Survivor of the S-21," by Som Sorya, *Searching for the Truth,* No. 22, October 2001.

75. This is a territory known as Cochin China; it was Cambodian but it was ceded by the French to Vietnam after they left Indochina. The Khmer Rouge made it their mission to recover the land, known in Cambodia as Kampuchea Krom or Lower Cambodia. The prisoners were not allowed to use Kampuchea Krom to make an emotional appeal to the guards or interrogators. Interestingly, when the Khmer Rouge invaded Vietnam in 1977, they paid more attention to the liberation of the "land" but killed any ethnic Cambodians in Kampuchea Krom they encountered. They sought to liberate only the land, not the "people." To the Khmer Rouge, they were all Vietnamese.

76. Dy Khamboly, *A History of Democratic Kampuchea.*

77. David Chandler, *Voices from S-21.*

78. Trial Chamber Judgement announced on July 26, 2010, *Case 001, Kaing Guek Eav, alias Duch.*

79. Marie Alexandrine Martin, *Le Mal Cambodgien*; David Chandler, *Pol Pot, Brother Number One*; François Ponchaud, *Cambodge année zero*; and Philip Short, *Pol Pot, A History of a Nightmare.* These works provided a very good description and overview.

80. David Chandler, *Pol Pot, Brother Number One.*

81. Dy Khamboly, *History of Democratic Kampuchea.*

82. "Interview with Nou Khav, living in Peam Chimiet village, Nankhiloek Sub-District, Koh Nhek District, Mondul Kiri," File: D24374, DC-Cam.

83. Dy Khamboly, *A History of Democratic Kampuchea.*

84. "Interview with Comrade Ung Sem, permanent member in Prey Kabas District," document D00011, DC-Cam.

85. Huy Vannak, *From Victory to Self-destruction.*

86. "A pure society is one without money," Huy Sophorn, *Searching for the Truth,* No. 26, February 2002.

87. Ibid.

88. Ibid.

89. Vann Nath, *A Cambodian Prison Portrait.*

90. Dy Khamboly, *A History of Democratic Kampuchea.*

CHAPTER 3

1. "Dear Beloved and Respected Angkar [from the Southwest Zone]," File: D01610, DC-Cam.

2. See "Telegram 1," File: D01971, DC-Cam. The telegram was sent to Office 870, which was the cabinet office of Pol Pot, but it was addressed to "Dear elder brother Por," in which it is highly likely that "Por" was an incomplete name for "Pol," an alias of Pol Pot. In the Khmer language, "Por" only needs another single consonant to produce "Pol." We did not know the detail, but it was either a spelling mistake or a contraction of the alias (which, in itself, was already a contraction of the real name).

3. "Telegram 98," May 7, 1977, File: N0001422, DC-Cam.

4. "Dear Beloved Office 870," August 14, 1977, File: D01757; "Situation along the border, Region 23," August 14, 1977, File: D01772; DC-Cam. The first one was the report about the arrest of one deserter and the second report was about the Vietnamese drifters.

5. Ralph Wetterhahn, *The Last Battle.*

6. Ibid.

7. Elizabeth Becker, *When the War Was Over.*

8. Ieng Sary's interview on September 6, 1975, in New York. Quoted in "Ieng Sary and the Mayaguez Incident," *Searching for the Truth,* No. 2, February 2000, p. 29.

9. Ibid.

10. Elizabeth Becker; *When the War Was Over.*

11. Peter Paret and Michael Howard, eds., *Makers of Modern Strategies.*

12. For a debate on this issue, see John J. Mearsheimer, "Assessing the Conventional Balance: The 3:1 Rule and Its Critics," *International Security* 13, No. 4 (Spring 1989); and Joshua M Epstein, "The 3:1 Rule, the Adaptive Dynamic Model, and the Future of Security Studies," *International Security* 13, No. 4 (Spring 1989).

13. Kenneth M. Pollack, *Arabs at War: Military Effectiveness, 1948-1991.* Lincoln: Bison Books, 2004.

14. U.S. Census Bureau, http://www.census.gov/population/international/data/idb/region.php, accessed on October 28, 2012.

15. For a definition and exposé on military effectiveness, see Allan Millet and Williamson Murray, eds., *Military Effectiveness.* Vol. 3. Cambridge: Cambridge University Press, 2010.

16. U.S. Census Bureau, http://www.census.gov/population/international/data/idb/region.php, accessed on October 28, 2012.

17. "Black Paper: The 'Indochina Federation Strategy' of Ho Chi Minh's Indochina Communist Party," Office of propaganda and information, Ministry of Foreign Affairs, Democratic Kampuchea, *Search for the Truth,* No. 9, September 2000.

18. Ibid., p. 41.

19. Deterrence might be a third possibility, and a smarter move that would involve the Khmer Rouge not attacking Vietnam but using other stronger powers like China to deter any Vietnamese initiative. But existing archives do not point to this possibility.

20. Please refer to the Appendix 4 on the radio broadcast concerning "DK's defensive strategy."

21. DC-Cam collections.

22. According to Michael Vickery (*Why Vietnam Invaded Cambodia*), the Khmer Rouge did not succeed in pushing the Vietnamese out during the campaign in late 1977 but it was Vietnam who withdrew.

23. Elizabeth Becker, *When the War Was Over.*

24. Ibid.

25. Ibid.

26. For the application of psychology in political science and international relations, see Deborah Welch Larson, *Origins of Containment: A Psychological Explanation.* Princeton: Princeton University Press, 1989; and Robert Jervis, Richard Ned Lebow, and Janice Gross Stein, *Psychology and Deterrence.* Baltimore: Johns Hopkins University Press, 1989.

27. Huy Vannak, *From Victory to Self-destruction.*

28. Ibid.

29. Duch himself claimed it was out of fear. See, Trial Chamber Judgement announced on July 26, 2010, *Case 001, Kaing Guek Eav, alias Duch.*

30. David Chandler, *Voices from S-21.*

31. Ibid.

32. Ibid.

33. Elizabeth Becker; *When the War Was Over.*

34. David Chandler, *Voices from S-21.*

35. Sann Kalyan, "Hu Nim, a Prisoner of Angkar," *Searching for the Truth,* No. 24, December 2001, pp. 2–4.

36. Elizabeth Becker, *When the War Was Over;* and David Chandler, *Voices from S-21.*

37. David Chandler, *Voices from S-21.*

38. Dy Camboly, *A History of Democratic Kampuchea.*

39. David Chandler, *Voices from S-21.*

40. Ibid.

41. Ibid.

42. Andrew Mertha, "Surrealpolitik: The Experience of Chinese Experts in Democratic Kampuchea, 1975–1979," *Cross-Current: East Asian History and Culture Review* E-journal No. 4 (September 2012).

43. David Chandler, *Voices from S-21.*

44. Nayan Chanda, *Brother Enemy.*

45. See the series of meetings on defense in the previous chapter.

46. Stephen Morris, *Why Vietnam Invaded Kampuchea: Political Culture and the Causes of War.* Stanford: Stanford University Press, 1999; and Huy Vannak, *From Victory to Self-destruction.*

47. Dy Camboly, *A History of Democratic Kampuchea.*

48. The full extent of the meeting can be gauged from "Telegram 79," File: L0001099, DC-Cam. Like other archive materials, each quote here is presented with the full context.

49. Ibid., p. 2.

50. "Telegram 20," March 3, 1976, File: L0001145, DC-Cam.

51. Telegram 25 suggests that division 920 was in the fight that led to a subsequent negotiation. See "Telegram 25," March 7, 1976, File: L0001151, DC-Cam.

52. Ibid.

53. Ibid.

54. "Report from division 801 to 89 (general staff office)," March 24, 1977, File: L0000058, DC-Cam. The report summed up activities in the East and Northeast Zones and it divided up the report into two parts, the internal enemy situation and the external enemy situation. The latter section reported about flights of enemy planes and alleged Vietnamese agents.

55. "Dear Office 870," File: N0001423, DC-Cam.

56. For a full content, please see "Dear beloved and respected brother, from Chhean," April 29, 1977, File:L0001435, DC-Cam.

57. Ibid., p. 2.

58. See for example, Nayan Chanda, *Brother Enemy.*

59. Dmitry Mosyakov, *Khmer Rouge and the Vietnamese Communists.*

60. Stephen Morris, *Why Vietnam Invaded Kampuchea.*

61. Ibid.

62. See report on "Border Situation, Region 23," dated May 21, 1977, File: D01620, and "Enemy situation along the border, Region 23," dated May 29, 1977, File: D01621, DC-Cam.

63. The Khmer Rouge reports always made it clear that the encounters were the result of the "Vietnamese encroaching on our territory." The Vietnamese delegates also accused the Khmer Rouge of similar actions. Here, when I quote the report, I will quote the original text. Personally, however, I think one should exercise caution when reading these reports because the border issue at that time was a complicated issue and there had been no resolution to the disagreement between Democratic Kampuchea and Vietnam. In this book, with the limited amount of archive that I have, I do not intend to judge who encroached on whose territory, an issue that I will leave to other historians specializing in the border issue. Here, I will focus only on the military situation.

64. "Enemy situation along the border, Region 23," May 29, 1977, File: D01621 and "Enemy situation along the border, Region 23," May 30, 1977, File: D01622, DC-Cam.

65. "Border situation, Region 23," June 1, 1977, File: D01623, DC-Cam.

66. Nayan Chanda, *Brother Enemy.*

67. Stephen Morris, *Why Vietnam Invaded Cambodia.*

68. Nayan Chanda, *Brother Enemy.*

69. "Telegram 46," June 15, 1977, File: D01650, DC-Cam.

70. "Situation along the border, from Region 20," June 17–25 1977, File: D01644; "Situation along the border, from Region 20," August 8–10 1977, File: D01761; "Situation along the border, from Region 21," June 20–24, 1977, File: D01645; and "Situation along the border, from Region 23," May 29 to June 6, 1977, File: D01641; and "Situation along the border, from Region 23," July 2–5, 1977, File:D01768. All documents were obtained from the DC-Cam.

71. "Telegram of division 920 dated June 25 1977," File:D01704, DC-Cam.

72. "Situation along the border," June 14–18, 1977, File: D01648, DC-Cam.

73. No content is quoted out of context. If something is omitted, the whole sentence or paragraph will also be omitted. I took great care in adhering to the original meaning in the letter.

74. "Telegram 56," July 20, 1977, File: D01749, DC-Cam.

75. Region 23 reported that they had received a letter from the district chief in Tay Ninh province on August 15, 1977. See document number: D01753, DC-Cam.

76. At this point, it was unclear what troops were used by the Khmer Rouge to attack Vietnam. We do not have the internal reports from the activities of the divisions of the Central Committee and the archive that is currently available contains mostly the reports of the regional and local troops. Therefore, I also relied on secondary literature to fill in the gaps.

77. "Telegram 68," August 30, 1977, File:D01780, DC-Cam. Based on the address and content, it is most likely that this is a message from the embassy of Democratic Kampuchea in Hanoi.

78. Ibid., p. 2.

79. Stephen Morris, *Why Vietnam Invaded Cambodia.*

80. "Dear beloved Office 81," undated (likely late 1977 because it mentioned a treaty between Vietnam and Germany in December 1977), File: D01830, DC-Cam.

81. Ibid.

82. Elizabeth Becker, *When the War Was Over.*

83. Interview with a former battalion commander of Region 20 (Phnom Penh, August 13, 2012).

84. They should be valid, until newly disclosed archives contradict them, which I think is unlikely.

85. "Blitzkrieg" is German for "lightning war." It was reportedly developed independently by English, French, and German thinkers but it was the Germans who were the first to apply such a tactic in World War II. The tactic called for fast movement to achieve breakthrough in narrow sectors and penetrate deep behind enemy lines and cause havoc on the logistics lines, communication and reserve. Once this occurs, the front line of the enemy will collapse not because they are beaten but because the command structure is broken down and thrown into confusion. This tactic therefore calls for the independent use of armored, mechanized units and motorized infantry. Artillery and air support must be constantly provided to compensate for the lack of infantry support.

86. "Telegram 54," October 26, 1977, File: D01893, DC-Cam.

87. "Telegram 55," October 26, 1977, File: D01888; "Telegram 56," October 26, 1977, File: D01889; "Telegram 57," October 27, 1977, File: D01892; "Telegram 58," October 27, 1977, File: D01891. All documents were obtained from the DC-Cam.

88. This technique and agility was later used by the Khmer Rouge with deadly efficiency when fighting in the 1980s and 1990s.

89. "Telegram 59," October 28, 1977, File: D01886, DC-Cam.

90. Telegram 60," October 29, 1977, File: D01887, DC-Cam.

91. "Telegram 76," November 13, 1977, File: D01798, DC-Cam.

92. "Telegram 82," November 18, 1977, File: D01816, DC-Cam.

93. "Telegram 85," November 19, 1977, File: D01855, DC-Cam.

94. "Telegram 83," December 6, 1977, File: D01845, DC-Cam.

95. "Telegram 85," December 7, 1977, File: D01844, DC-Cam.

96. "Telegram 1," December 22, 1977, File: D01971, DC-Cam.

97. "Telegram 07," December 23, 1977 (19:30), File: D01975, DC-Cam.

98. "Telegram 06," December 23, 1977 (19:45), File: D01972, DC-Cam. This telegram was sent later than the previous one but was received by Office 870 one day earlier. That is the reason why this one was marked Telegram 06.

99. "Telegram 08," December 24, 1977, File: D01974, DC-Cam.

100. "Telegram 3," December 24, 1977, File: D01973, DC-Cam.

101. "Le Cambodge aurait lancé une offensive dans la province vietnamienne de Tay Ninh," *Le Monde*, February 26–27, 1978. The newspaper mentioned that the number was given by a "reliable source" to a representative of AFP.

102. Stephen Morris, *Why Vietnam Invaded Cambodia.*

103. See *Searching for the Truth* magazine, Special Issue 107, November 2008.

104. Interview with a former battalion commander of Region 20 (Phnom Penh, August 13, 2012).

105. Ibid.

106. Alexander Hinton, *Why Did They Kill? Cambodia in the Shadow of Genocide.* Vol. 11. Berkeley: University of California Press, 2004.

107. "Telegram 11," May 6, 1978, File: D02127, DC-Cam.

108. "Le Cambodge aurait lancé une offensive dans la province vietnamienne de Tay Ninh," *Le Monde,* February 26–27, 1978.

CHAPTER 4

1. Speech by *Samdech* Hun Sen, "Comments at the graduation in Vanda Institute," December 22, 2008.

2. Harish and Julie Mehta, *Hun Sen: Strongman of Cambodia.* Singapore: Graham Brash, 1999.

3. Speech of *Samdech Techo* Prime Minister Hun Sen, during the "Commemoration ceremony of fallen veterans and the inauguration of the historical Memory Statue at the former location of Unit 125, the source of the armed forces of Cambodia under the command of comrade Hun Sen," Dong Nai province, January 2, 2012.

4. "Telegram 79," dated January 7, 1976, from comrade Buth, File: L0001099, DC-Cam.

5. Speech of *Samdech Techo* Prime Minister Hun Sen, "Commemoration ceremony of fallen veterans."

6. Harish and Julie Mehta, *Hun Sen: Strongman of Cambodia.*

7. Speech of *Samdech Techo* Prime Minister Hun Sen, "Commemoration ceremony of fallen veterans."

8. Ibid.

9. Ibid.

10. See previous chapter.

11. Comrade Hun Sen would only reunite with his family after 1979.

12. Speech of *Samdech Techo* Prime Minister Hun Sen, "Commemoration ceremony of fallen veterans."

13. Ibid.

14. Nayan Chanda, *Brother Enemy.*

15. Ibid., p. 216.

16. "Instructions of [Office] 870," January 3, 1978, File: D01993, DC-Cam.

17. "Telegram 18," January 19, 1978, File: D02017, DC-Cam.

18. Huy Vannak, *From Victory to Self-destruction.*

19. "Le Cambodge aurait lancé une offensive dans la province vietnamienne de Tay Ninh," *Le Monde,* February 26–27, 1978. The newspaper mentioned that the number was given by a "reliable source" to a representative of AFP.

20. Huy Vannak, *From Victory to Self-destruction.*

21. "Telegram 20," April 26, 1978, File:D02120, DC-Cam.

22. Nayan Chanda, *Brother Enemy.*

23. See for example, "Telegram 2," April 12, 1978, File:D02107, DC-Cam.

24. Speech of *Samdech Techo* Prime Minister Hun Sen, "Commemoration ceremony of fallen veterans."

25. Ibid.

26. Ibid.

27. The descriptions reveal that these units probably performed as armed reconnaissance units.

28. Ibid.

29. Ibid.

30. Nem Sowath, *The Tea Banh Story.*

31. Ibid.

32. "Confessions and Telegrams related to Ke Pauk," *Searching for the Truth*, No. 27, March 2002, p. 11.

33. Antitank ammunitions, recoilless rifle rounds, antitank mines and antipersonnel mines figured prominently on the list of requests to the Central Committee. See "Telegram 3," April 12, 1978, File: D02109, and "Telegram 20," April 26, 1978, File: D02120, DC-Cam.

34. Huy Vannak, *From Victory to Self-destruction.*

35. "Telegram 19," April 8, 1978, File: D02103, DC-Cam.

36. "Telegram 20," April 26, 1978, File: D02120, DC-Cam.

37. "Telegram 11," May 6, 1978, File: D02127, DC-Cam.

38. Huy Vannak, *From Victory to Self-destruction.*

39. "Telegram 54," April 23, 1978, File: D02118, DC-Cam.

40. Huy Vannak, *From Victory to Self-destruction.*

41. Ibid.

42. Ibid.

43. Interview, PP-KR-R20-C-130812.

44. Nayan Chanda, *Brother Enemy.* My interviews and conversations with various former commanders and cadres who were also victims in the same wave of purges confirmed Chanda's accounts.

45. Ibid.

46. Ibid., and Stephen Morris, *Why Vietnam Invaded Cambodia.* This account of what happened to Sor Phim was confirmed by many eyewitness interviews.

47. Speech of *Samdech Techo* Prime Minister Hun Sen, "Commemoration ceremony of fallen veterans."

48. Ibid.

49. Ibid.

50. Nayan Chanda, *Brother Enemy.*

51. Sihanouk, Norodom, and Simonne Lacouture. *Prisonnier des Khmers Rouges.* Paris: Hachette littérature générale, 1986.

52. Ibid.

53. Ibid.

54. Ibid.

55. Ibid., pp. 358–59.

56. Ibid.

57. Ibid., p. 359.

58. Nayan Chanda, *Brother Enemy.* According to Chanda, one team of Vietnamese special forces was sent in after the prince had already been evacuated out of the country by the Khmer Rouge. Chanda claimed the team was decimated. But my conversation with a relative of a Vietnamese soldier involved in the operation revealed that before the combat team went in, a forward, noncombat, reconnaissance team had already gone in to scout the approach. This team survived but lacked the capability to change the situation.

59. Nicholas Regaud, *Le Cambodge dans la tourmente: Le Troisième Conflit Indochinois 1978-1991.* Paris: Harmattan, 1992.

About the Author

Lt. Col. BORADEN NHEM is deputy director of the Institute of Military History, General Department of Policy and Foreign Affairs, Ministry of National Defense, Kingdom of Cambodia. He also serves as assistant to Gen. Tea Banh, deputy prime minister and minister of national defense. Nhem is a doctoral candidate in political science and international relations with a focus on national security affairs, University of Delaware, Newark, after previous studies in France and Cambodia. His published works include the monograph *A Continuation of Politics by Other Means: The "Politics" of a Peacekeeping Mission in Cambodia (1992–93)*, published by the Peacekeeping and Stability Operations Institute and Strategic Studies Institute at the U.S. Army War College, Carlisle, PA. He is also the English translator of many Khmer books including *Civil War Termination in Cambodia: Win-Win Policy of Samdech Techo Hun Sen in International Context, Research into Guerilla Warfare in Pailin,* and the forthcoming second volume of Gen. Tea Banh's biography.